[best__]
[there_]

[is__]
[bub_]

WOLVERINE BY BENJAMIN PERCY VOL. 3. Contains material originally published in magazine form as WOLVERINE (2020) #14-19. First printing 2021. ISBN 978-1-302-92725-7. Published by MARVEL WORLDWIDE, INC., a subsidiary of MARVEL ENTERTAINMENT, LLC. OFFICE OF PUBLICATION: 1290 Avenue of the Americas, New York, NY 10104. © 2021 MARVEL No similarity between any of the names, characters, persons, and/or institutions in this book with those of any living or dead person or institution is intended, and any such similarity which may exist is purely coincidental. **Printed in Canada.** KEVIN FEIGE, Chief Creative Officer; DAN BUCKLEY, President, Marvel Entertainment; JOE QUESADA, EVP & Creative Director; DAVID BOGART, Associate Publisher & SVP of Talent Affairs; TOM BREVOORT, VP, Executive Editor; NICK LOWE, Executive Editor, VP of Content, Digital Publishing; DAVID GABRIEL, VP of Print & Digital Publishing; JEFF YOUNGQUIST, VP of Production & Special Projects; ALEX MORALES, Director of Publishing Operations; DAN EDINGTON, Managing Editor; RICKEY PURDIN, Director of Talent Relations; JENNIFER GRÜNWALD, Senior Editor, Special Projects; SUSAN CRESPI, Production Manager; STAN LEE, Chairman Emeritus. For information regarding advertising in Marvel Comics or on Marvel.com, please contact Vit DeBellis, Custom Solutions & Integrated Advertising Manager, at vdebellis@ marvel.com. For Marvel subscription inquiries, please call 888-511-5480. **Manufactured between 12/10/2021 and 1/11/2022 by SOLISCO PRINTERS, SCOTT, QC, CANADA.**

10 9 8 7 6 5 4 3 2 1

WOLVERINE

Writer:	Benjamin Percy
Pencilers:	Adam Kubert (#14-16),
	Lan Medina (#17),
	Paco Diaz (#18) &
	Javi Fernández (#19)
Inkers:	Adam Kubert (#14-16),
	Cam Smith (#17),
	Paco Diaz (#18) &
	Javi Fernández (#19)
Colorists:	Frank Martin (#14-16),
	Espen Grundetjern (#16),
	Java Tartaglia (#17-18),
	Dijjo Lima (#18) &
	Matthew Wilson (#19)
Letterer:	VC's Cory Petit
Cover Art:	Adam Kubert &
	Frank Martin
Head of X:	Jonathan Hickman
Design:	Tom Muller
Assistant Editors:	Lauren Amaro &
	Drew Baumgartner
Editor:	Mark Basso
Senior Editor:	Jordan D. White

Collection Editor:	Jennifer Grünwald
Assistant Editor:	Daniel Kirchhoffer
Assistant Managing Editor:	Maia Loy
Associate Manager, Talent Relations:	Lisa Montalbano
VP Production & Special Projects:	Jeff Youngquist
SVP Print, Sales & Marketing:	David Gabriel
Editor in Chief:	C.B. Cebulski

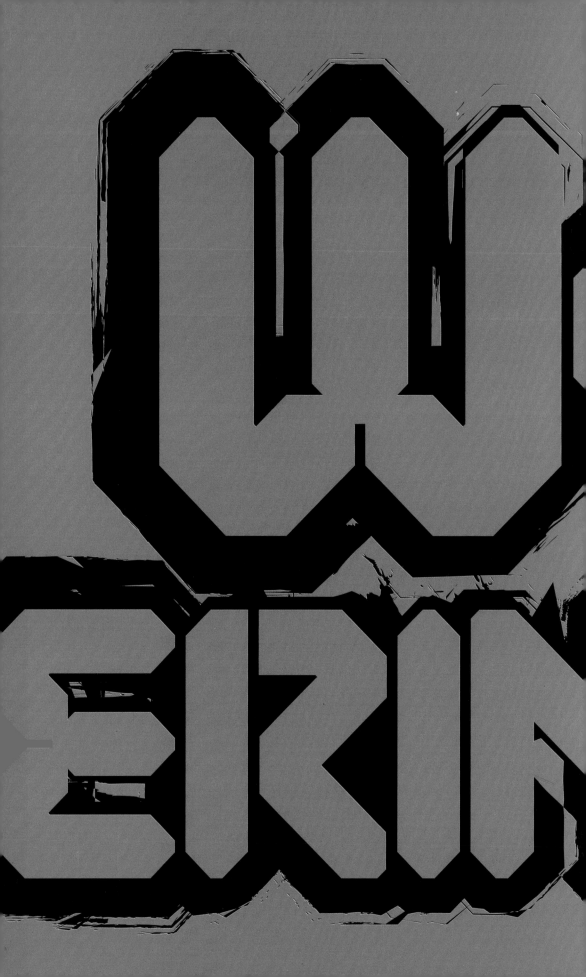

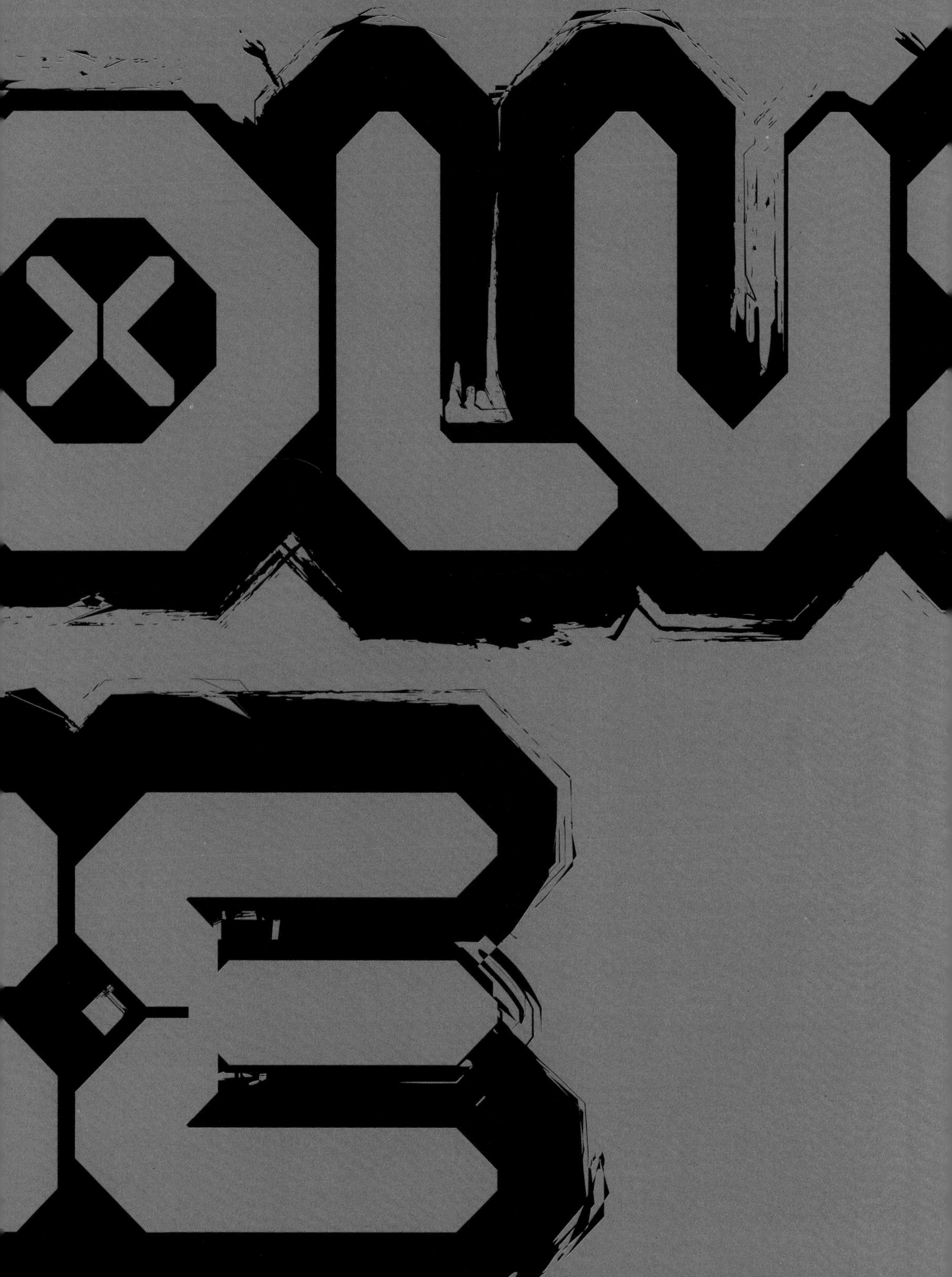

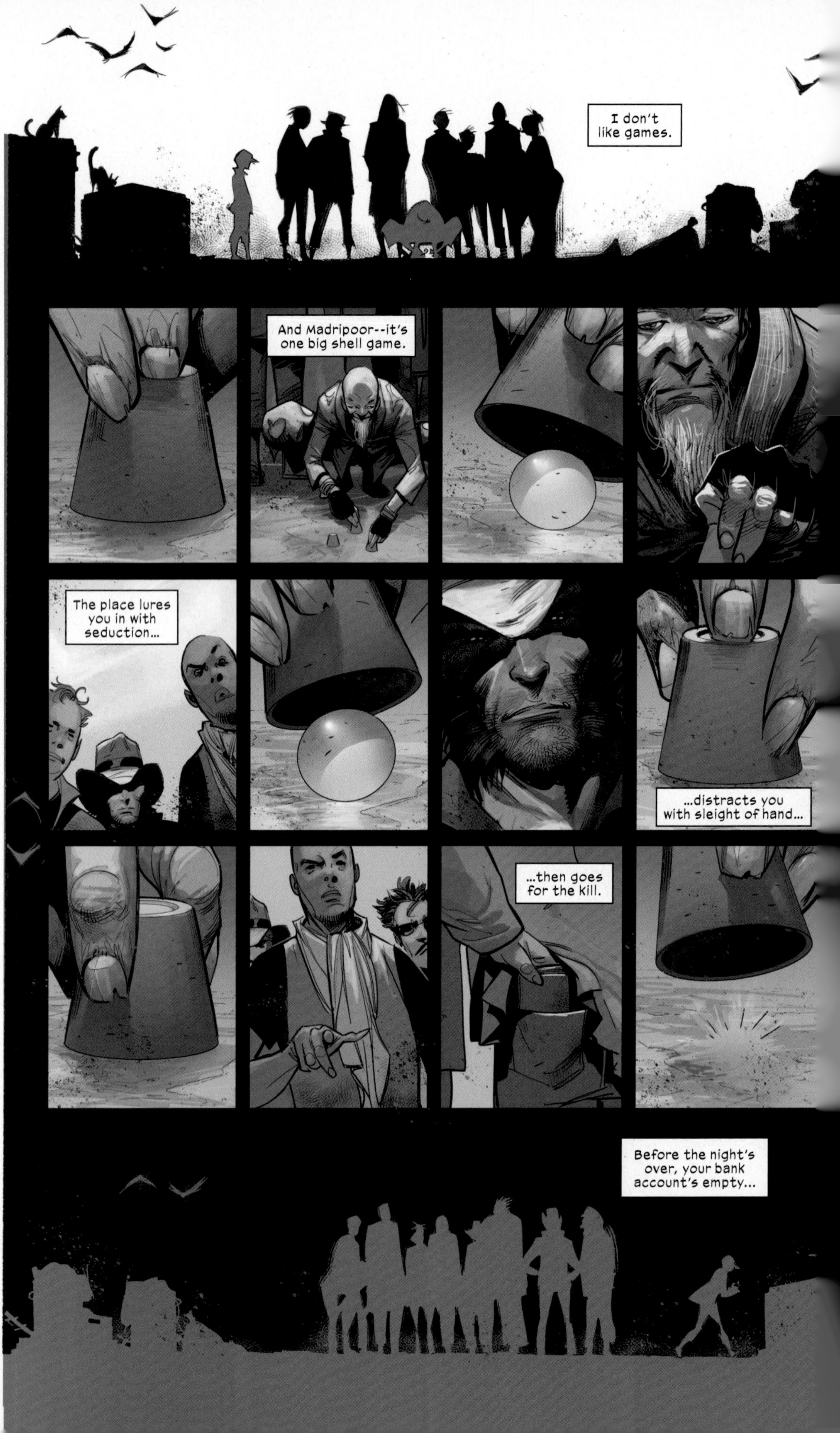
I don't like games.
And Madripoor--it's one big shell game.
The place lures you in with seduction...
...distracts you with sleight of hand...
...then goes for the kill.
Before the night's over, your bank account's empty...

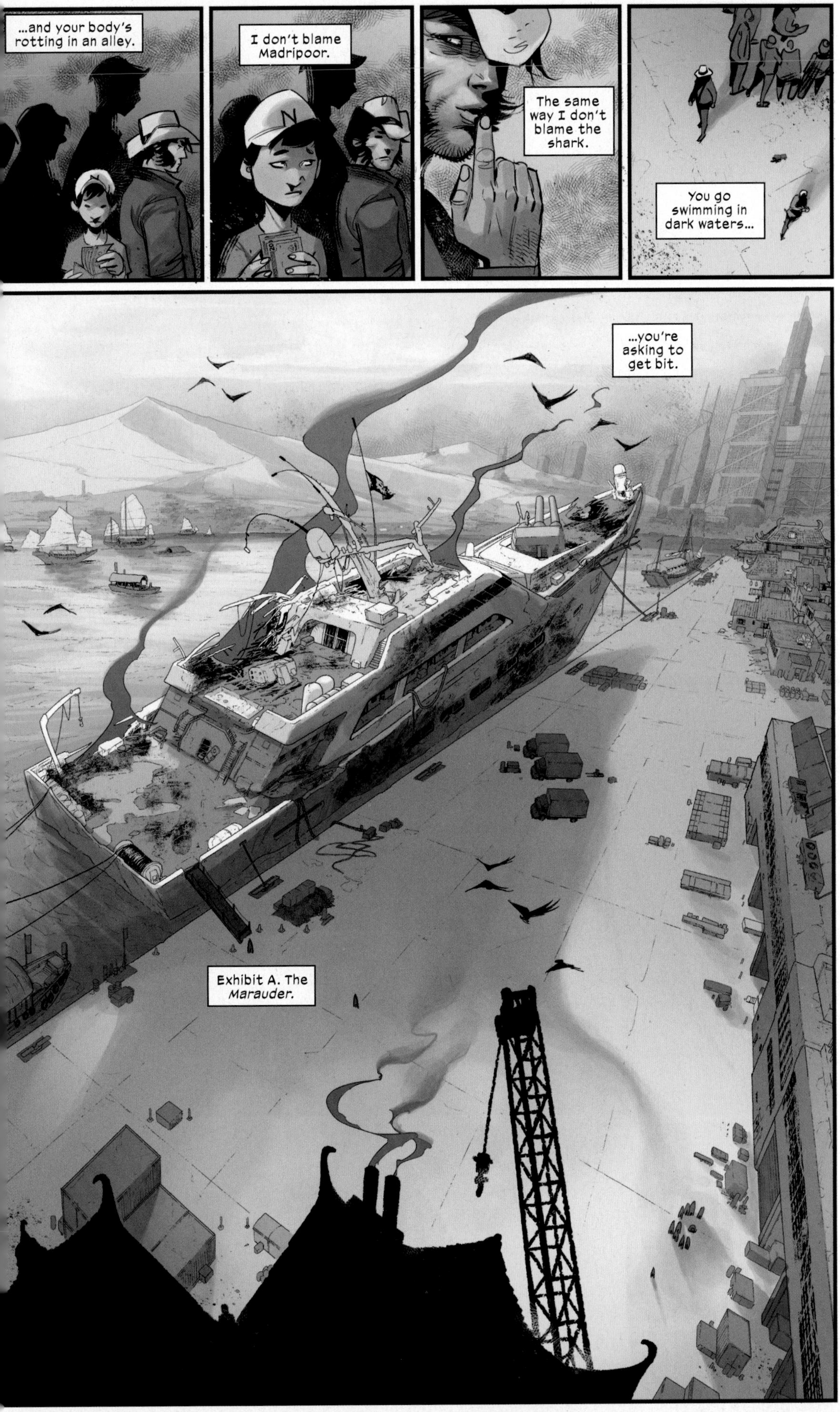
...and your body's rotting in an alley.
I don't blame Madripoor.
The same way I don't blame the shark.
You go swimming in dark waters...
...you're asking to get bit.
Exhibit A. The *Marauder*.

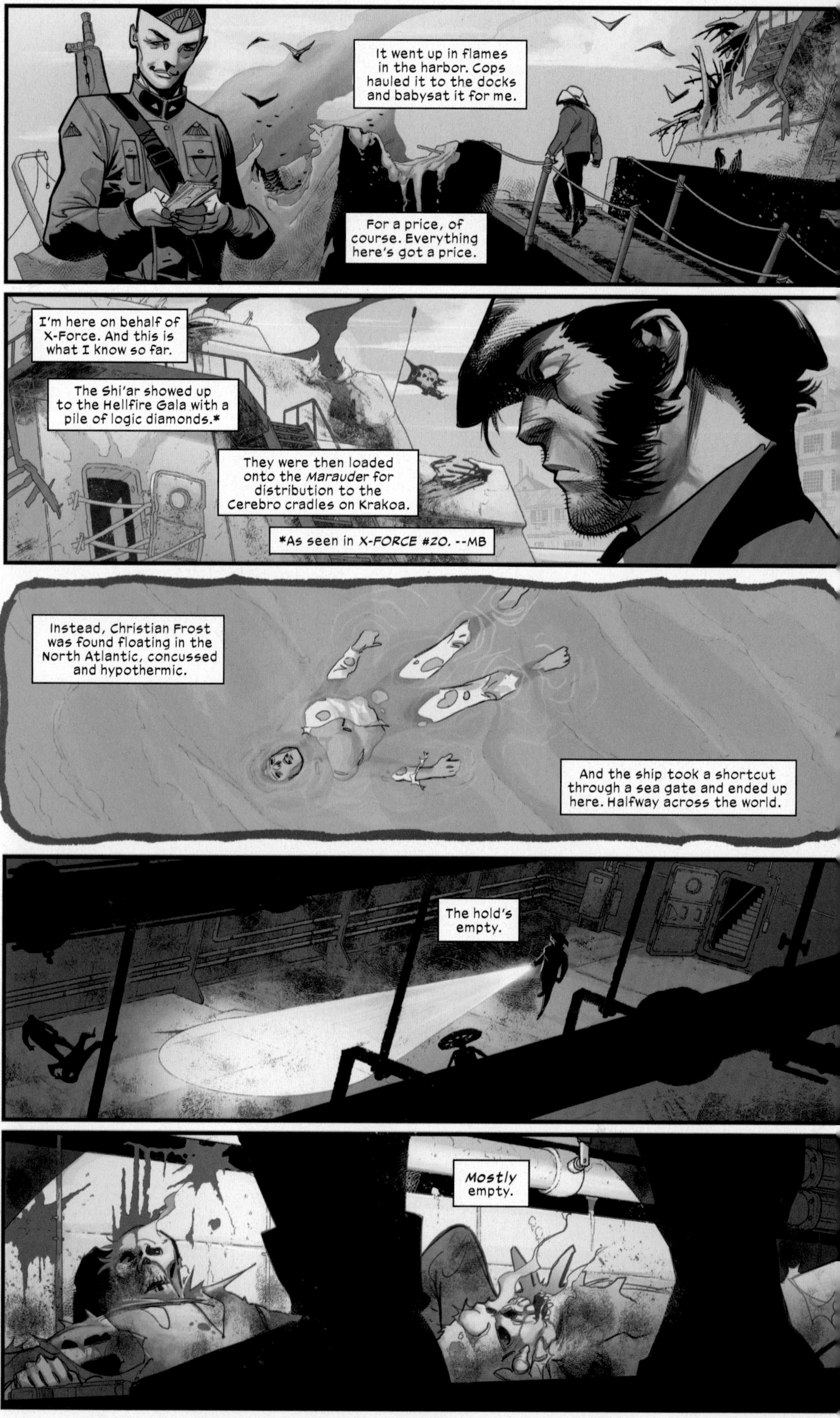
It went up in flames in the harbor. Cops hauled it to the docks and babysat it for me.
For a price, of course. Everything here's got a price.
I'm here on behalf of X-Force. And this is what I know so far.
The Shi'ar showed up to the Hellfire Gala with a pile of logic diamonds.*
They were then loaded onto the *Marauder* for distribution to the Cerebro cradles on Krakoa.
*As seen in *X-FORCE #20.* --MB
Instead, Christian Frost was found floating in the North Atlantic, concussed and hypothermic.
And the ship took a shortcut through a sea gate and ended up here. Halfway across the world.
The hold's empty.
Mostly empty.

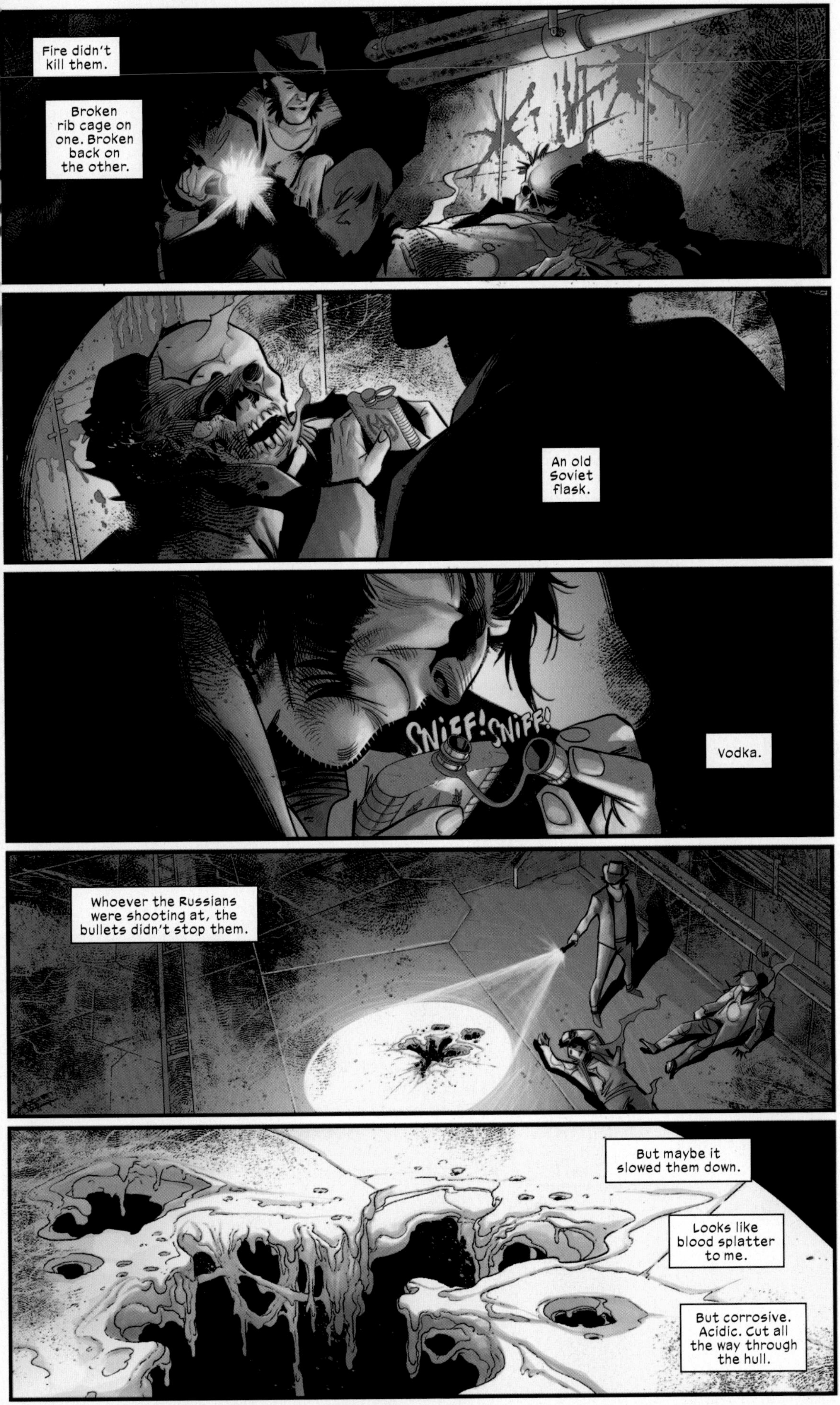

Fire didn't kill them.
Broken rib cage on one. Broken back on the other.
An old Soviet flask.
SNIFF! SNIFF!
Vodka.
Whoever the Russians were shooting at, the bullets didn't stop them.
But maybe it slowed them down.
Looks like blood splatter to me.
But corrosive. Acidic. Cut all the way through the hull.

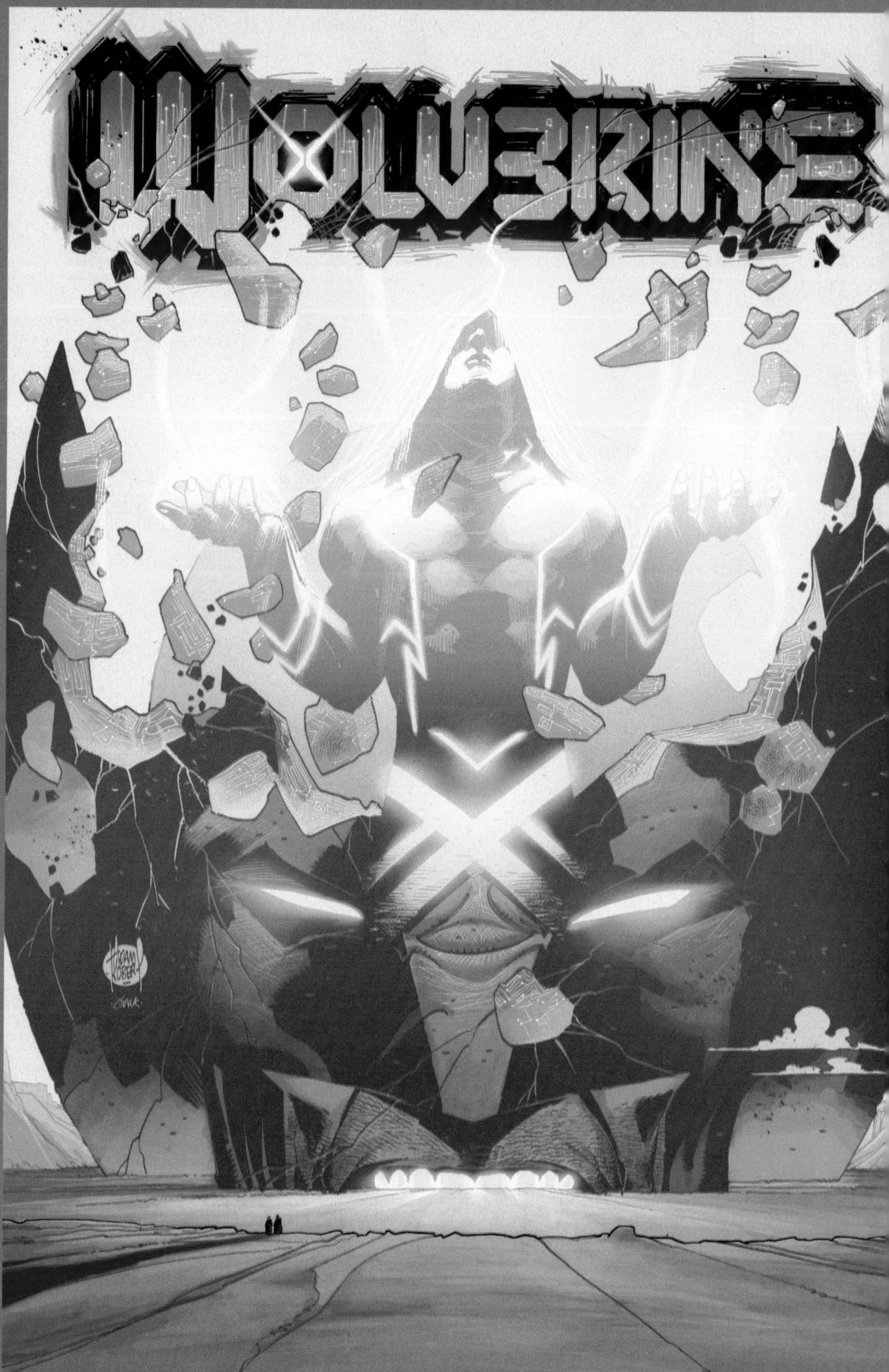
WOLVERINE

The Unusual Suspects

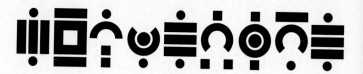

FOX HUNT

During the Hellfire Gala, Wolverine and the rest of X-Force managed to narrowly avoid an international disaster following the failure of Beast's telefloronic programming of Terra Verde's ambassadors. But while the team was distracted, someone managed to ambush the *Marauder* and left one of their fellow mutants for dead. With that culprit still out in the wind and no leads, there's only one man for the job, and he's the best there is at what he does...

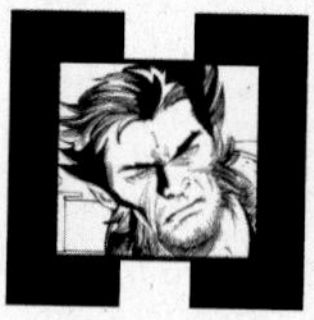
Wolverine

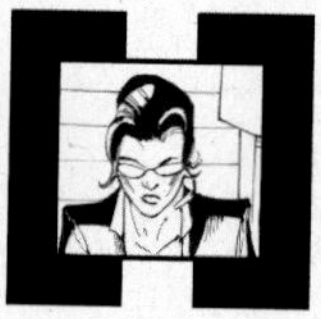
Sage

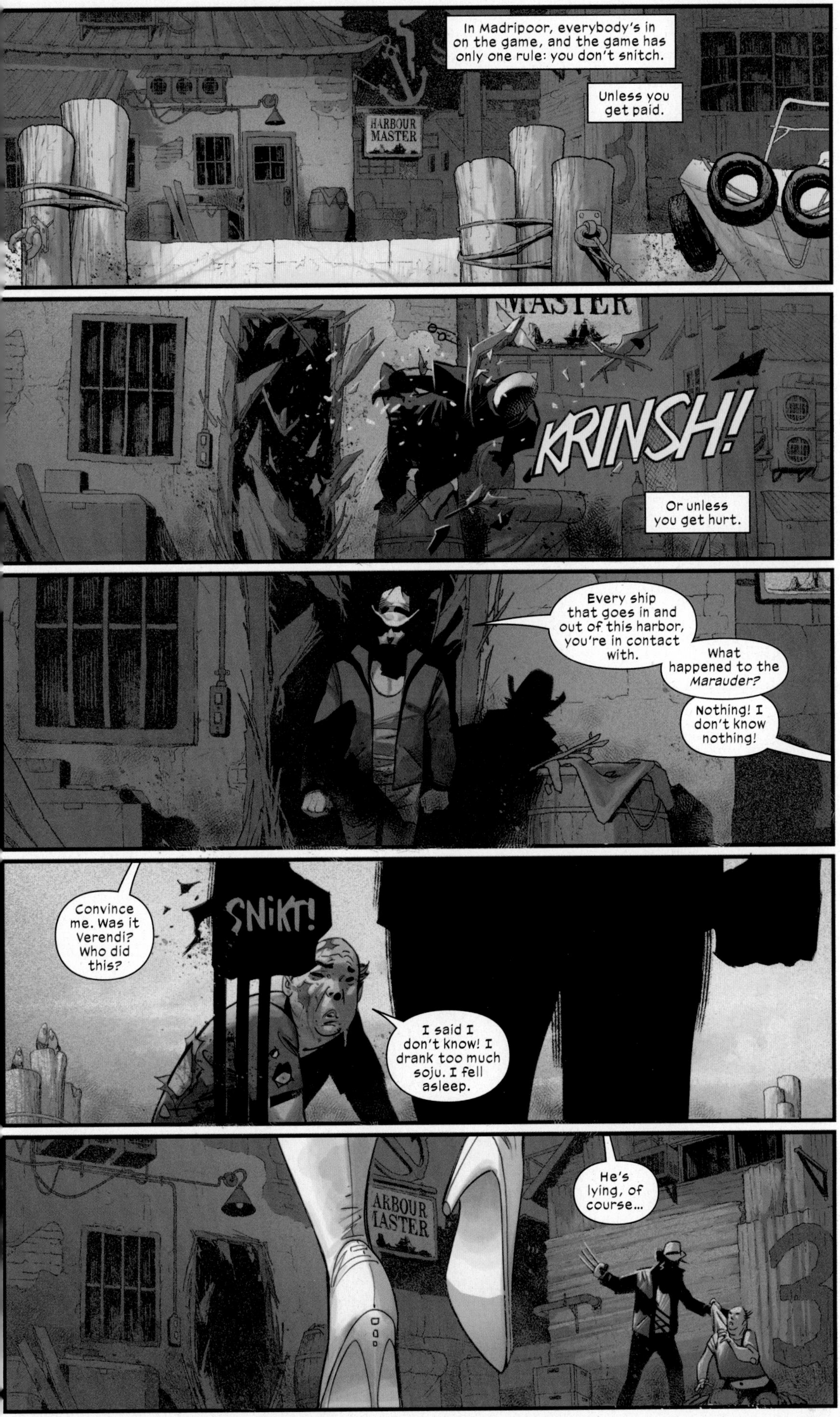

In Madripoor, everybody's in on the game, and the game has only one rule: you don't snitch.
Unless you get paid.
HARBOUR MASTER
KRINSH!
Or unless you get hurt.
Every ship that goes in and out of this harbor, you're in contact with.
What happened to the *Marauder?*
Nothing! I don't know nothing!
Convince me. Was it Verendi? Who did this?
SNIKT!
I said I don't know! I drank too much soju. I fell asleep.
He's lying, of course...

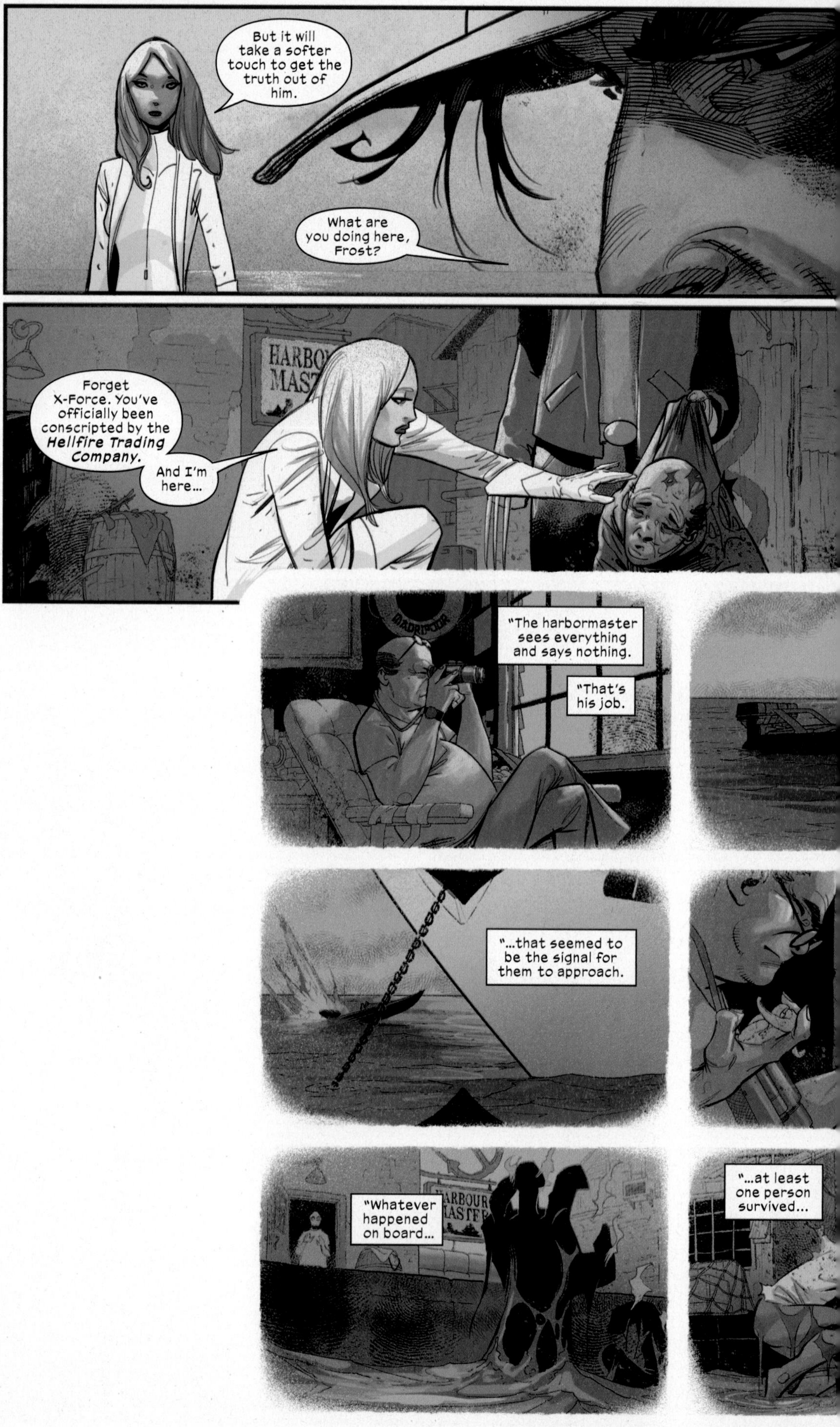
But it will take a softer touch to get the truth out of him.
What are you doing here, Frost?
HARBOUR MAST
Forget X-Force. You've officially been conscripted by the *Hellfire Trading Company.*
And I'm here...
MADRIPOOR
"The harbormaster sees everything and says nothing.
"That's his job.
"...that seemed to be the signal for them to approach.
"Whatever happened on board...
"...at least one person survived...

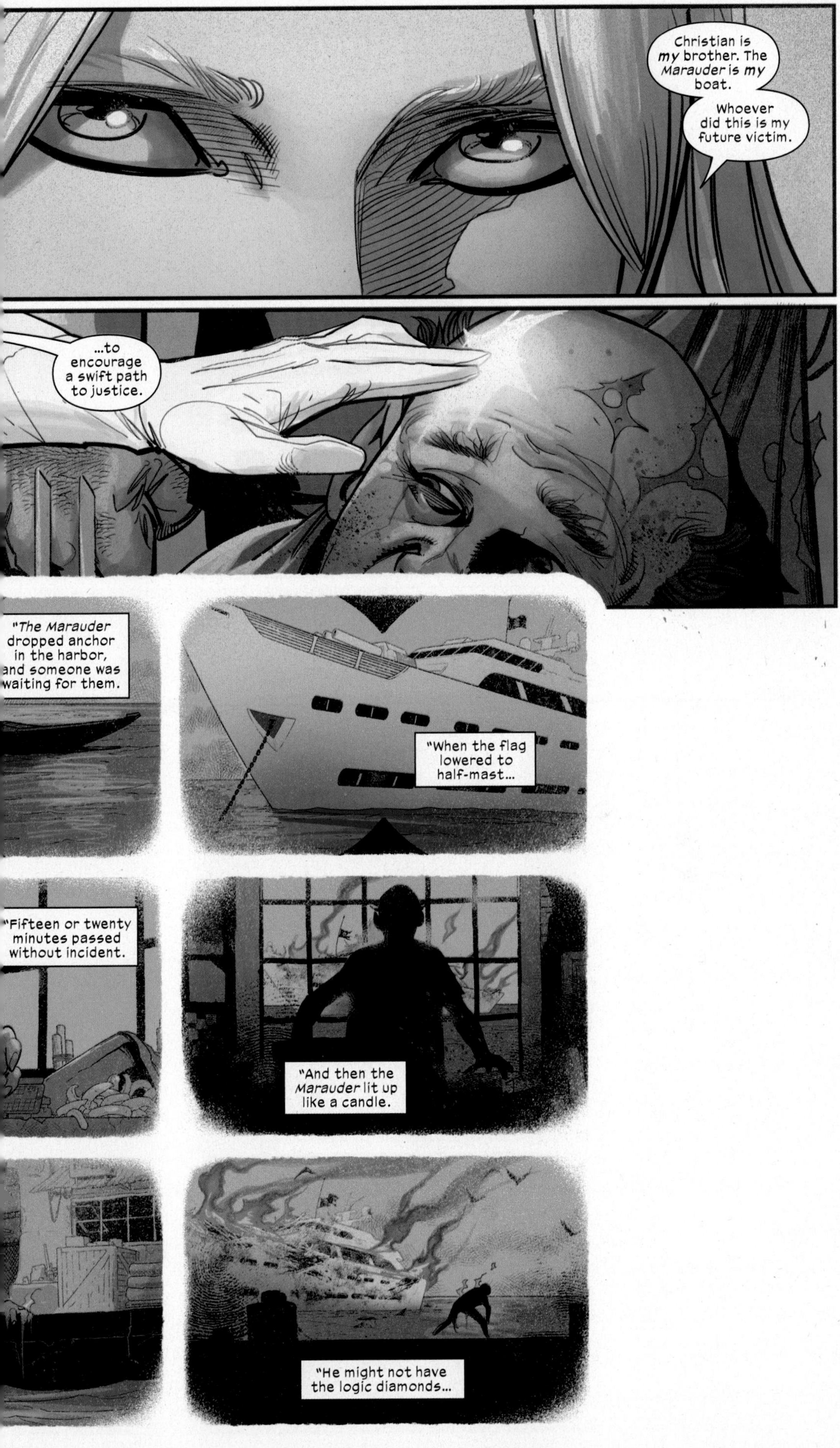
Christian is *my* brother. The *Marauder* is *my* boat.
Whoever did this is my future victim.
...to encourage a swift path to justice.
"*The Marauder* dropped anchor in the harbor, and someone was waiting for them.
"When the flag lowered to half-mast...
"Fifteen or twenty minutes passed without incident.
"And then the *Marauder* lit up like a candle.
"He might not have the logic diamonds...

"...but he knows something.

"Find him."

Emma's not my boss.

But for now, I'll let her think that's the case.

Far as I'm concerned, as the queen of the black market...

RTL

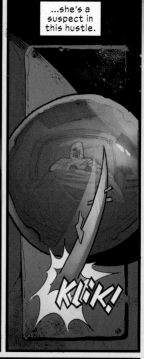

...she's a suspect in this hustle.

KLIK!

That's him!

I told you he was here! Now let me go.

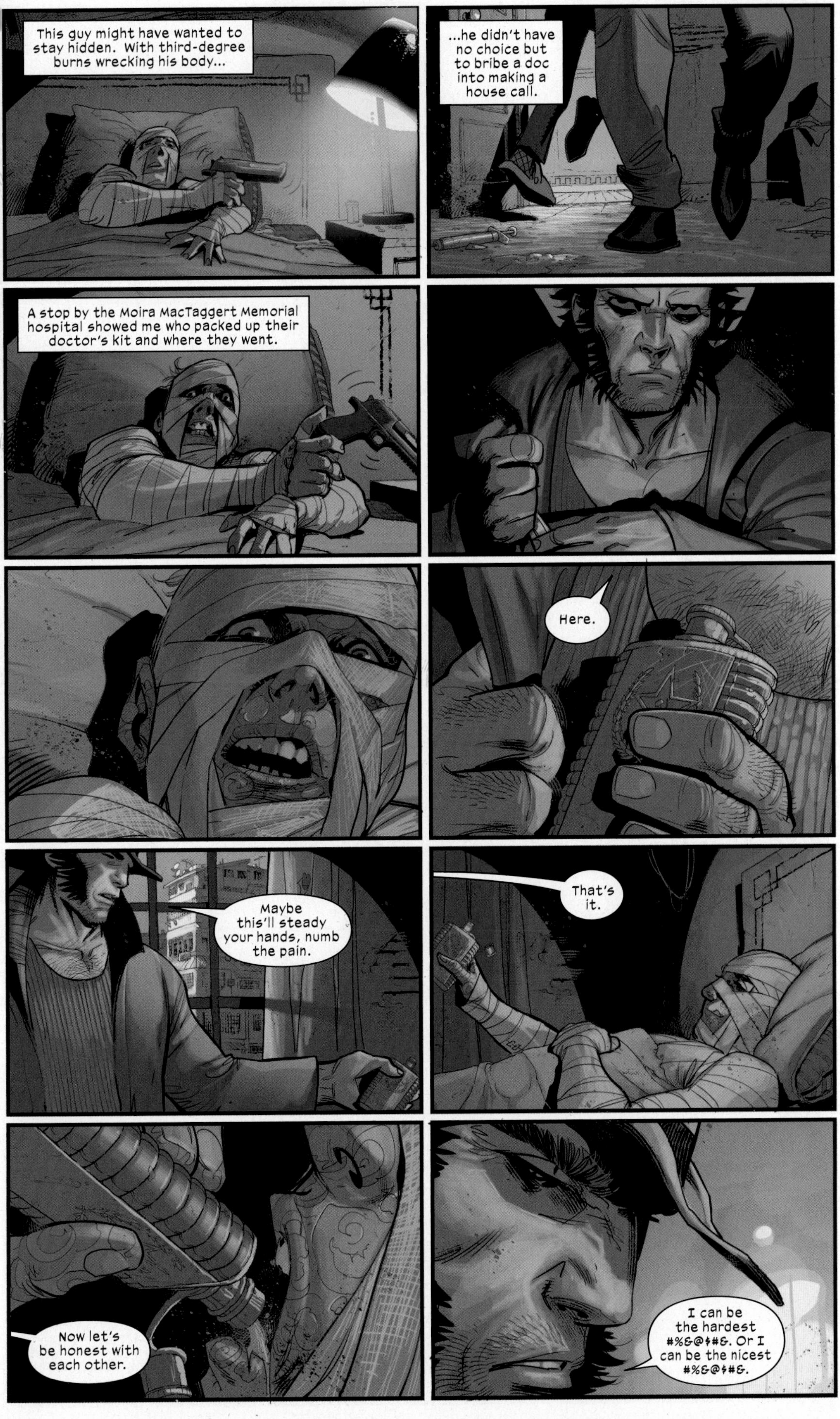
This guy might have wanted to stay hidden. With third-degree burns wrecking his body...
...he didn't have no choice but to bribe a doc into making a house call.
A stop by the Moira MacTaggert Memorial hospital showed me who packed up their doctor's kit and where they went.
Here.
Maybe this'll steady your hands, numb the pain.
That's it.
Now let's be honest with each other.
I can be the hardest #%&@$#&. Or I can be the nicest #%&@$#&.

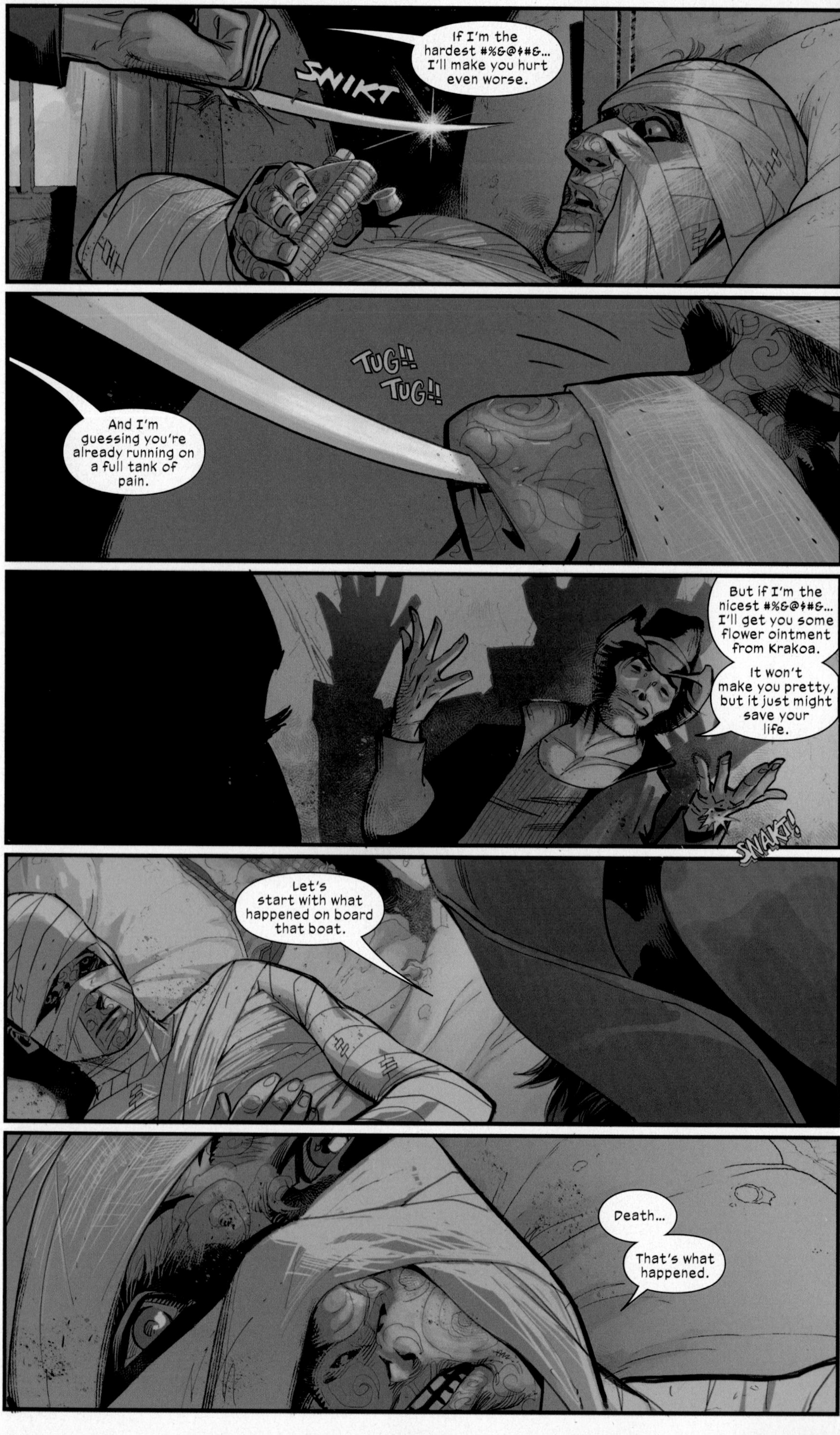
If I'm the hardest #%&@$#&... I'll make you hurt even worse.
SNIKT
TUG!! TUG!!
And I'm guessing you're already running on a full tank of pain.
But if I'm the nicest #%&@$#&... I'll get you some flower ointment from Krakoa.
It won't make you pretty, but it just might save your life.
SNAKT!
Let's start with what happened on board that boat.
Death...
That's what happened.

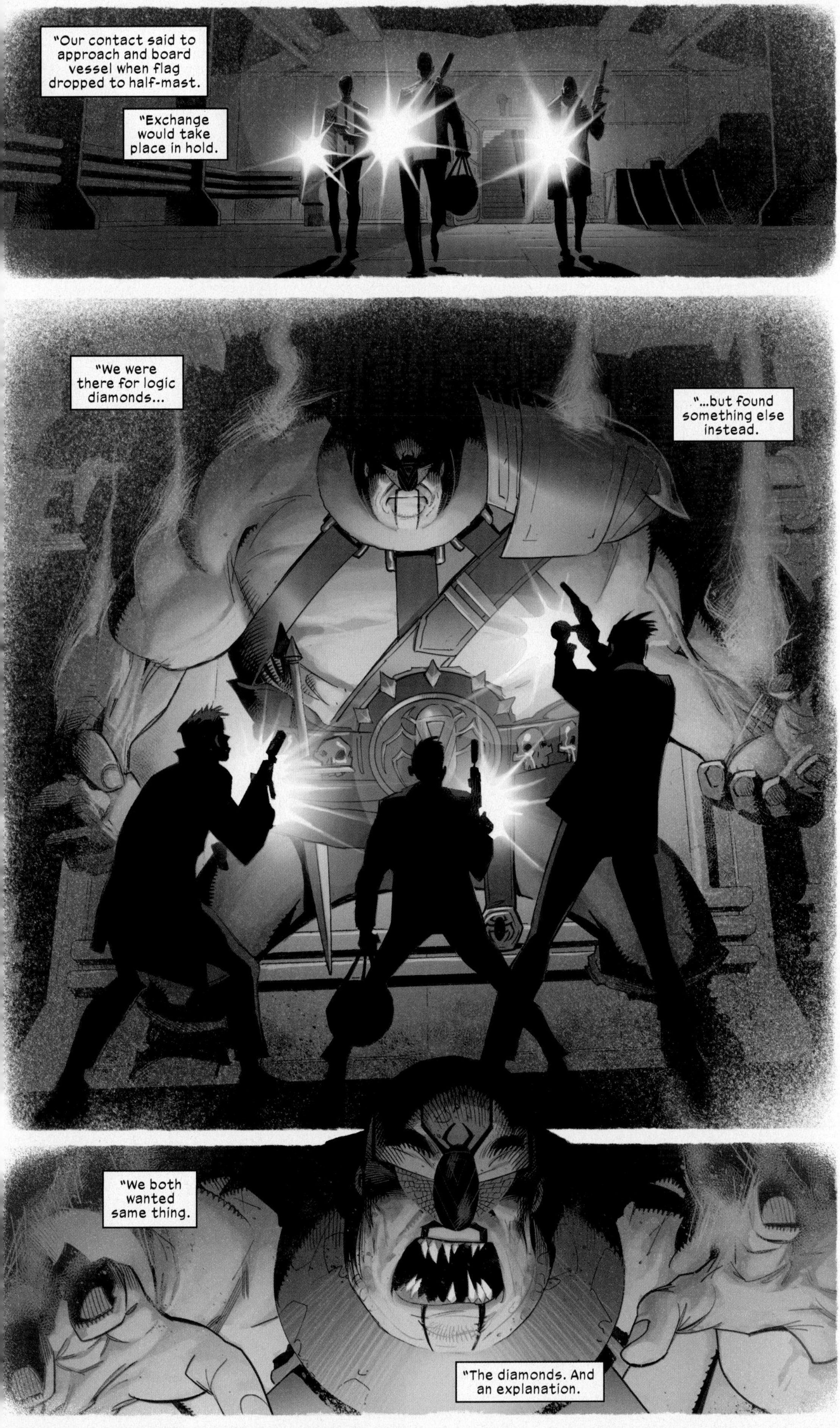
"Our contact said to approach and board vessel when flag dropped to half-mast.
"Exchange would take place in hold.
"We were there for logic diamonds...
"...but found something else instead.
"We both wanted same thing.
"The diamonds. And an explanation.

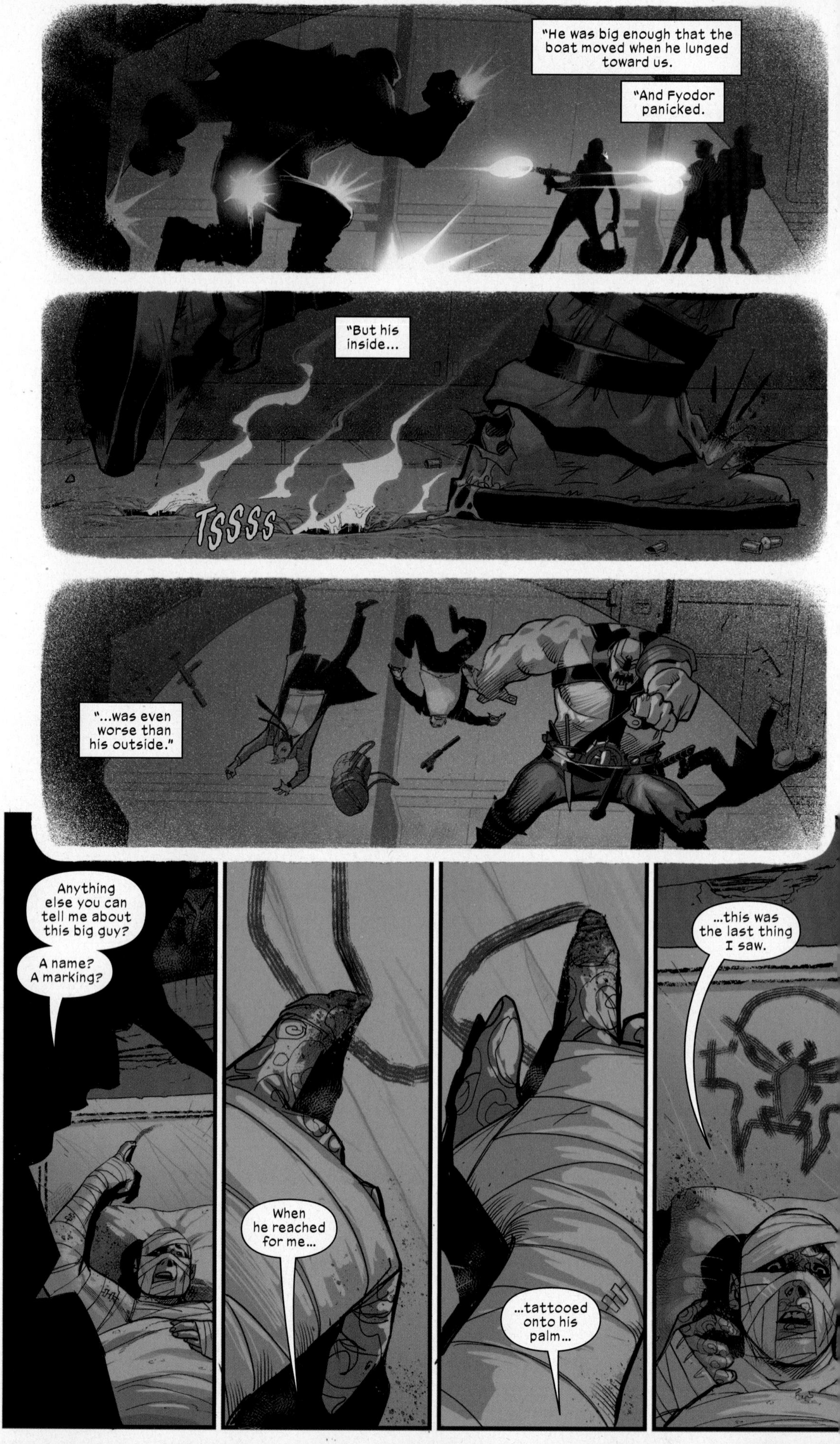
"He was big enough that the boat moved when he lunged toward us.
"And Fyodor panicked.
"But his inside...
TSSSS
"...was even worse than his outside."
Anything else you can tell me about this big guy?
A name? A marking?
When he reached for me...
...tattooed onto his palm...
...this was the last thing I saw.

SAGE'S LOGBOOK:

:::Interrogation Transcript /// Comm Relay:::

Subject: Antony Kriev

KRIEV: You told us to come.

WOLVERINE: My memory's not the best, but I think I'd remember that one.

KRIEV: The mutants...Hellfire...

KRIEV: It was a black-market negotiation.

WOLVERINE: Who did you speak to?

KRIEV: Like I said. One of you. A mutant.

WOLVERINE: Where?

KRIEV: I have reputation, yes? My crew? We move packages. Anything. Across borders. Very discreet. Very big-time.

<coughing fit>

KRIEV: But with Krakoa, this has been problem. So when I see opportunity, I take.

WOLVERINE: "Where" is what I asked. Where did this mutant speak to you?

KRIEV: In my home. I live in very nice apartment. People always say they like view of park. I wake up with blade to throat.

WOLVERINE: What did he look like?

KRIEV: It was too dark for me to say. He looked like shadow.

WOLVERINE: How'd you know he was a mutant?

KRIEV: Because he said he was one of you. He said that if Antony did good job, I would become big horse for Hellfire Club Moscow.

WOLVERINE: You mean mule?

KRIEV: Horse is better.

WOLVERINE: I'm getting the sense that you're kind of a #%&@ idiot.

Profile:
Antony Kriev never earned his certificate for secondary education. He has served time in three different prisons for crimes ranging from burglary to manslaughter to credit card fraud. The payment for the logic diamonds came on loan from the Russian Brotherhood at a rate of 50% in ten days. He can hardly be considered proficient enough to be earnestly solicited for this kind of exclusive work. He is challenged intellectually and criminally. He is, in every respect, a failure.

<<<<PRELIMINARY CONCLUSION>>>>

Kriev was hired to fail. He was expected to die.

<<<<FURTHER QUERIES>>>>

Why? By whom? And is the status of the Hellfire Club in Moscow currently active? If so, who is the local captain?

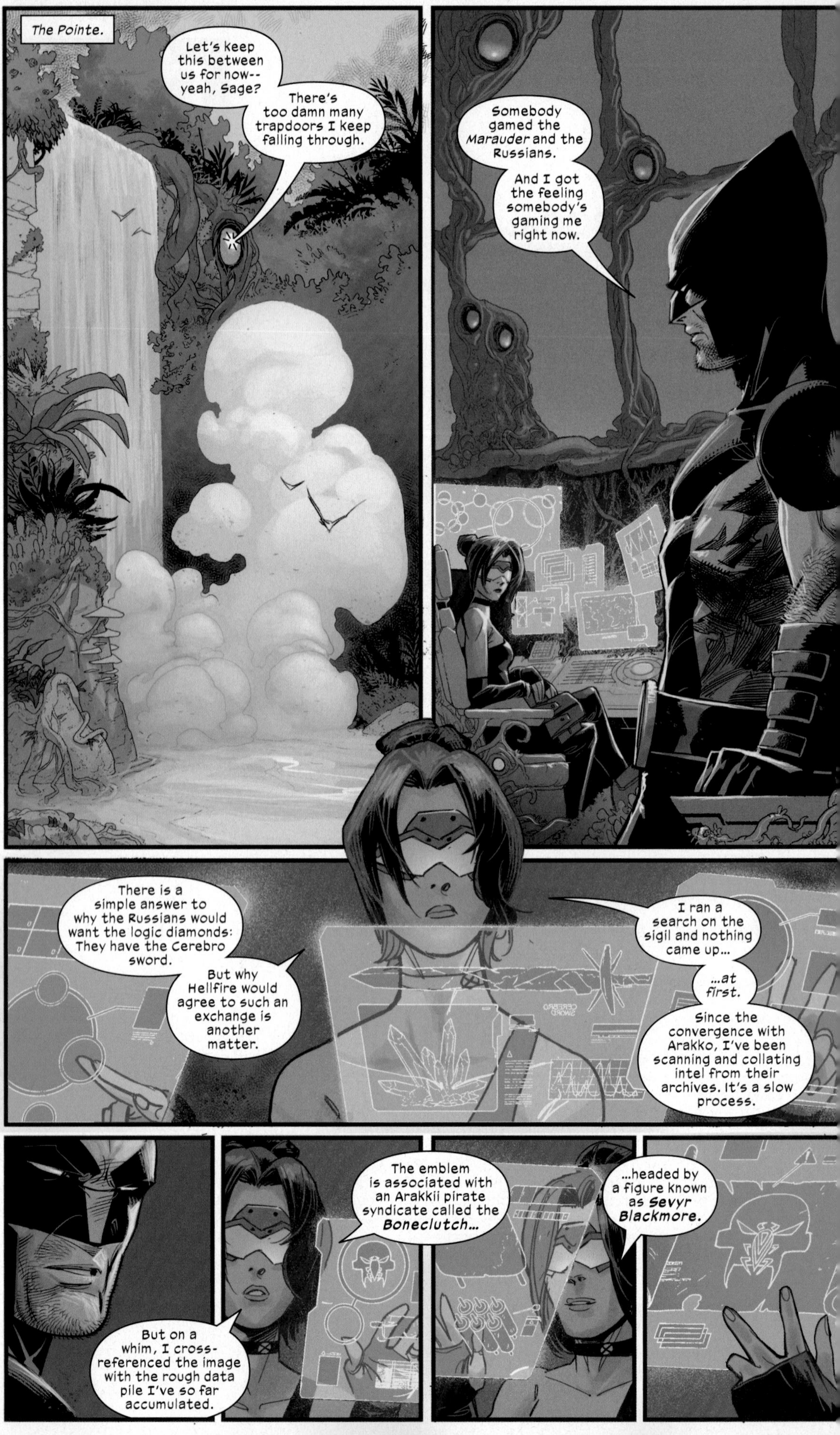
The Pointe.
Let's keep this between us for now-- yeah, Sage?
There's too damn many trapdoors I keep falling through.
Somebody gamed the Marauder and the Russians.
And I got the feeling somebody's gaming me right now.
There is a simple answer to why the Russians would want the logic diamonds: They have the Cerebro sword.
But why Hellfire would agree to such an exchange is another matter.
I ran a search on the sigil and nothing came up...
...at first.
Since the convergence with Arakko, I've been scanning and collating intel from their archives. It's a slow process.
But on a whim, I cross-referenced the image with the rough data pile I've so far accumulated.
The emblem is associated with an Arakkii pirate syndicate called the Boneclutch...
...headed by a figure known as Sevyr Blackmore.

SAGE'S LOGBOOK:

Outstanding Queries from the Hellfire Gala

1) The Shi'ar Question:

//Further investigation has revealed the Shi'ar invitation to the Hellfire Gala was accompanied by a request for logic diamonds. What was initially believed to be a gift to the mutants was in fact a requested donation.

//Emma Frost denies any knowledge of this.

//The message's origin has so far proved untraceable.

2) The Terra Verdean Question:

//Whoever cut off the telefloronic feed -- making the Terra Verdeans go rogue during the gala -- could have been acting out of benevolence (encouraging the nation's freedom) and/or hostility (hoping to undercut any Krakoan diplomatic efforts).

//Or it might have been a distraction, so that the trouble in Madripoor could play out before X-Force became aware of what was going on.

3) The Madripoor Question:

//Does the same logic then extend to the burned *Marauder*, the dead Russians, and the Arakkii pirate? Is there another sort of distraction at play? A misdirection? Like a shell game?

//Upon relaying these questions to Wolverine by comm, I received the following response:

"There's only one way to be sure, and that's to hunt this Arakkii #%$@ down."

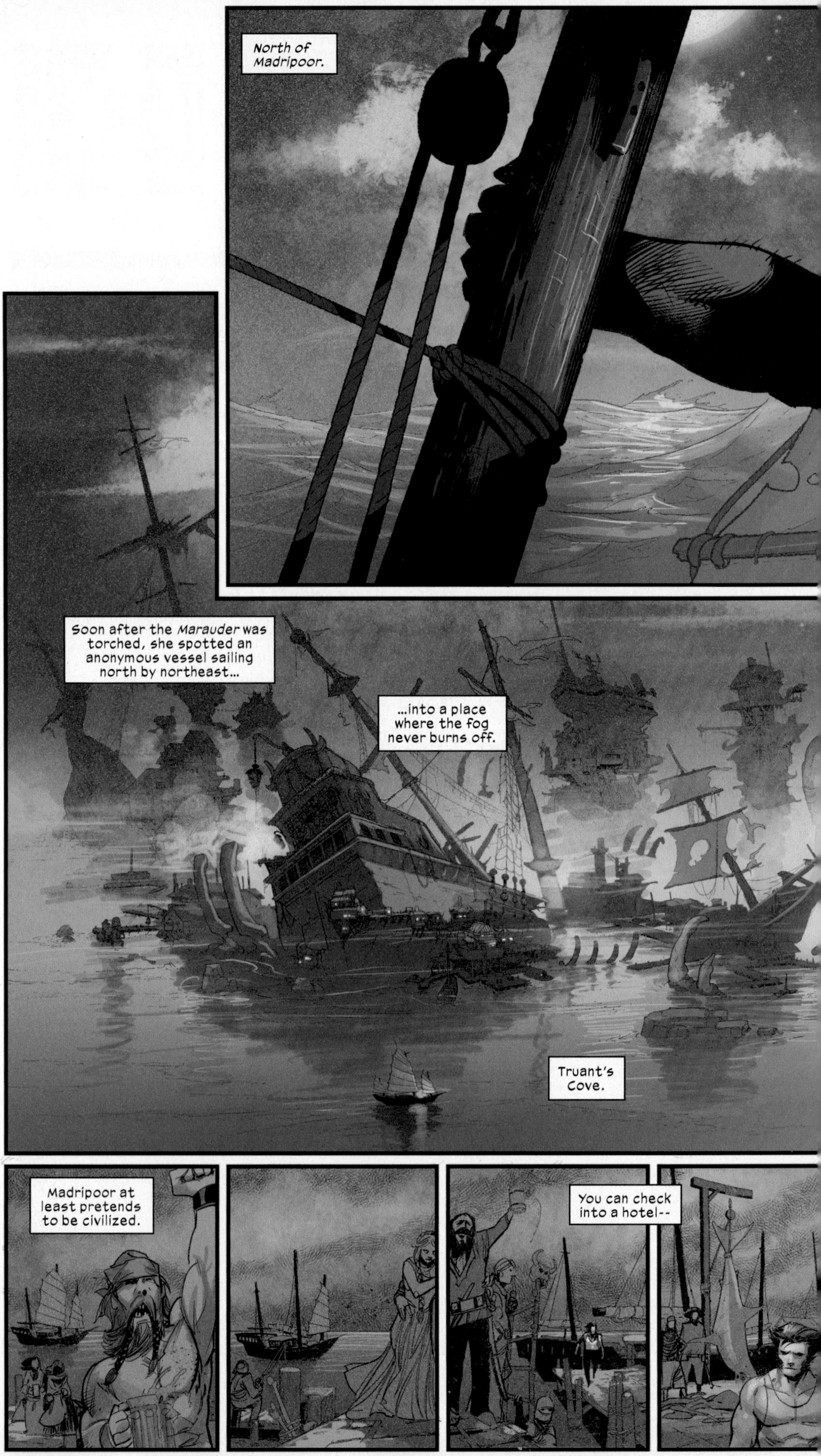
North of Madripoor.
Soon after the Marauder was torched, she spotted an anonymous vessel sailing north by northeast...
...into a place where the fog never burns off.
Truant's Cove.
Madripoor at least pretends to be civilized.
You can check into a hotel--

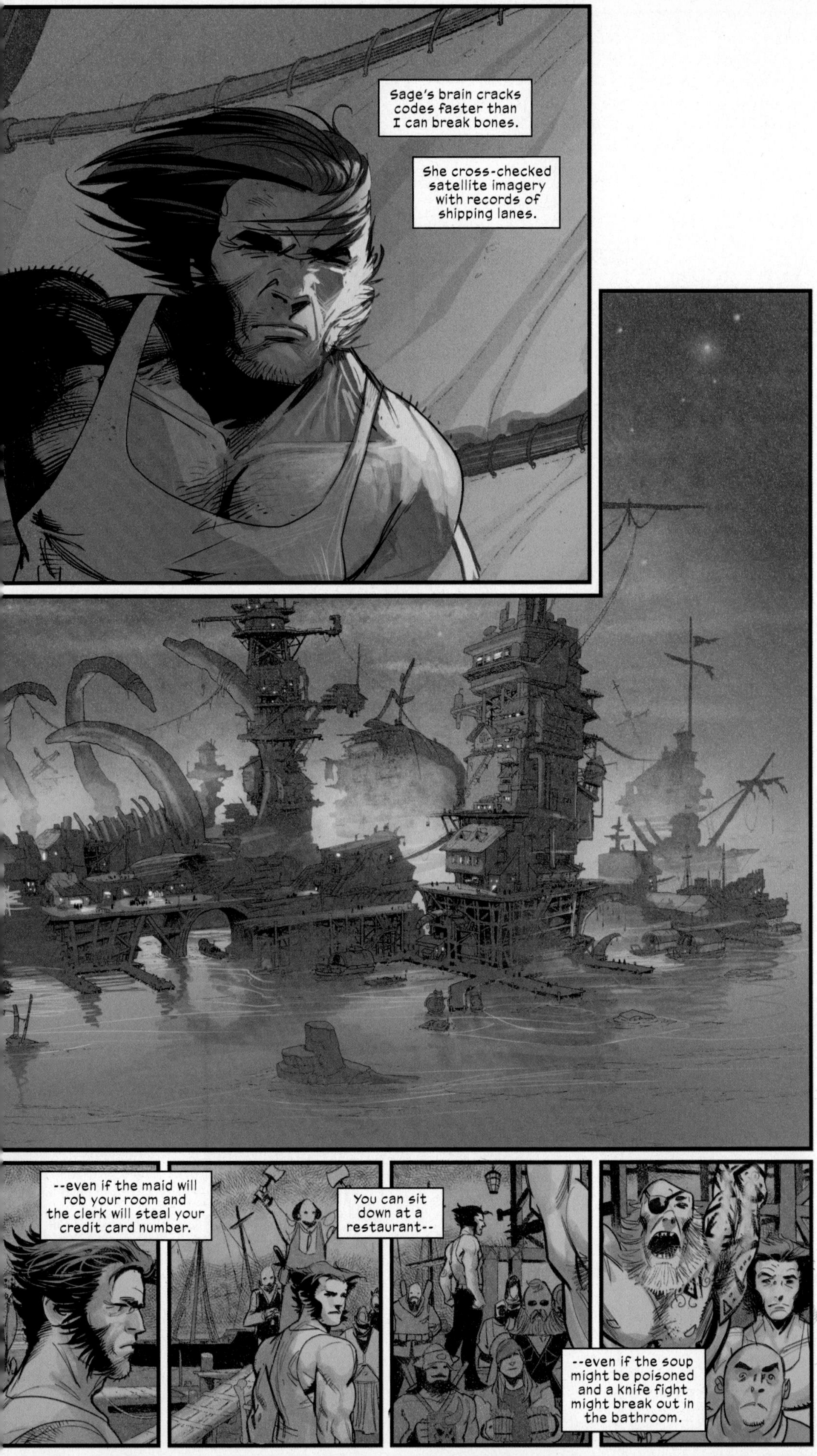
Sage's brain cracks codes faster than I can break bones.
She cross-checked satellite imagery with records of shipping lanes.
--even if the maid will rob your room and the clerk will steal your credit card number.
You can sit down at a restaurant--
--even if the soup might be poisoned and a knife fight might break out in the bathroom.

This place doesn't even try to pretend it's anything other than...

...a bloodbath.

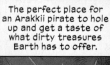
The perfect place for an Arakkii pirate to hole up and get a taste of what dirty treasures Earth has to offer.

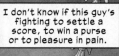
I don't know if this guy's fighting to settle a score, to win a purse or to pleasure in pain.

This ain't the first time I've faced an Arakkii in the ring without a clear sense of the rules.

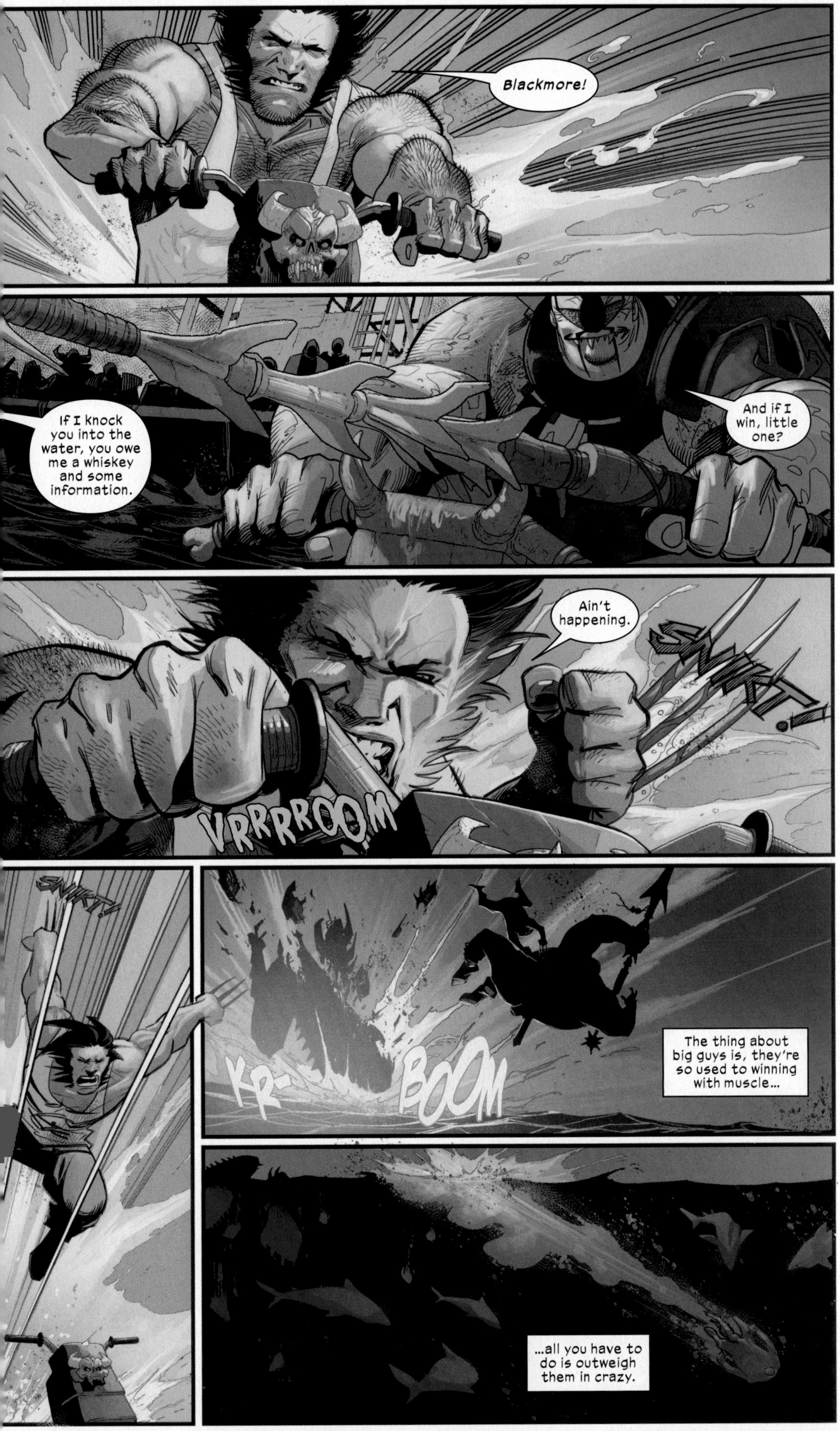
Blackmore!
If I knock you into the water, you owe me a whiskey and some information.
And if I win, little one?
Ain't happening.
SNIKT!
VRRRROOM
SNIKT!
KR-BOOM
The thing about big guys is, they're so used to winning with muscle...
...all you have to do is outweigh them in crazy.

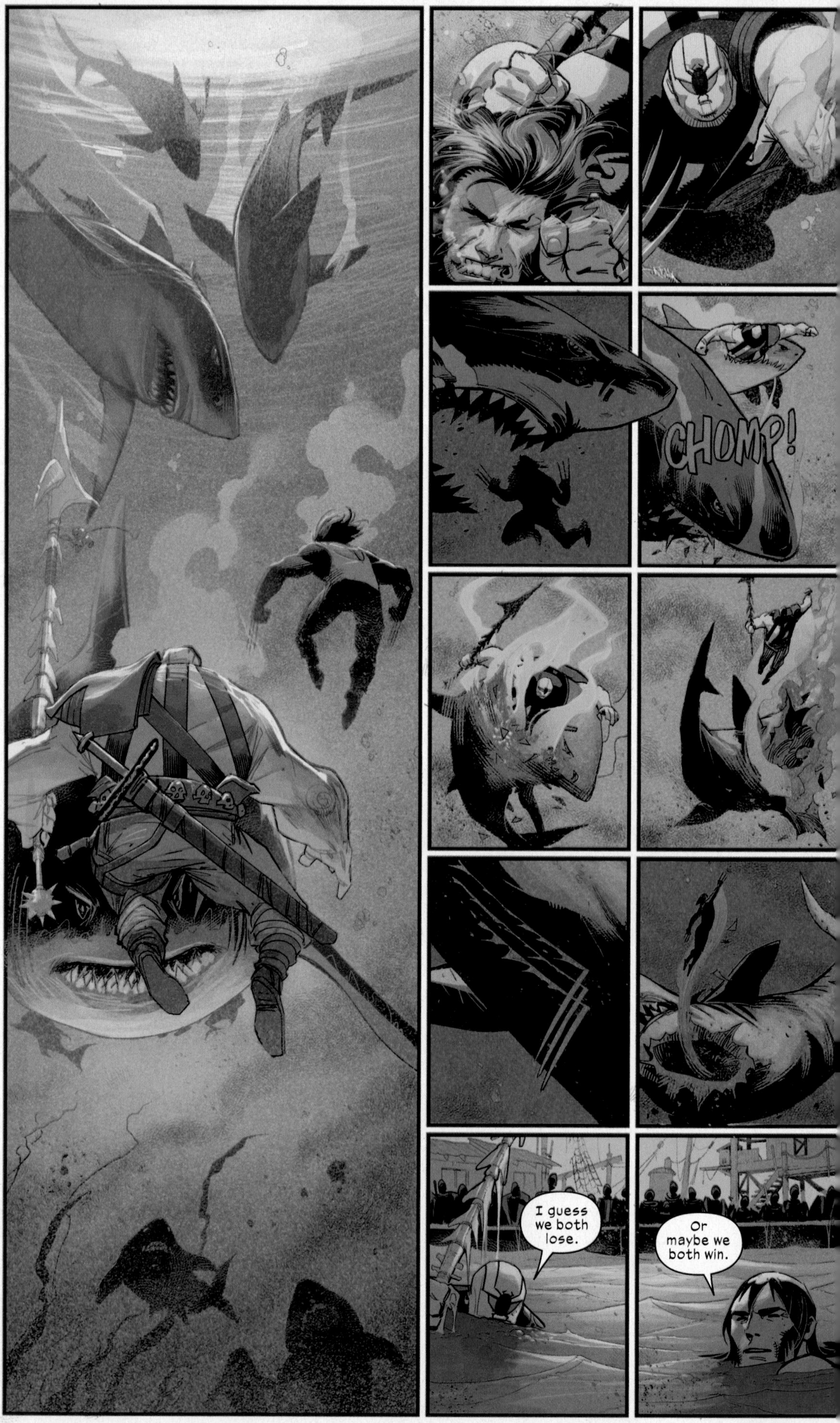
CHOMP!
I guess we both lose.
Or maybe we both win.

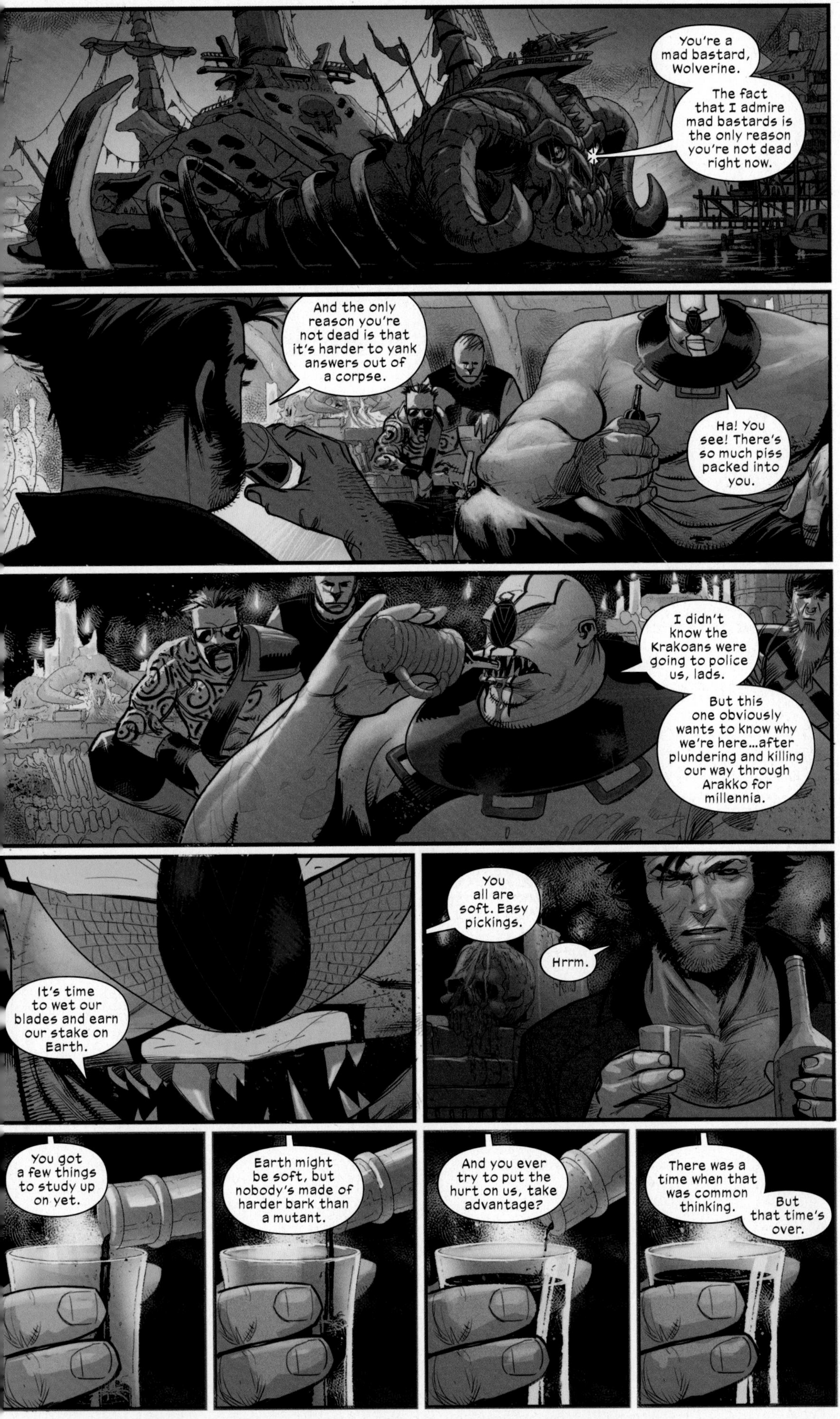

You're a mad bastard, Wolverine.
The fact that I admire mad bastards is the only reason you're not dead right now.
And the only reason you're not dead is that it's harder to yank answers out of a corpse.
Ha! You see! There's so much piss packed into you.
I didn't know the Krakoans were going to police us, lads.
But this one obviously wants to know why we're here...after plundering and killing our way through Arakko for millennia.
It's time to wet our blades and earn our stake on Earth.
You all are soft. Easy pickings.
Hrrm.
You got a few things to study up on yet.
Earth might be soft, but nobody's made of harder bark than a mutant.
And you ever try to put the hurt on us, take advantage?
There was a time when that was common thinking.
But that time's over.

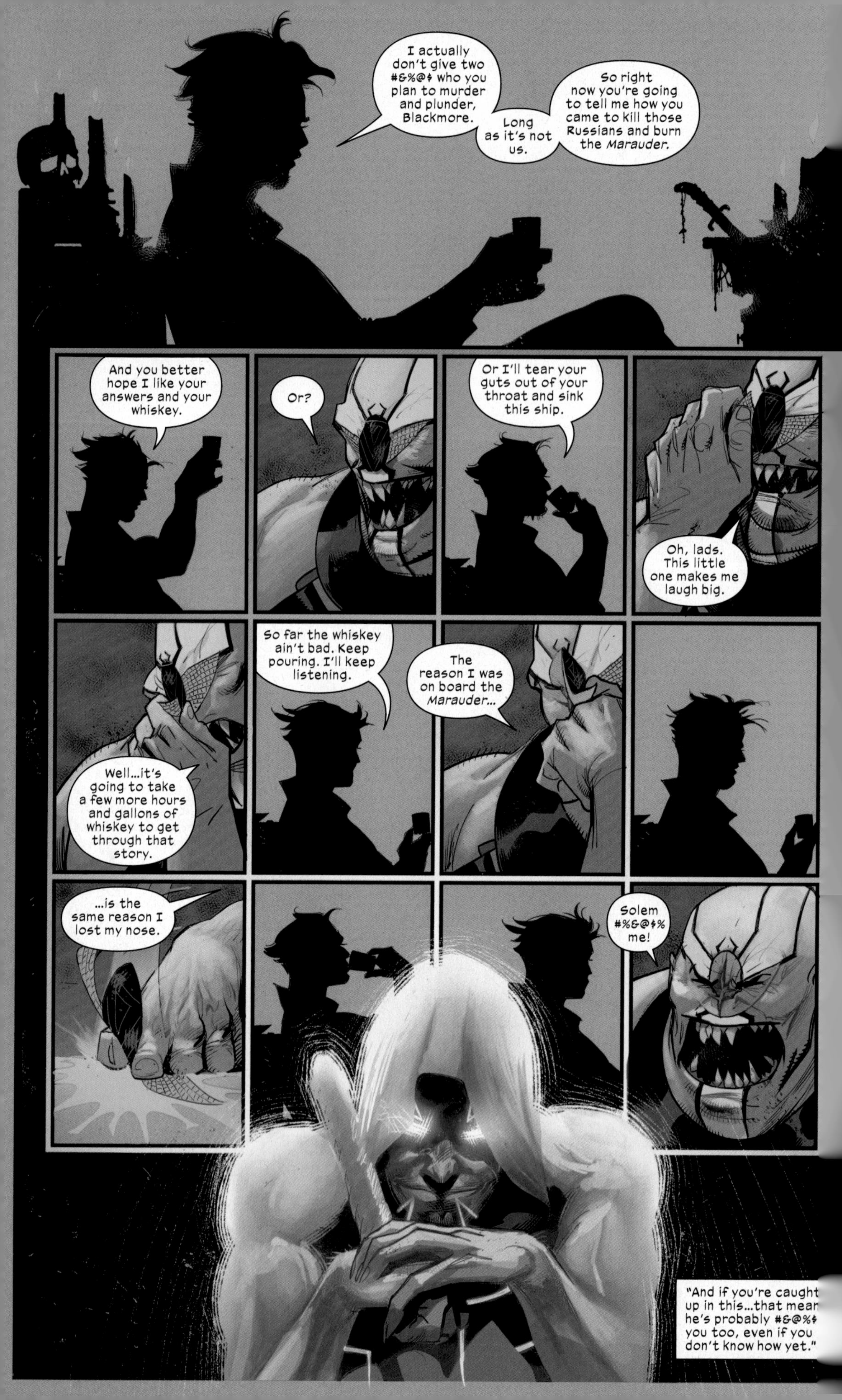
I actually don't give two #&%@$ who you plan to murder and plunder, Blackmore.
Long as it's not us.
So right now you're going to tell me how you came to kill those Russians and burn the *Marauder.*
And you better hope I like your answers and your whiskey.
Or?
Or I'll tear your guts out of your throat and sink this ship.
Oh, lads. This little one makes me laugh big.
Well...it's going to take a few more hours and gallons of whiskey to get through that story.
So far the whiskey ain't bad. Keep pouring. I'll keep listening.
The reason I was on board the *Marauder...*
...is the same reason I lost my nose.
Solem #%&@$% me!
"And if you're caught up in this...that mear he's probably #&@%$ you too, even if you don't know how yet."

[reign_of_x]

[best__]
[there_]

[is__]
[bub_]

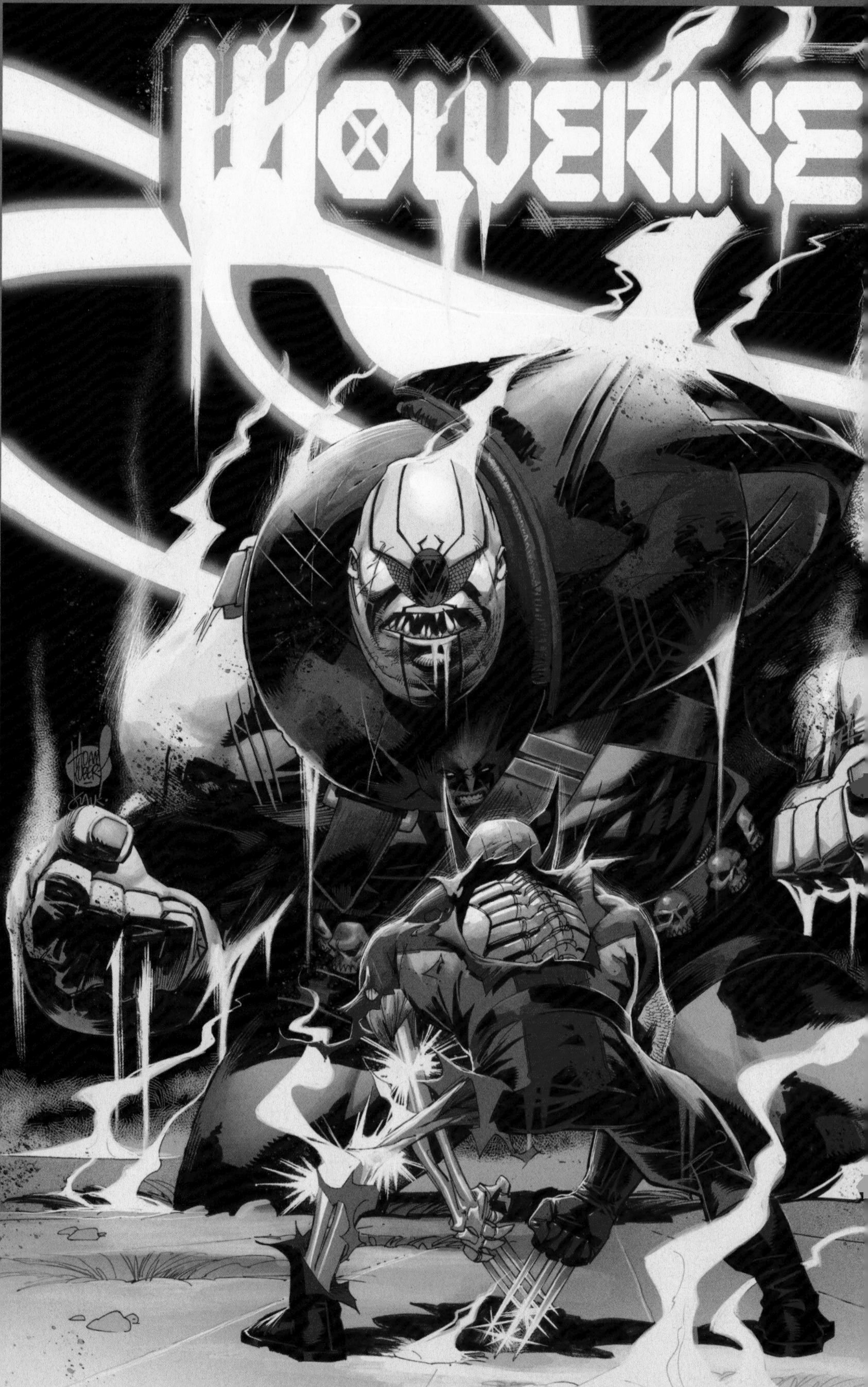
WOLVERINE

Deceiver

15

[reign_of_x]

[best__]
[there_]

[is__]
[bub_]

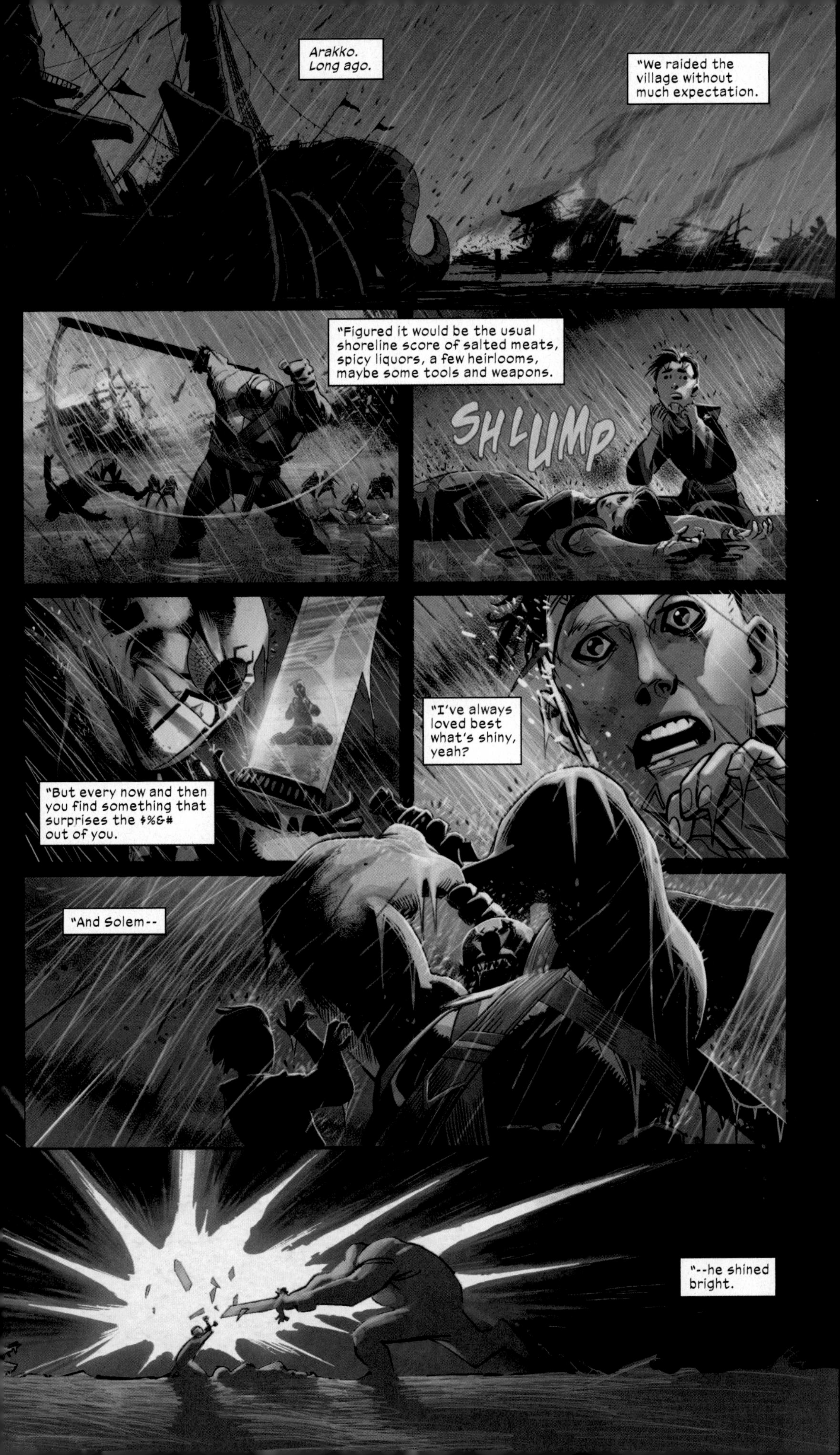

Arakko.
Long ago.
"We raided the village without much expectation.
"Figured it would be the usual shoreline score of salted meats, spicy liquors, a few heirlooms, maybe some tools and weapons.
SHLUMP
"I've always loved best what's shiny, yeah?
"But every now and then you find something that surprises the $%&# out of you.
"And Solem--
"--he shined bright.

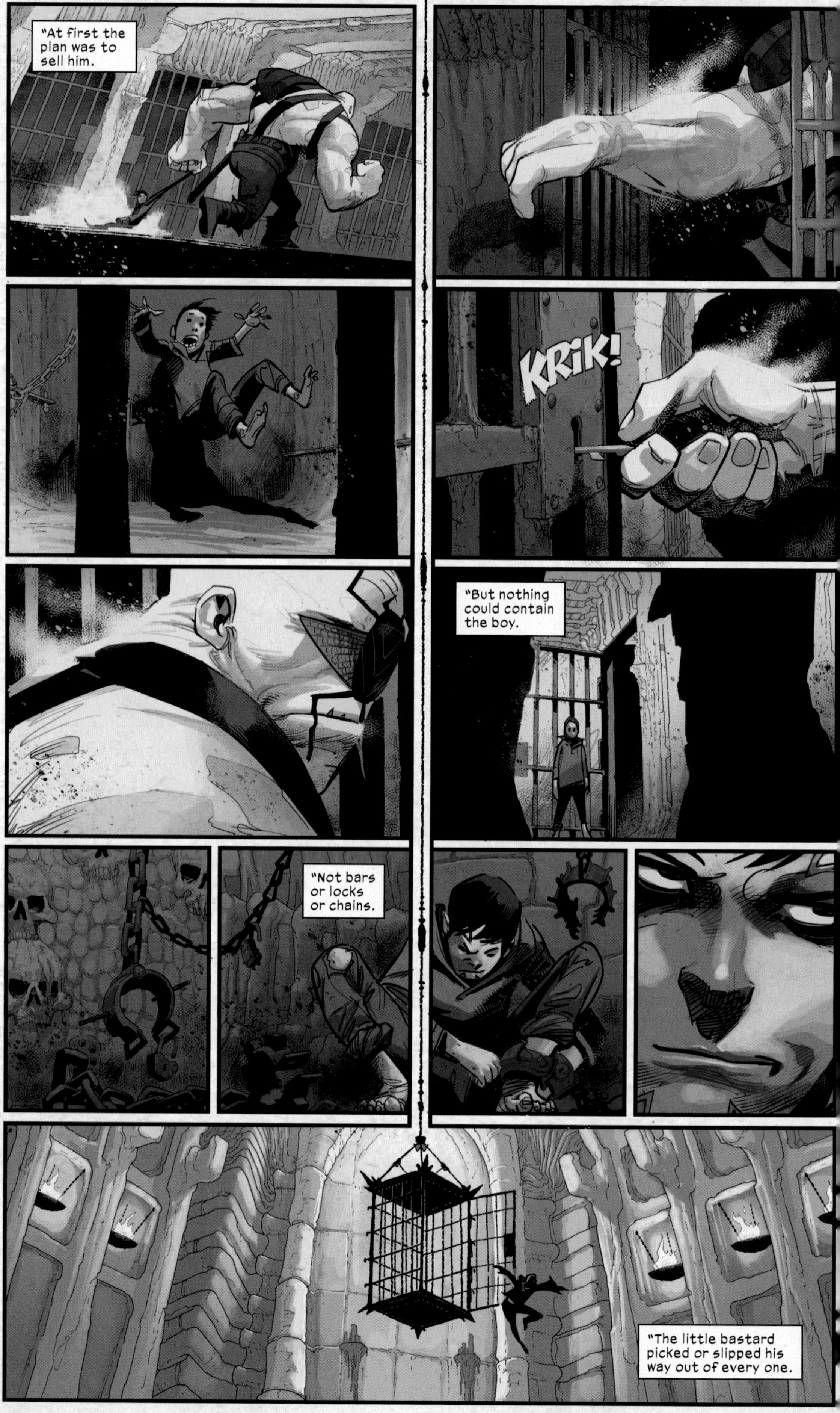
"At first the plan was to sell him.
KRIK!
"But nothing could contain the boy.
"Not bars or locks or chains.
"The little bastard picked or slipped his way out of every one.

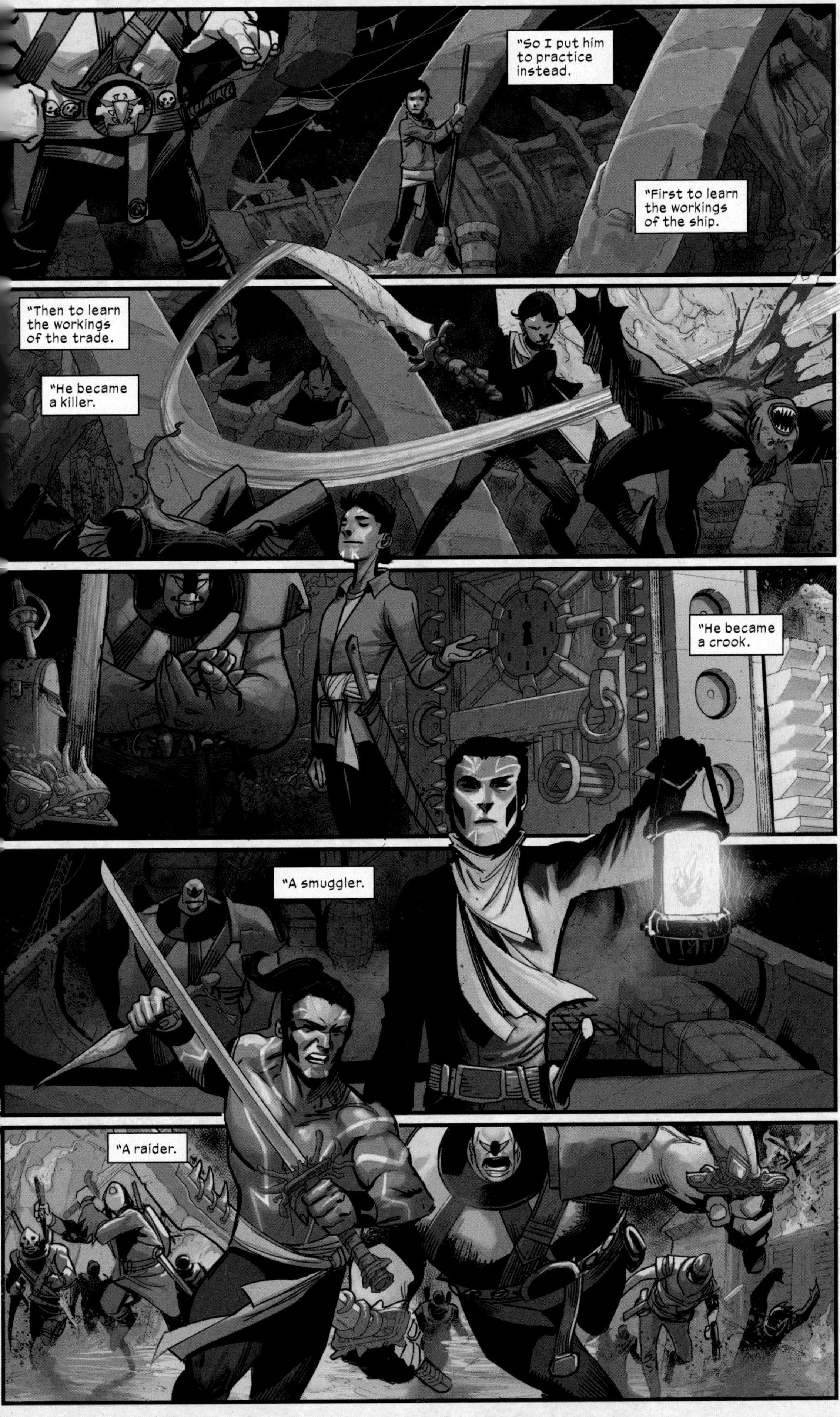
"So I put him to practice instead.
"First to learn the workings of the ship.
"Then to learn the workings of the trade.
"He became a killer.
"He became a crook.
"A smuggler.
"A raider.

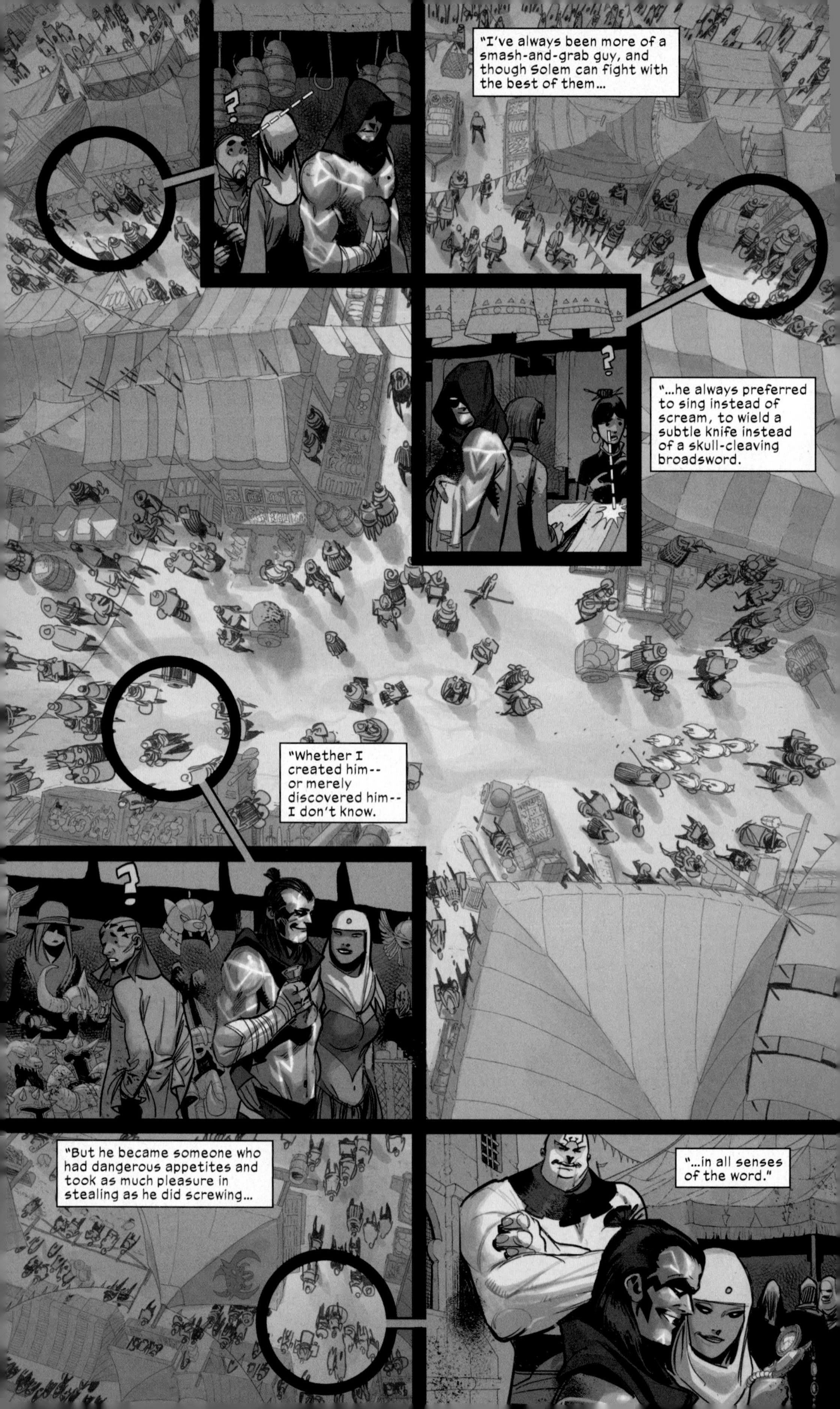
"I've always been more of a smash-and-grab guy, and though Solem can fight with the best of them...
?
?
"...he always preferred to sing instead of scream, to wield a subtle knife instead of a skull-cleaving broadsword.
"Whether I created him--or merely discovered him--I don't know.
?
"But he became someone who had dangerous appetites and took as much pleasure in stealing as he did screwing...
"...in all senses of the word."

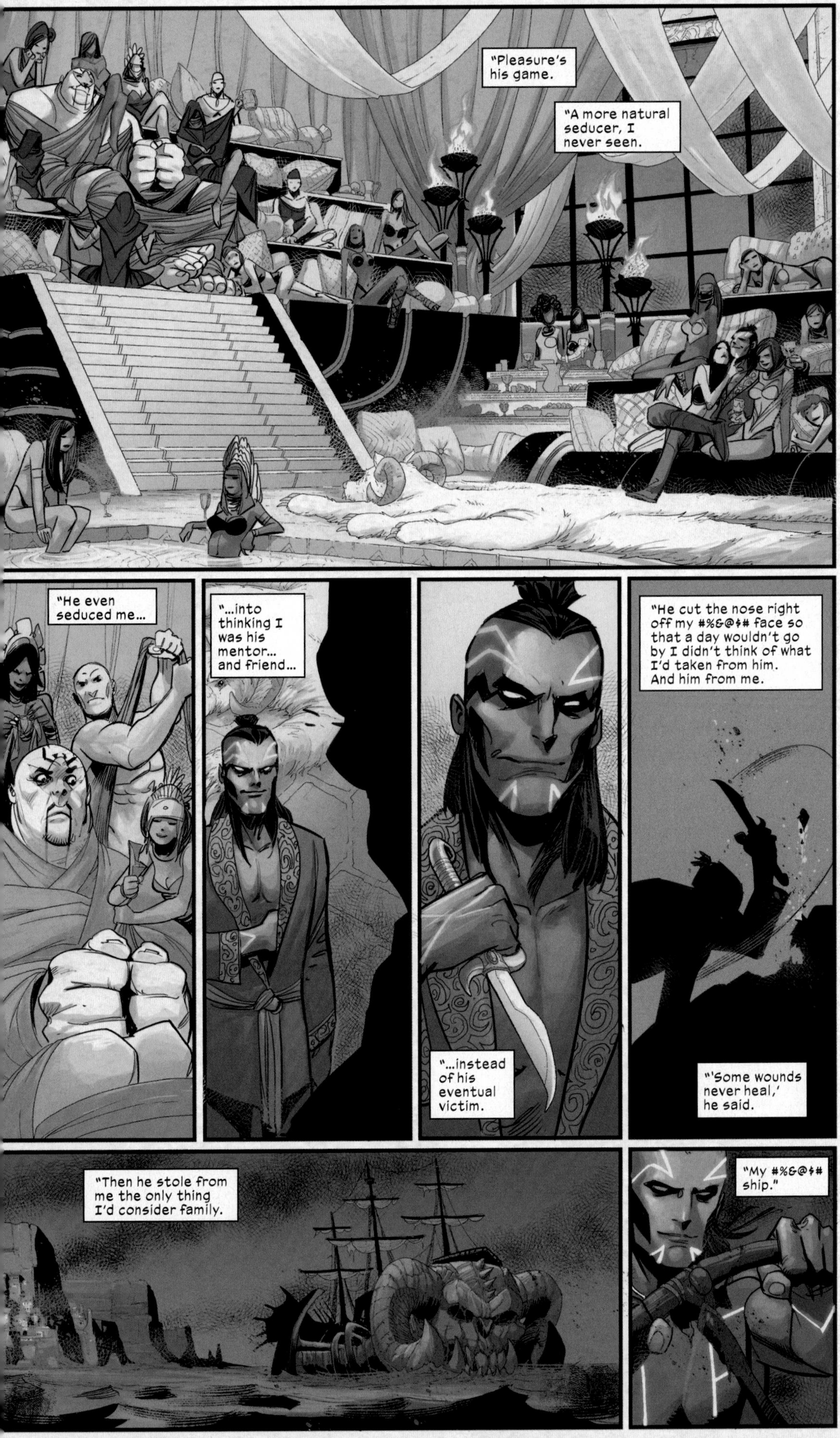
"Pleasure's his game.
"A more natural seducer, I never seen.
"He even seduced me...
"...into thinking I was his mentor... and friend...
"...instead of his eventual victim.
"He cut the nose right off my #%&@$# face so that a day wouldn't go by I didn't think of what I'd taken from him. And him from me.
"'Some wounds never heal,' he said.
"Then he stole from me the only thing I'd consider family.
"My #%&@$# ship."

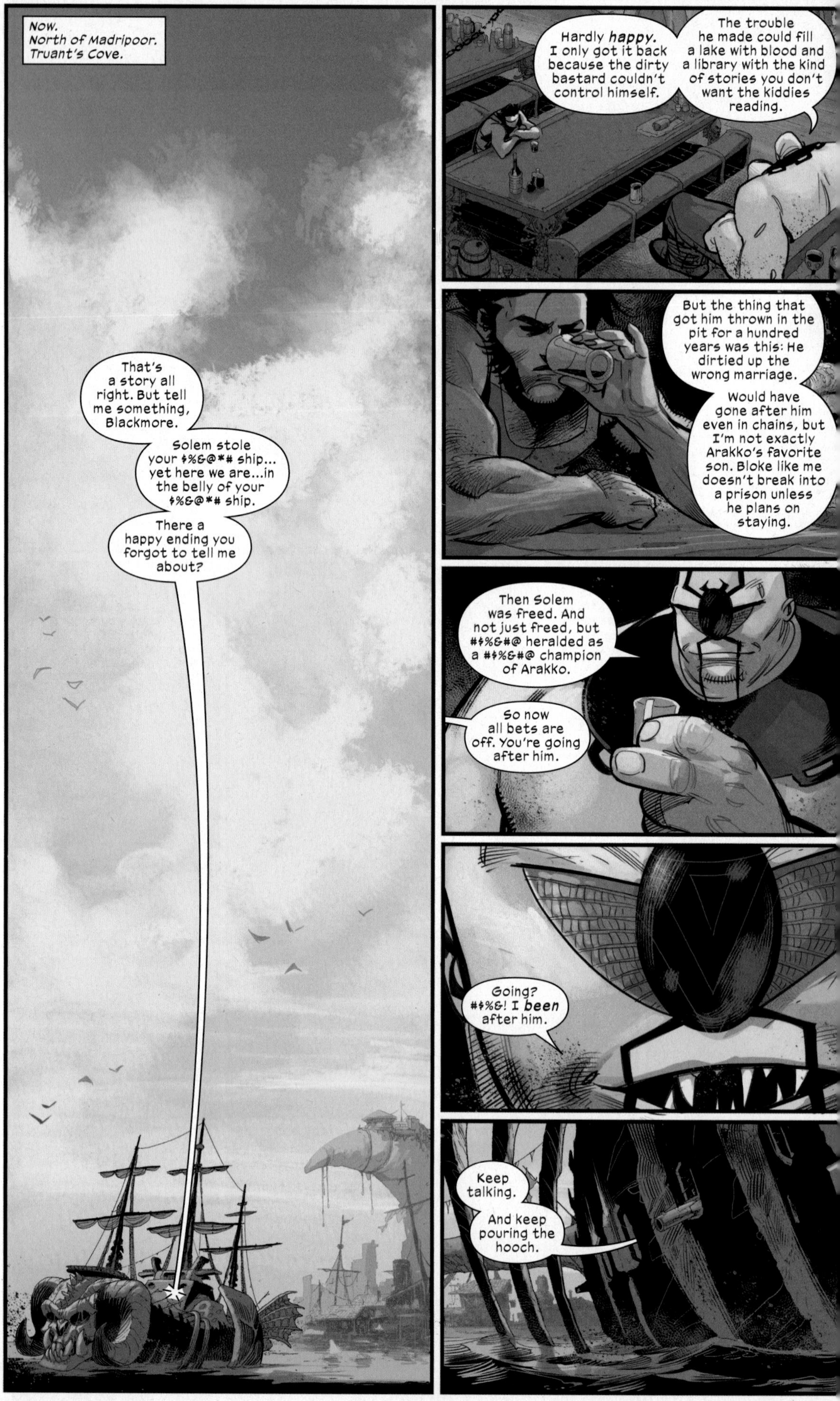
Now.
North of Madripoor.
Truant's Cove.
That's a story all right. But tell me something, Blackmore.
Solem stole your $%&@*# ship... yet here we are...in the belly of your $%&@*# ship.
There a happy ending you forgot to tell me about?
Hardly *happy.* I only got it back because the dirty bastard couldn't control himself.
The trouble he made could fill a lake with blood and a library with the kind of stories you don't want the kiddies reading.
But the thing that got him thrown in the pit for a hundred years was this: He dirtied up the wrong marriage.
Would have gone after him even in chains, but I'm not exactly Arakko's favorite son. Bloke like me doesn't break into a prison unless he plans on staying.
Then Solem was freed. And not just freed, but #$%&#@ heralded as a #$%&#@ champion of Arakko.
So now all bets are off. You're going after him.
Going? #$%&! I *been* after him.
Keep talking.
And keep pouring the hooch.

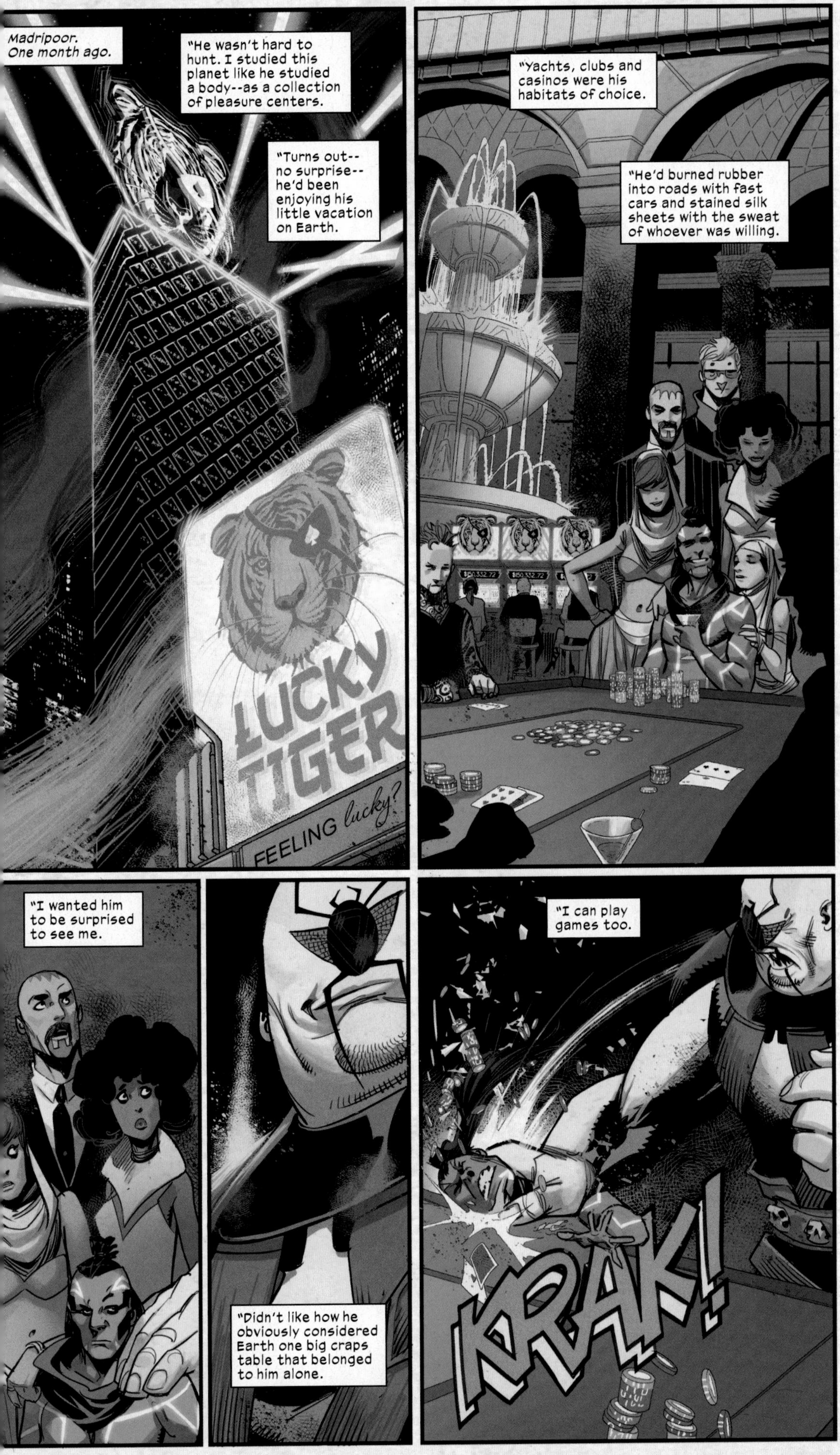

Madripoor. One month ago.
"He wasn't hard to hunt. I studied this planet like he studied a body--as a collection of pleasure centers.
"Turns out--no surprise--he'd been enjoying his little vacation on Earth.
LUCKY TIGER
FEELING lucky?
"Yachts, clubs and casinos were his habitats of choice.
"He'd burned rubber into roads with fast cars and stained silk sheets with the sweat of whoever was willing.
"I wanted him to be surprised to see me.
"Didn't like how he obviously considered Earth one big craps table that belonged to him alone.
"I can play games too.
KRAK!

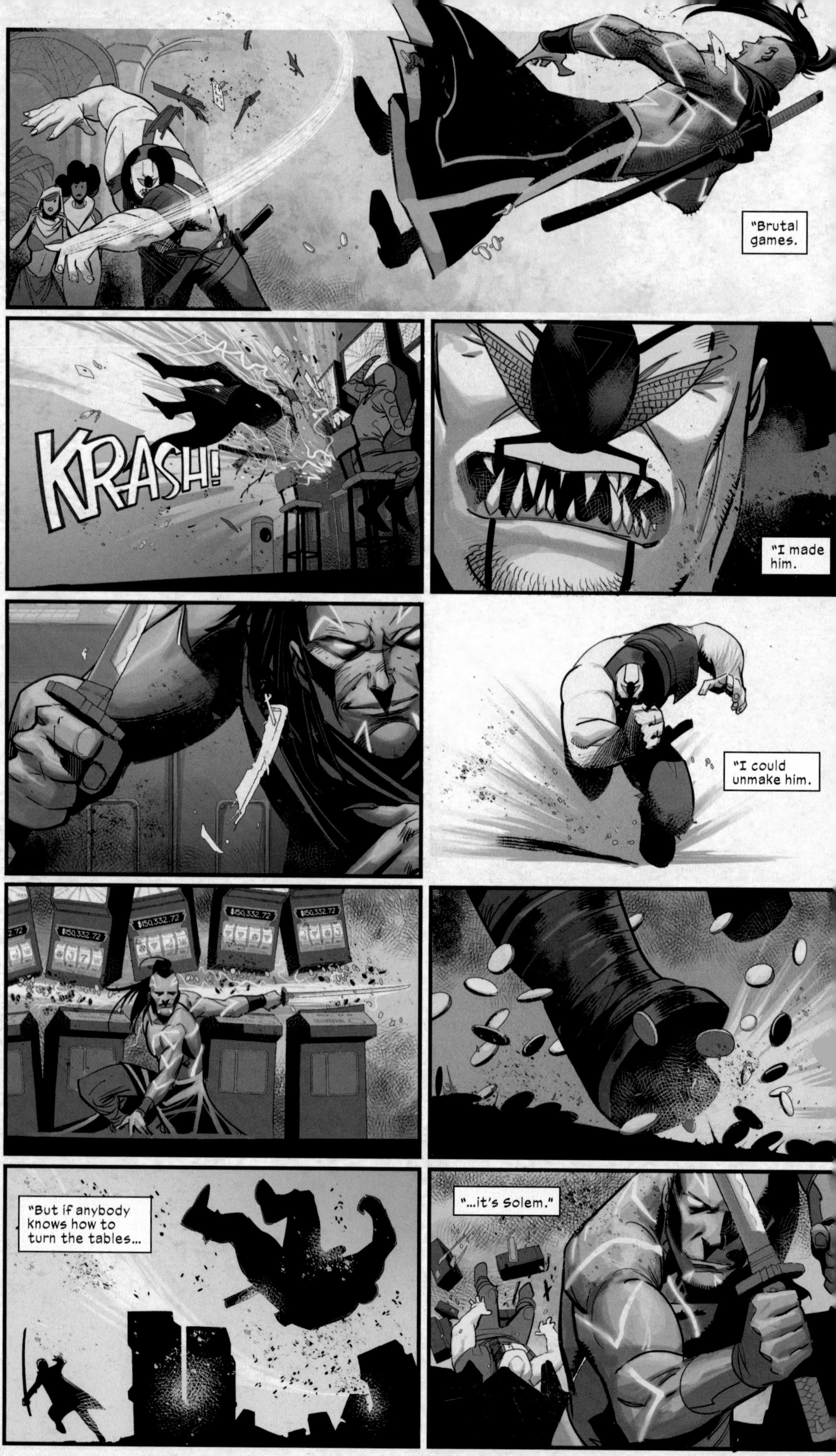
"Brutal games.
KRASH!
"I made him.
"I could unmake him.
$150,332.72
$150,332.72
$150,332.72
$150,332.72
"But if anybody knows how to turn the tables...
"...it's Solem."

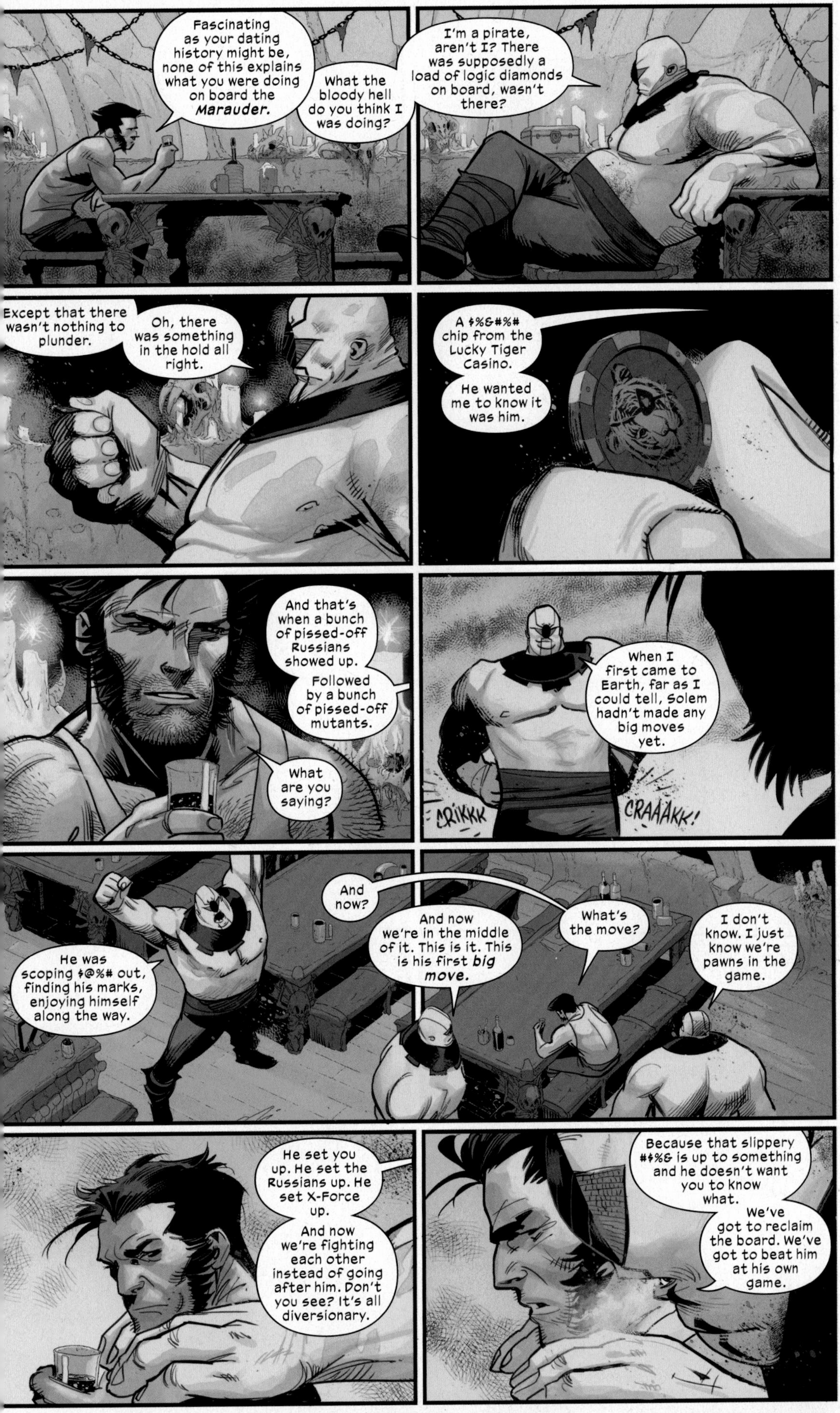

Fascinating as your dating history might be, none of this explains what you were doing on board the *Marauder.*
What the bloody hell do you think I was doing?
I'm a pirate, aren't I? There was supposedly a load of logic diamonds on board, wasn't there?
Except that there wasn't nothing to plunder.
Oh, there was something in the hold all right.
A $%&#%# chip from the Lucky Tiger Casino.
He wanted me to know it was him.
And that's when a bunch of pissed-off Russians showed up.
Followed by a bunch of pissed-off mutants.
What are you saying?
When I first came to Earth, far as I could tell, Solem hadn't made any big moves yet.
CRIKKK
CRAAAKK!
He was scoping $@%# out, finding his marks, enjoying himself along the way.
And now?
And now we're in the middle of it. This is it. This is his first *big move.*
What's the move?
I don't know. I just know we're pawns in the game.
He set you up. He set the Russians up. He set X-Force up.
And now we're fighting each other instead of going after him. Don't you see? It's all diversionary.
Because that slippery ##%& is up to something and he doesn't want you to know what.
We've got to reclaim the board. We've got to beat him at his own game.

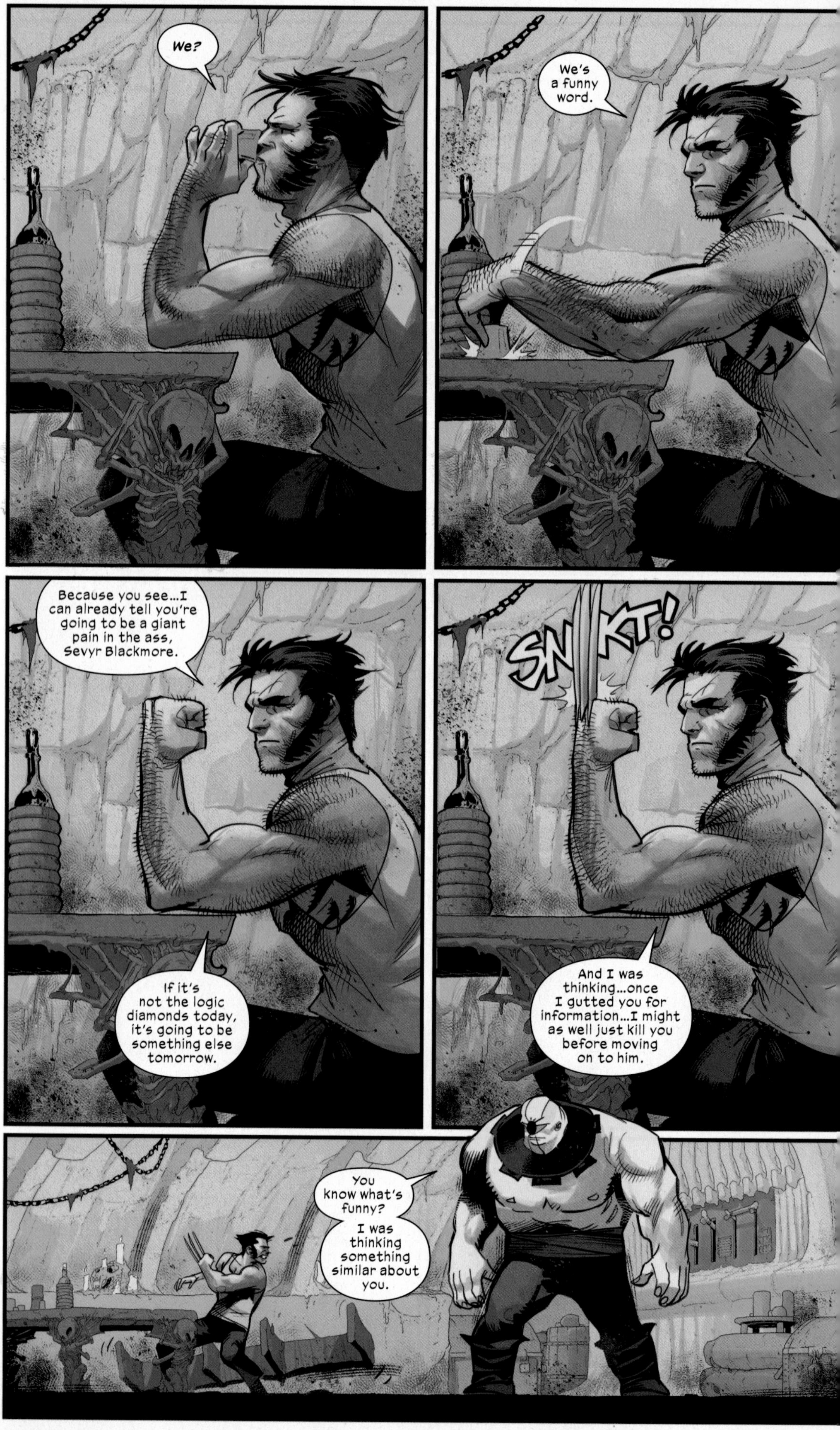
We?
We's a funny word.
Because you see...I can already tell you're going to be a giant pain in the ass, Sevyr Blackmore.
If it's not the logic diamonds today, it's going to be something else tomorrow.
SNIKT!
And I was thinking...once I gutted you for information...I might as well just kill you before moving on to him.
You know what's funny?
I was thinking something similar about you.

I made some modifications to the ship when I got it back.

To protect me from Solem.

K-CHNK

The hell?

Magnetic flooring.

You two couldn't be more different, could you? But you're made of the same stuff.

KRAK-CHOMP

And do you know what stuff I'm made of?

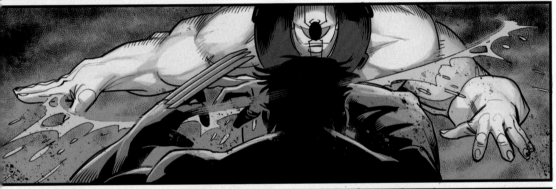

TSSSSS

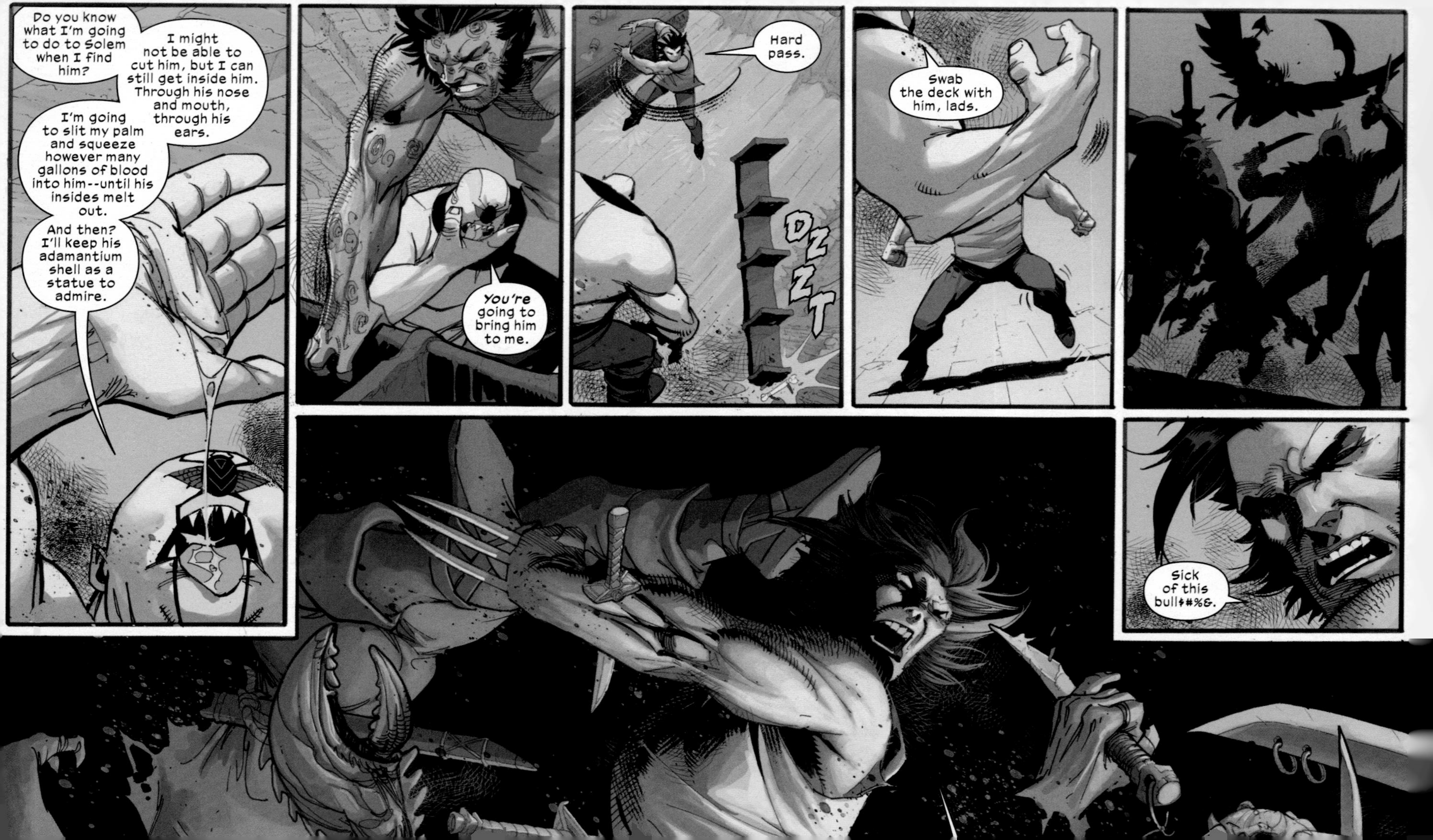
Do you know what I'm going to do to Solem when I find him?
I might not be able to cut him, but I can still get inside him. Through his nose and mouth, through his ears.
I'm going to slit my palm and squeeze however many gallons of blood into him--until his insides melt out.
And then? I'll keep his adamantium shell as a statue to admire.
You're going to bring him to me.
Hard pass.
DZZT
Swab the deck with him, lads.
Sick of this bull$#%&.

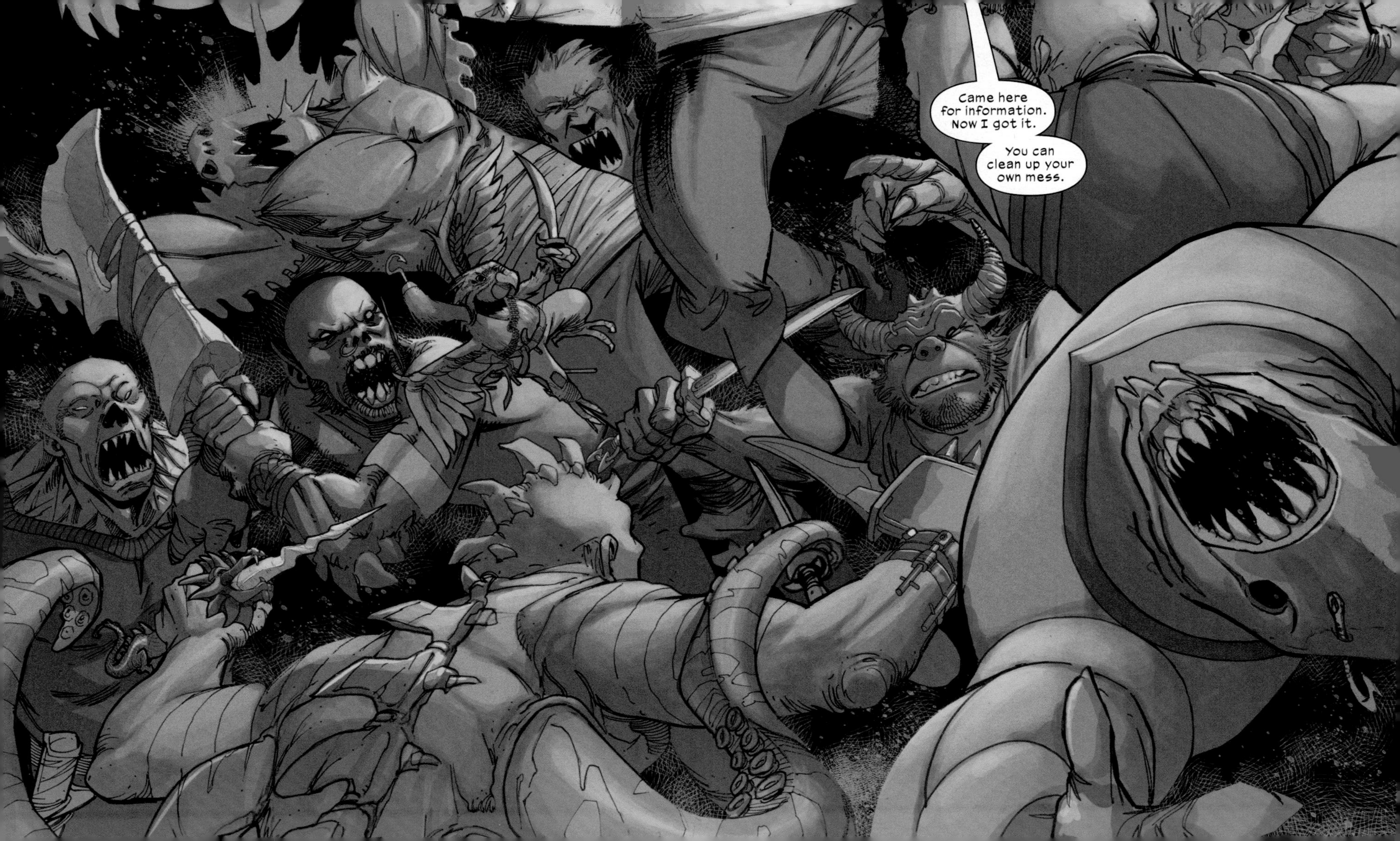
Came here for information. Now I got it.
You can clean up your own mess.

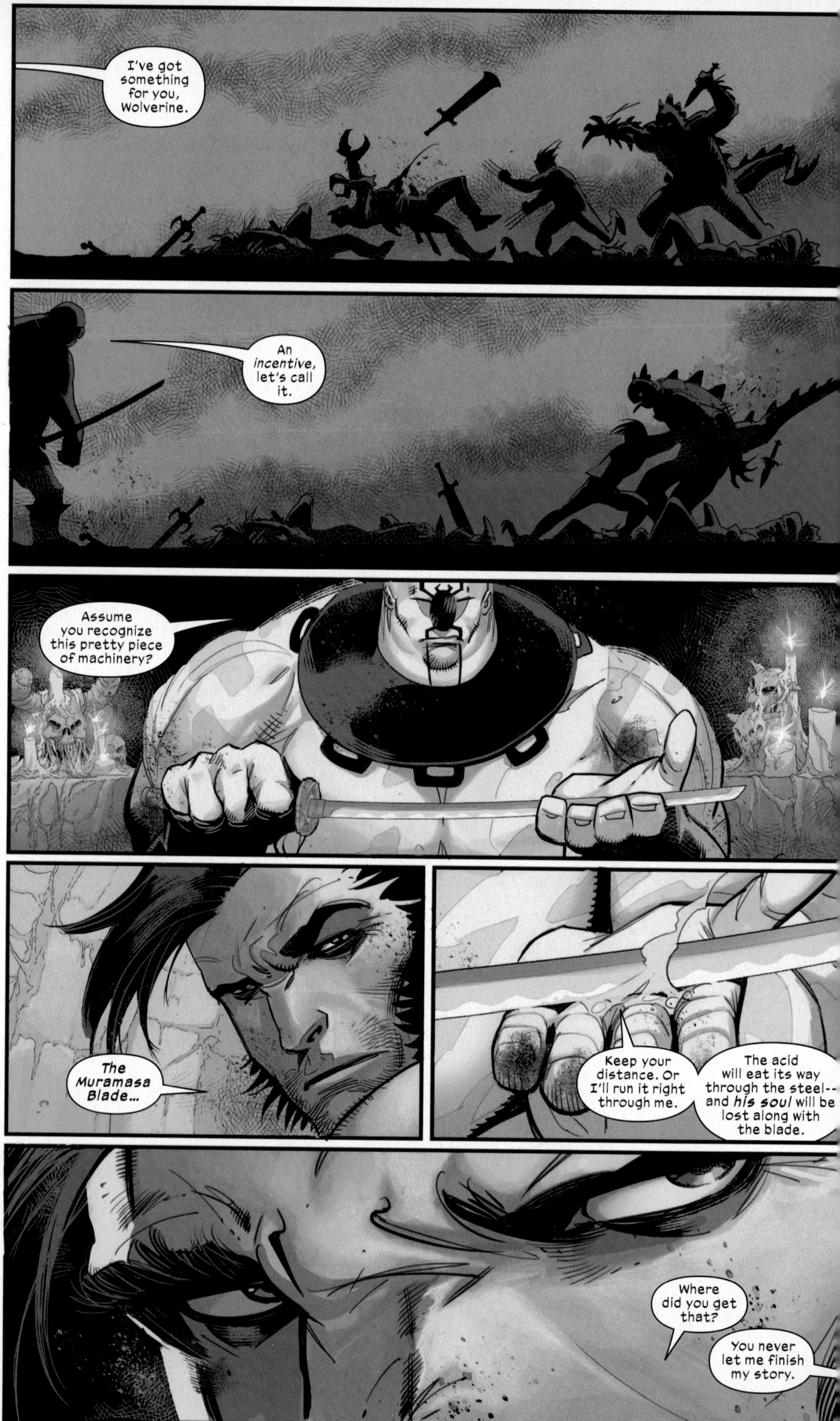
I've got something for you, Wolverine.
An *incentive,* let's call it.
Assume you recognize this pretty piece of machinery?
The Muramasa Blade...
Keep your distance. Or I'll run it right through me.
The acid will eat its way through the steel-- and ***his soul*** will be lost along with the blade.
Where did you get that?
You never let me finish my story.

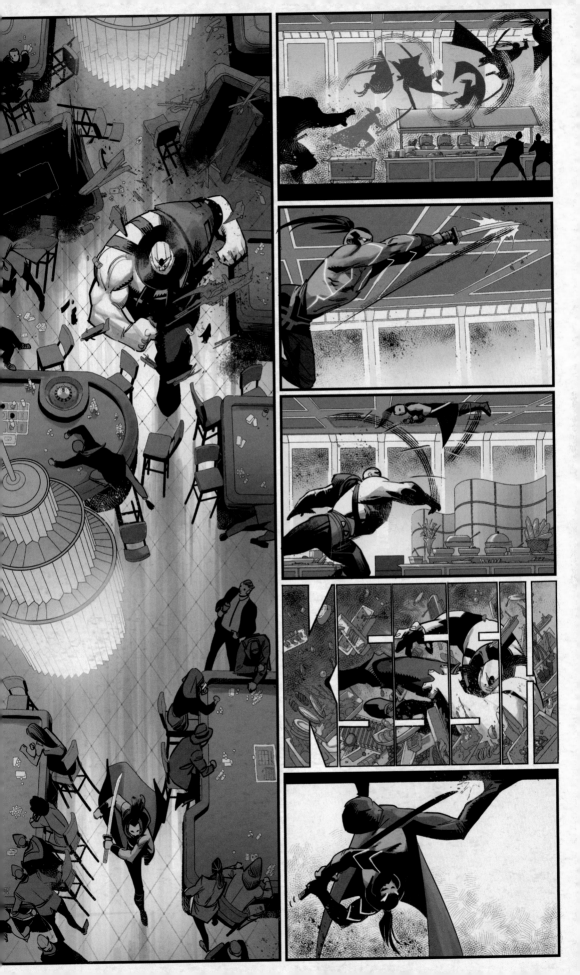

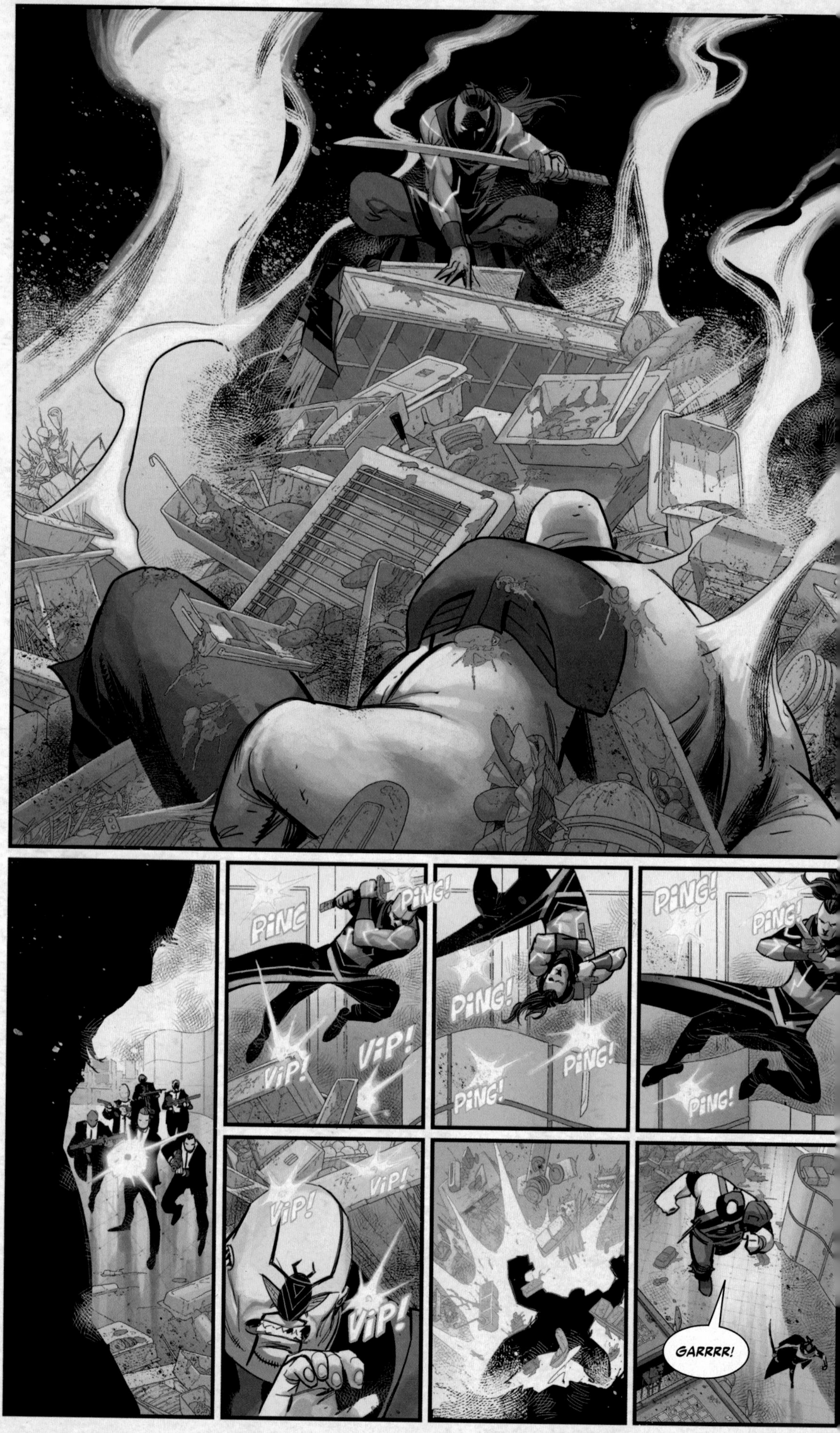
PING
PING!
VIP!
VIP!
PING!
PING!
PING!
PING!
PING!
PING!
VIP!
VIP!
VIP!
GARRRR!

"The thing about Solem is...

"...he'd rather slip like water through your fingers than take a punch.

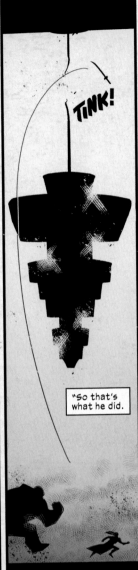

TiNK!

"So that's what he did.

KRINSH

"He might have gotten away..."

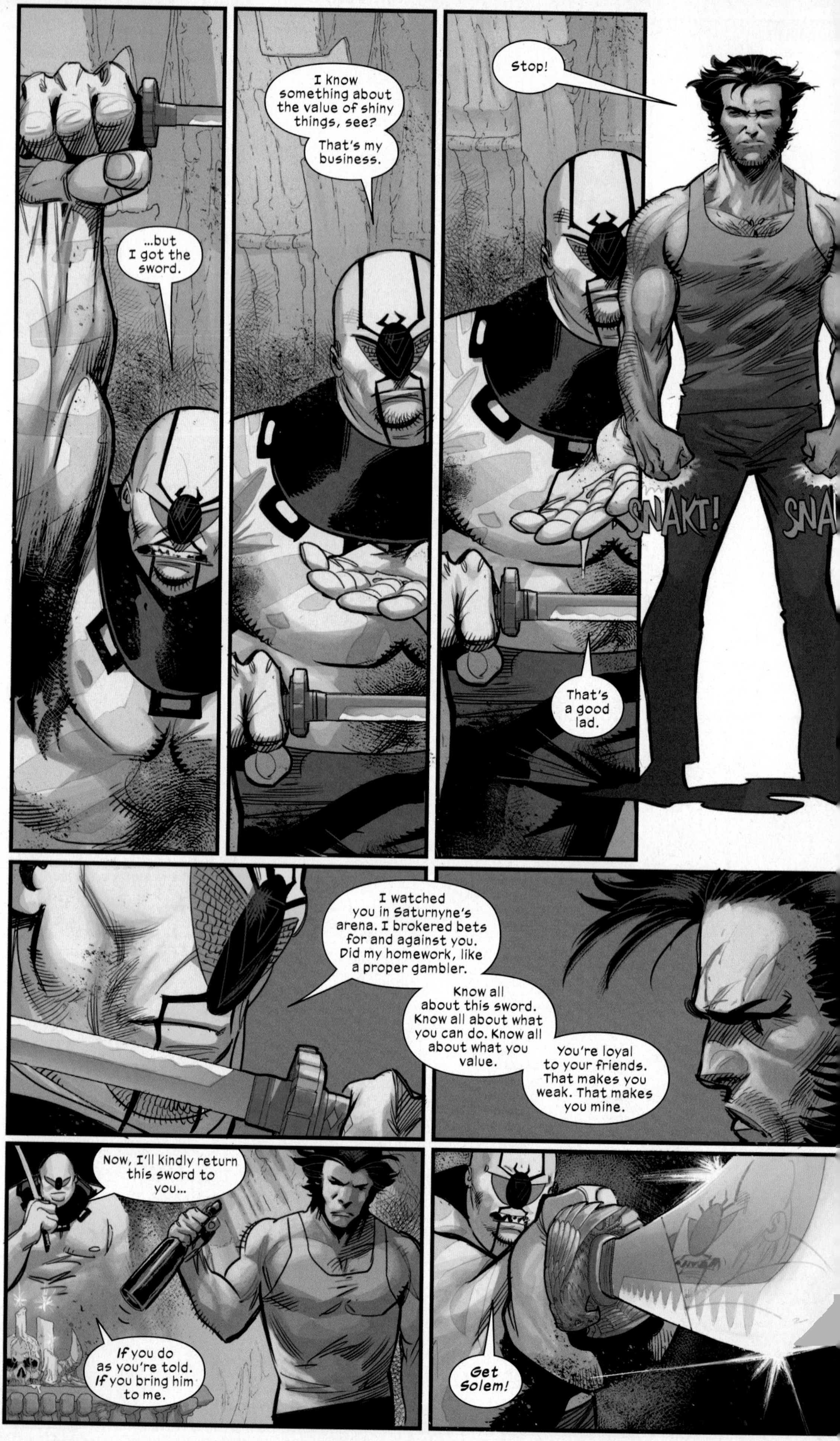
...but I got the sword.
I know something about the value of shiny things, see?
That's my business.
Stop!
SNAKT!
SNA
That's a good lad.
I watched you in Saturnyne's arena. I brokered bets for and against you. Did my homework, like a proper gambler.
Know all about this sword. Know all about what you can do. Know all about what you value.
You're loyal to your friends. That makes you weak. That makes you mine.
Now, I'll kindly return this sword to you...
If you do as you're told. *If* you bring him to me.
Get Solem!

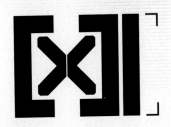

SAGE'S LOGBOOK: SOLEM CASE FILE

Suspected transgressions
Page 344 of 10,128

<data culled from Arakko>
::primary sources::

—>scrolls currently scanned and archived by X-Force
—>ciphers etched on cave walls
—>oral storytelling divined from songs and
wandering chroniclers

/A figure identified as S. was burned at the stake after stealing the sacred pearls from the Temple of the Mariner in the port town of Karna Blu, but after the flames melted his restraints, S. stepped out of the inferno with his skin glowing silver and slit the necks of his prosecutors/

/Solem is named as secondarily responsible for the death of a tribal judge. He allegedly had congress with the wife, son and daughter of Emil Raver and somehow convinced them to kill their patriarch in his sleep/

/A bay named Solem is notable for its shipwrecks and unpredictable currents/

/In one season, all the child-bearers of Dorn -- male and female -- became pregnant and gave birth to silver-skinned children/

/The Seven Holds -- the most elaborate labyrinth vault in Arakko -- was allegedly breached by Solem, who stole only one thing from its vast riches: a thousand-year-old bottle of wine that fermented its grapes in the blood of the Mad Queen Vesper/

<data culled from Earth>
::primary sources::

—> facial recognition algorithms
—>police reports
—> cellular data scans
—>social media scans

/Solem has been banned from every casino in Nevada and New Jersey/
/Solem has been banned from six dating apps/
/Solem is suspected of stealing no fewer than thirty luxury sports cars worth an estimated 20 million U.S. dollars/
/Solem ordered champagne for every table in the exclusive Cloud Lounge and then walked out on the tab/
/Several nude paintings of Solem were discovered inside the Palace of Versailles and a mural of him inside the Louvre/
/Solem was photographed inside the skybox of ███████ at the Super Bowl/
/The Crown Jewels disappeared for twelve hours from the Tower of London, after which time they were returned in a brown paper bag that read, "Now THAT was a fun night."/

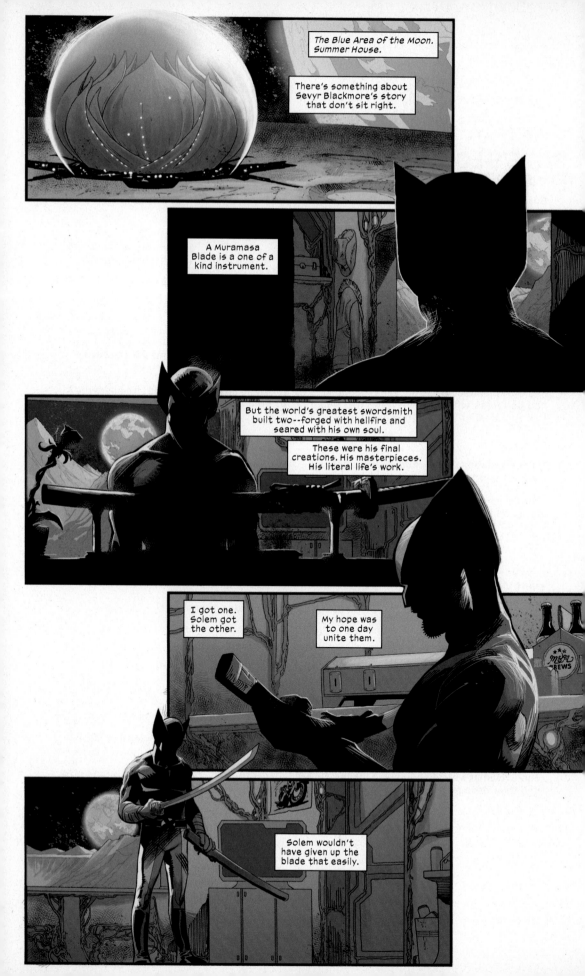

*The Blue Area of the Moon.
Summer House.*

There's something about Sevyr Blackmore's story that don't sit right.

A Muramasa Blade is a one of a kind instrument.

But the world's greatest swordsmith built two--forged with hellfire and seared with his own soul.

These were his final creations. His masterpieces. His literal life's work.

I got one. Solem got the other.

My hope was to one day unite them.

Solem wouldn't have given up the blade that easily.

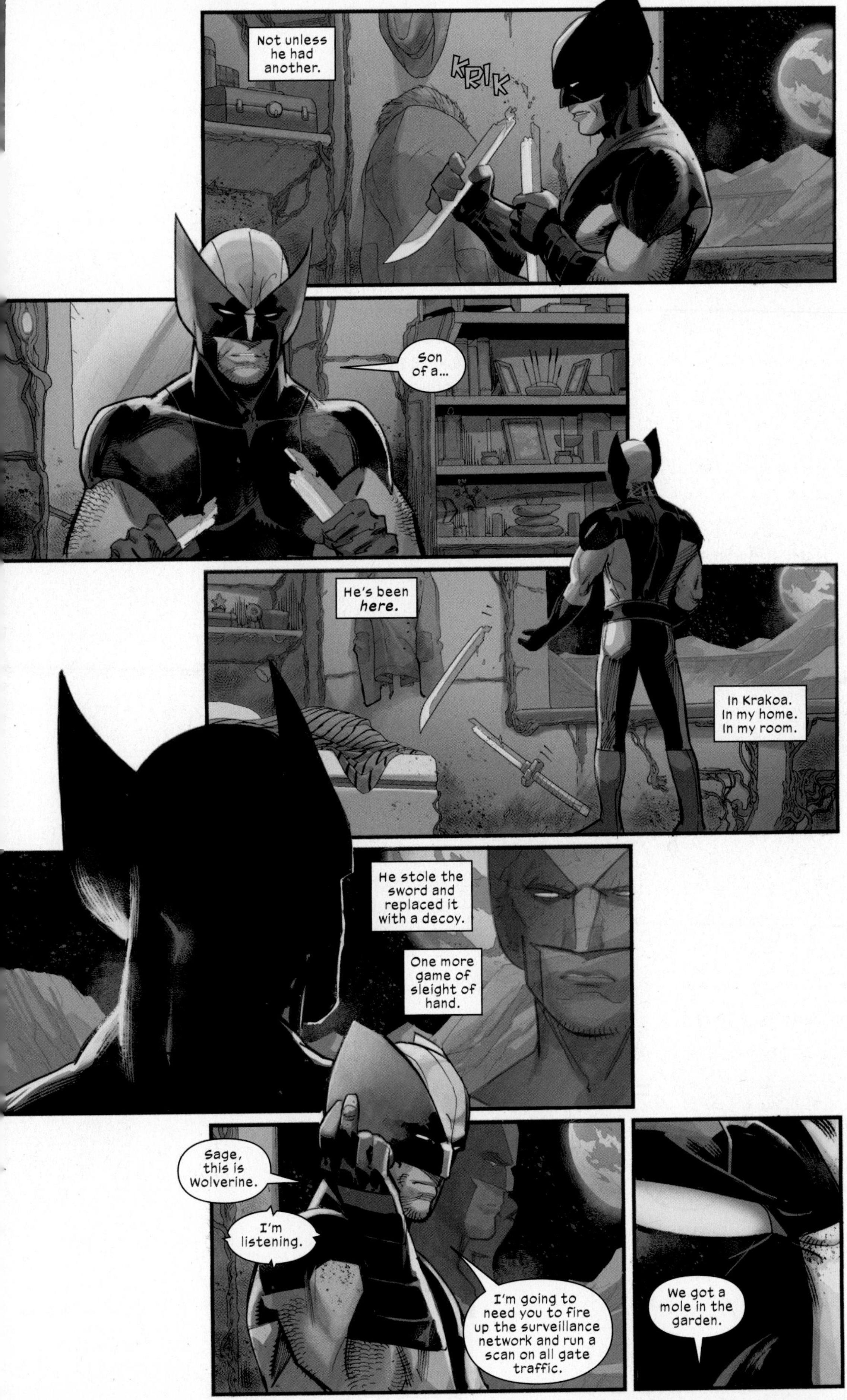
Not unless he had another.
KRIK
Son of a...
He's been *here.*
In Krakoa. In my home. In my room.
He stole the sword and replaced it with a decoy.
One more game of sleight of hand.
Sage, this is Wolverine.
I'm listening.
I'm going to need you to fire up the surveillance network and run a scan on all gate traffic.
We got a mole in the garden.

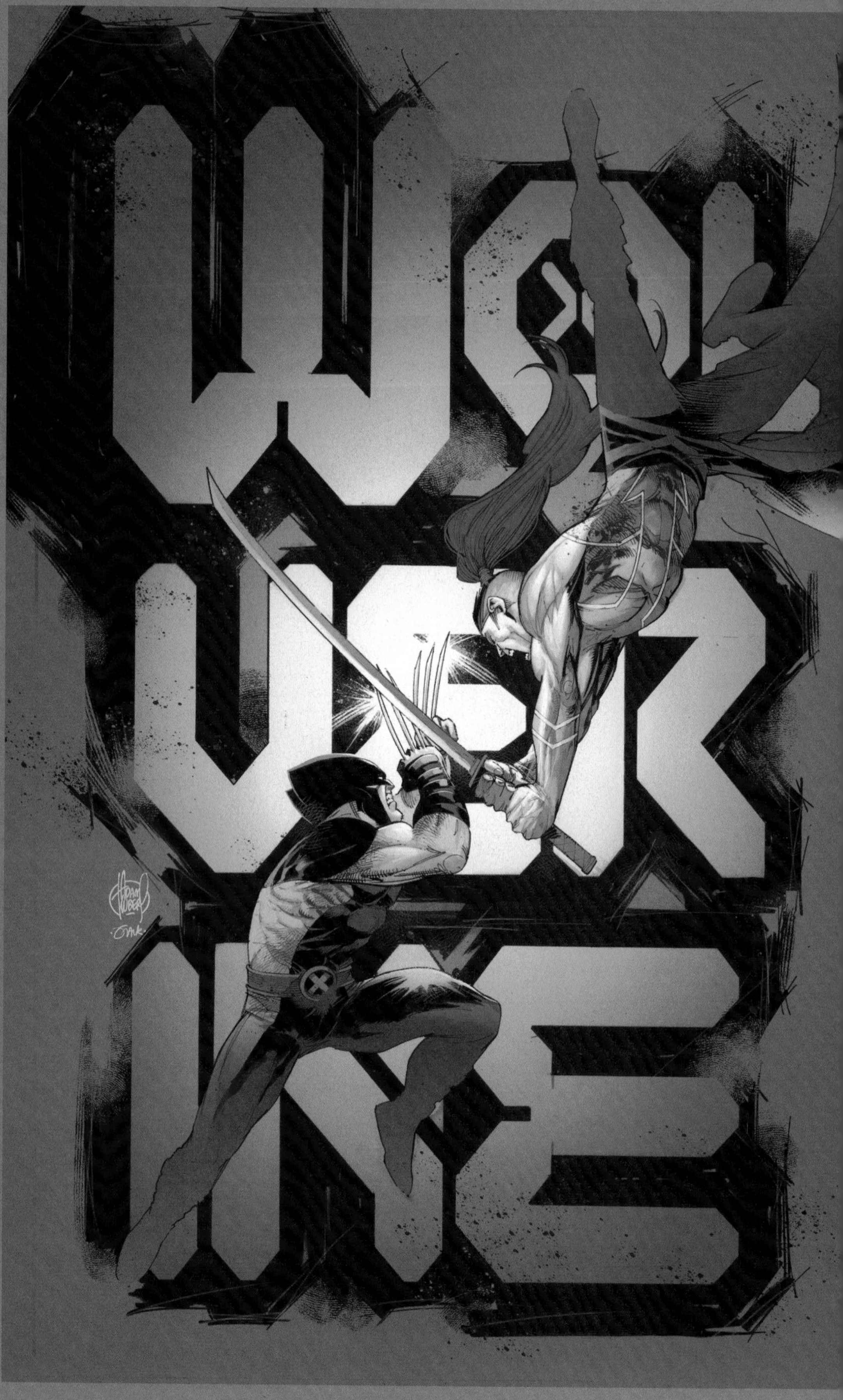

Ill-Gotten Gains

16

[reign_of_x]

[best__]
[there_]

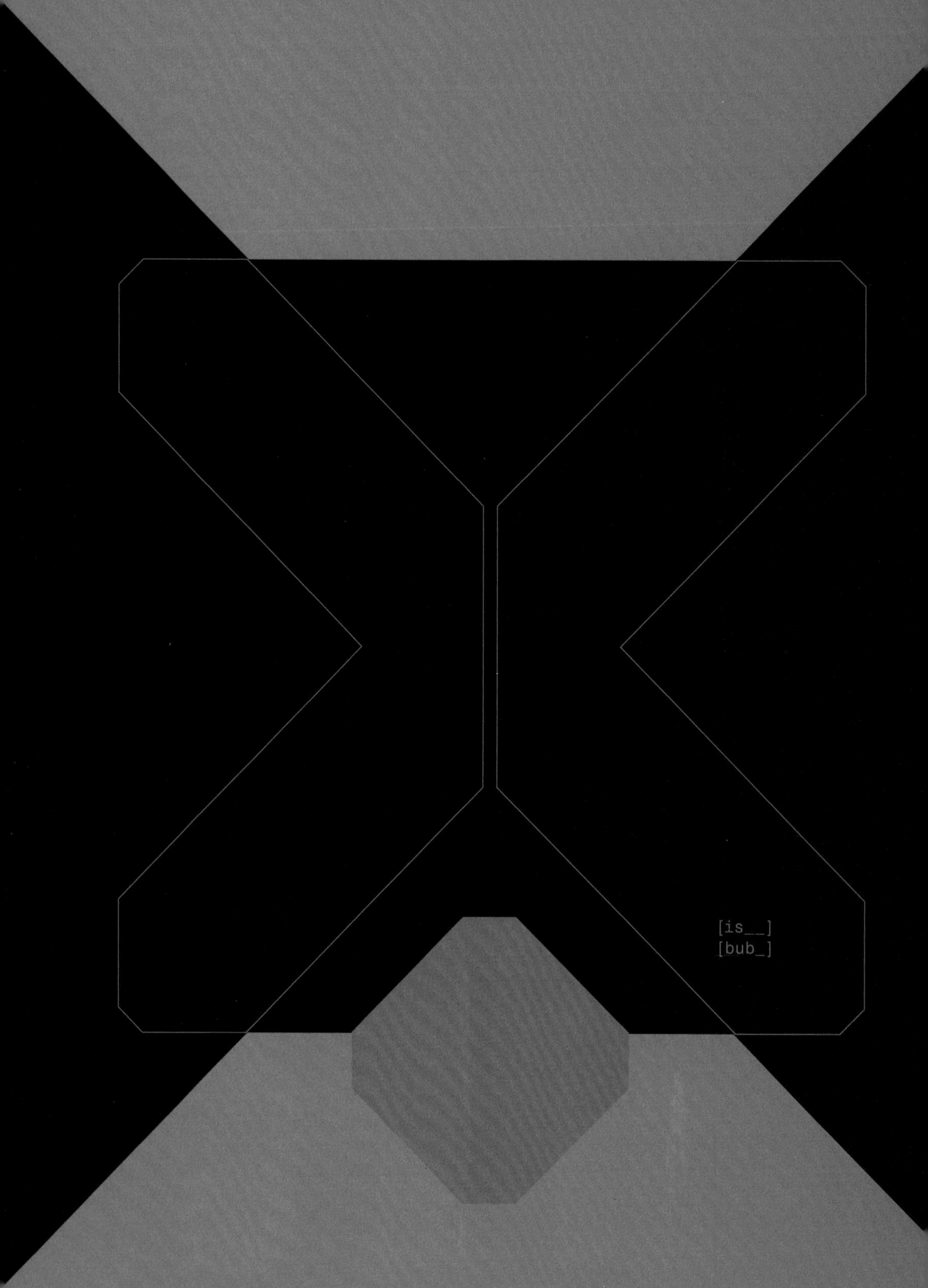
[is__]
[bub_]

The Green Lagoon.
Krakoa.

Everywhere I look--everyone I talk to--knots up the story further.

Maybe Solem's a victim or maybe he's a predator.

Maybe he's a mischievous little ‡&@# or maybe he's a sick bastard who enjoys causing other people pain.

Maybe he's just stupidly lucky or maybe...

...he's a mastermind.

Mind if I join you?

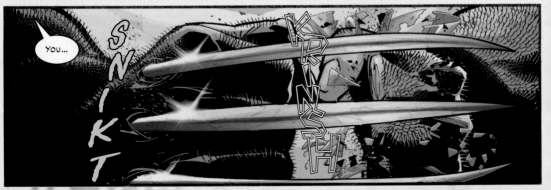

You...

SNIKT

KRINSH

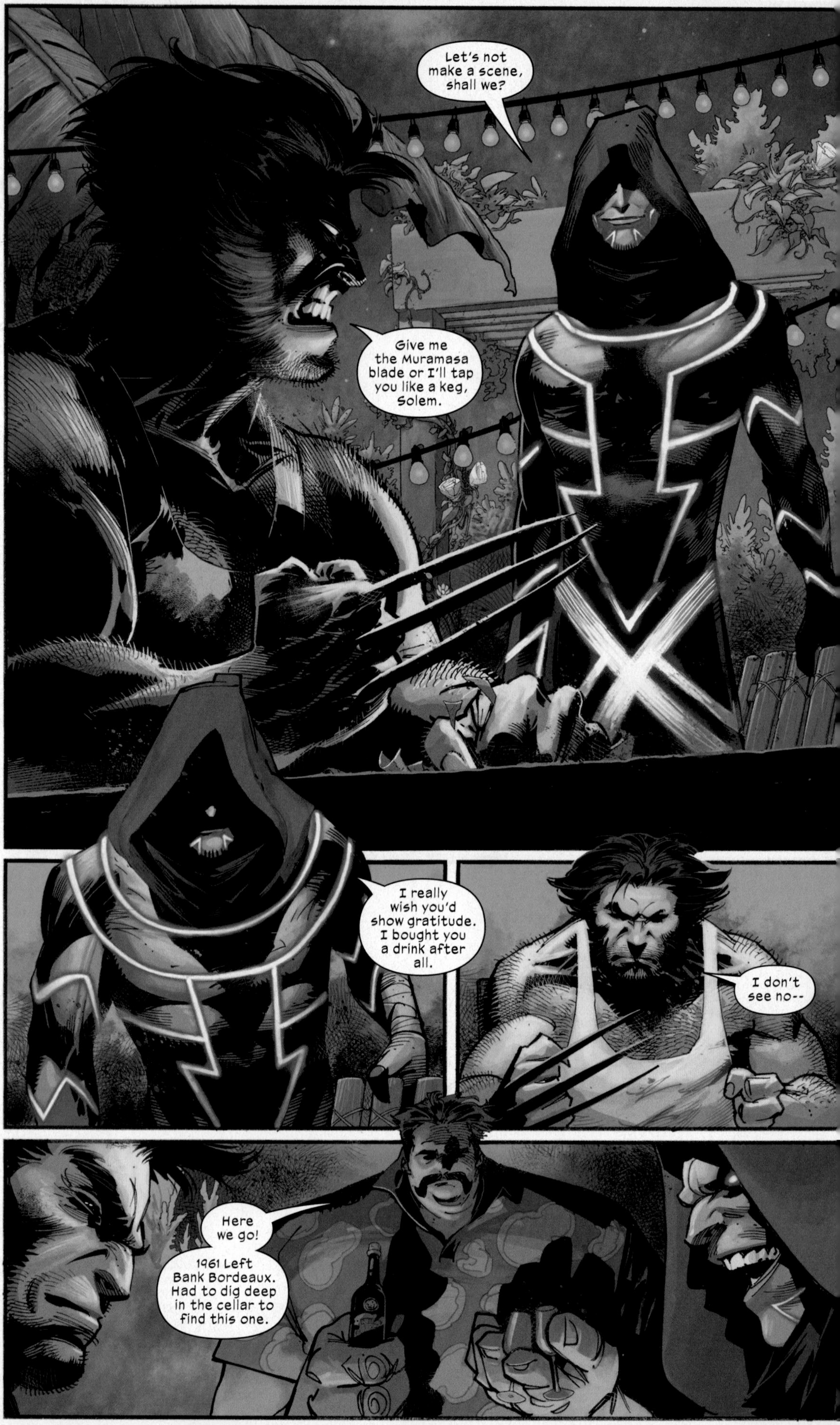
Let's not make a scene, shall we?
Give me the Muramasa blade or I'll tap you like a keg, Solem.
I really wish you'd show gratitude. I bought you a drink after all.
I don't see no--
Here we go!
1961 Left Bank Bordeaux. Had to dig deep in the cellar to find this one.

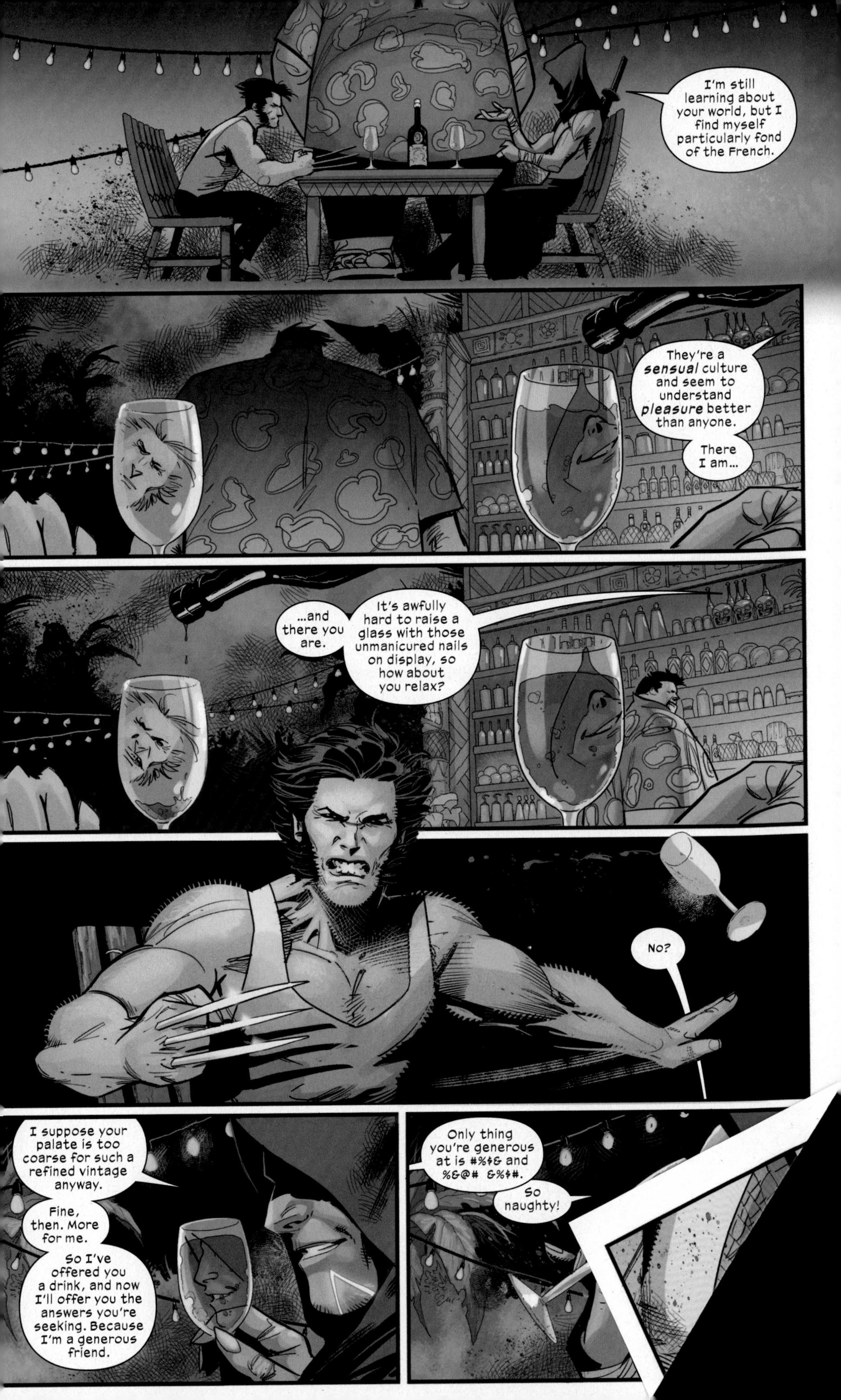
I'm still learning about your world, but I find myself particularly fond of the French.
They're a sensual culture and seem to understand pleasure better than anyone.
There I am...
...and there you are.
It's awfully hard to raise a glass with those unmanicured nails on display, so how about you relax?
No?
I suppose your palate is too coarse for such a refined vintage anyway.
Fine, then. More for me.
So I've offered you a drink, and now I'll offer you the answers you're seeking. Because I'm a generous friend.
Only thing you're generous at is #%$& and %&@# &%$#.
So naughty!

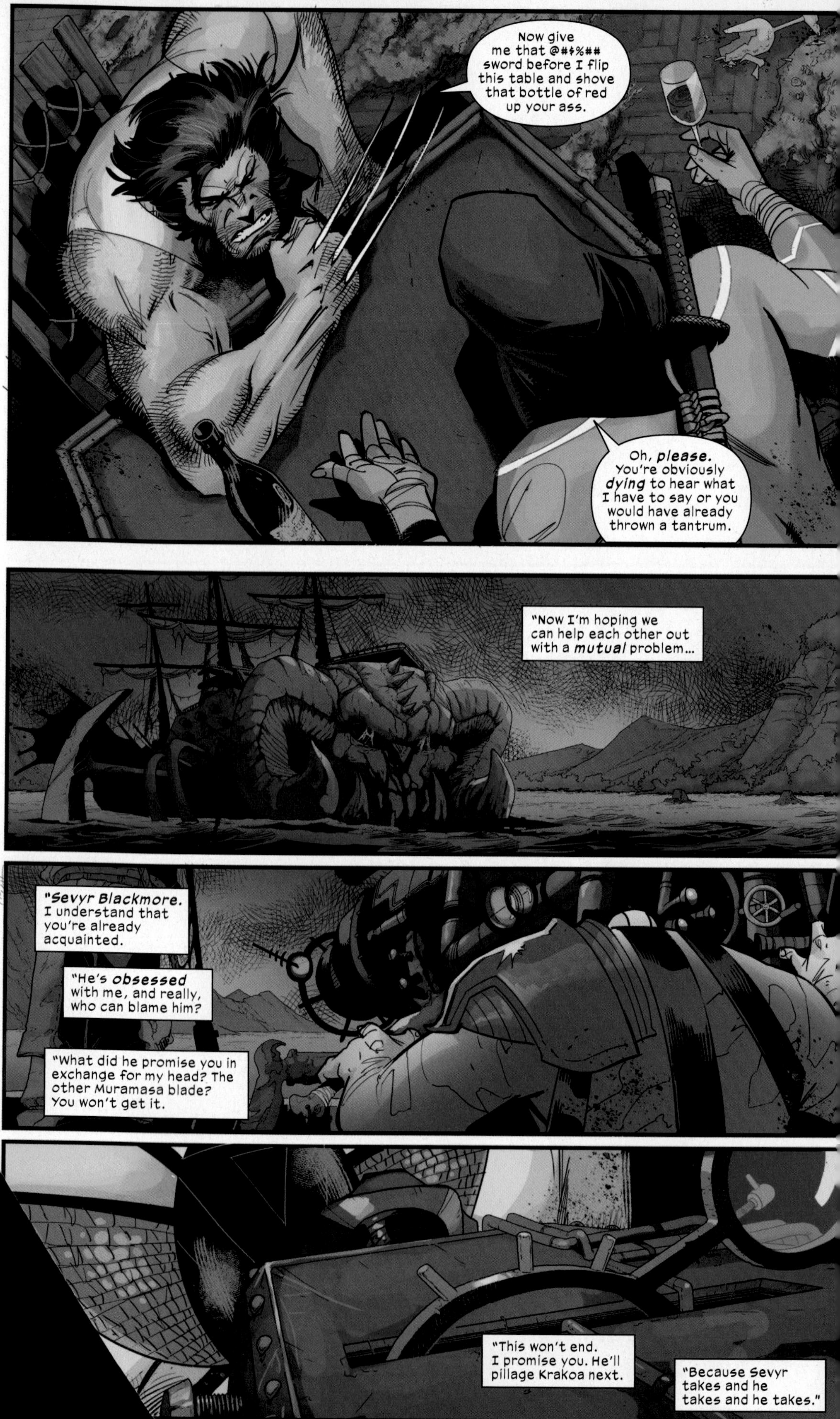
Now give me that @#$%## sword before I flip this table and shove that bottle of red up your ass.
Oh, please. You're obviously dying to hear what I have to say or you would have already thrown a tantrum.
"Now I'm hoping we can help each other out with a mutual problem...
"Sevyr Blackmore. I understand that you're already acquainted.
"He's obsessed with me, and really, who can blame him?
"What did he promise you in exchange for my head? The other Muramasa blade? You won't get it.
"This won't end. I promise you. He'll pillage Krakoa next.
"Because Sevyr takes and he takes and he takes."

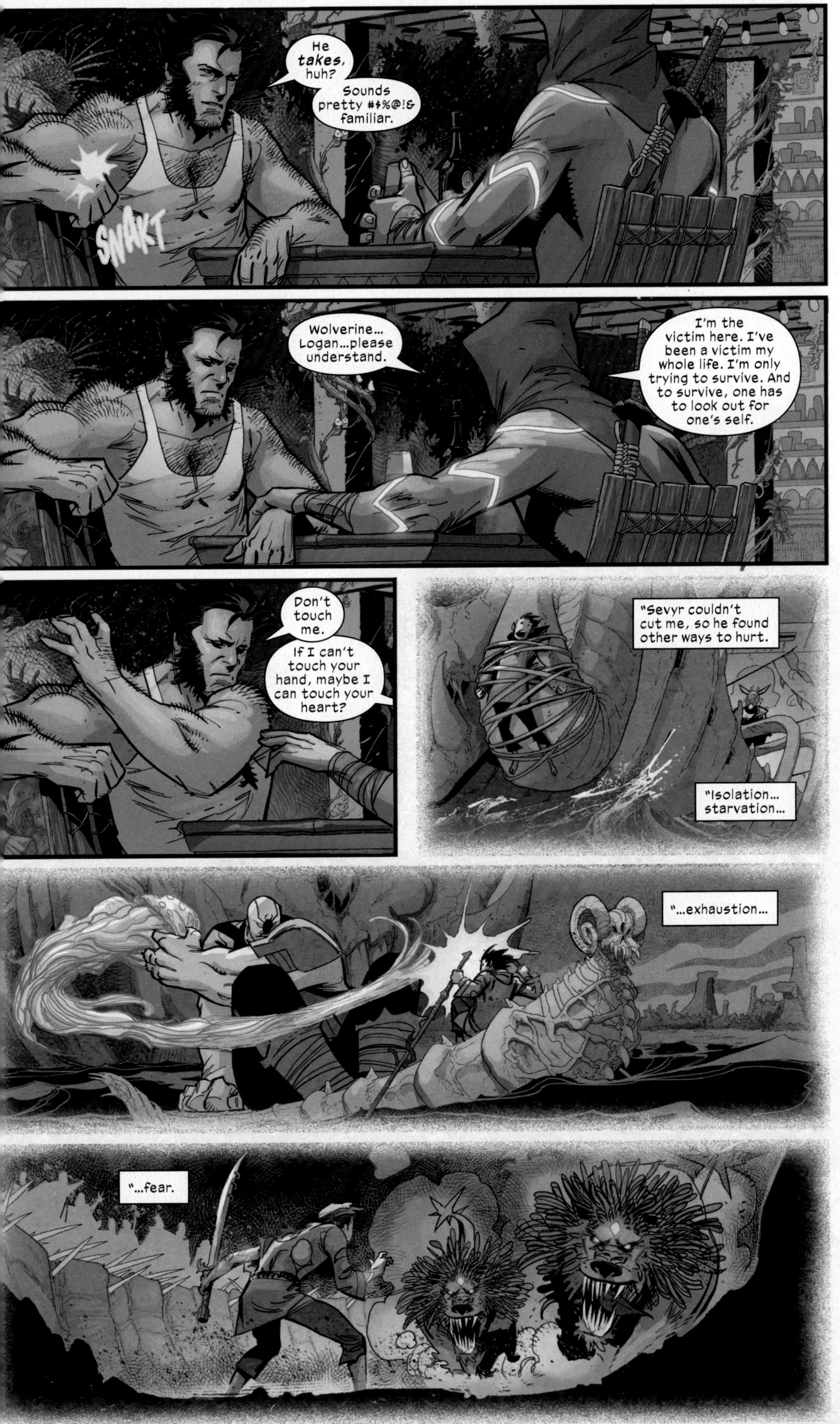
He *takes,* huh?
Sounds pretty #$%@!& familiar.
SNAKT
Wolverine... Logan...please understand.
I'm the victim here. I've been a victim my whole life. I'm only trying to survive. And to survive, one has to look out for one's self.
Don't touch me.
If I can't touch your hand, maybe I can touch your heart?
"Sevyr couldn't cut me, so he found other ways to hurt.
"Isolation... starvation...
"...exhaustion...
"...fear.

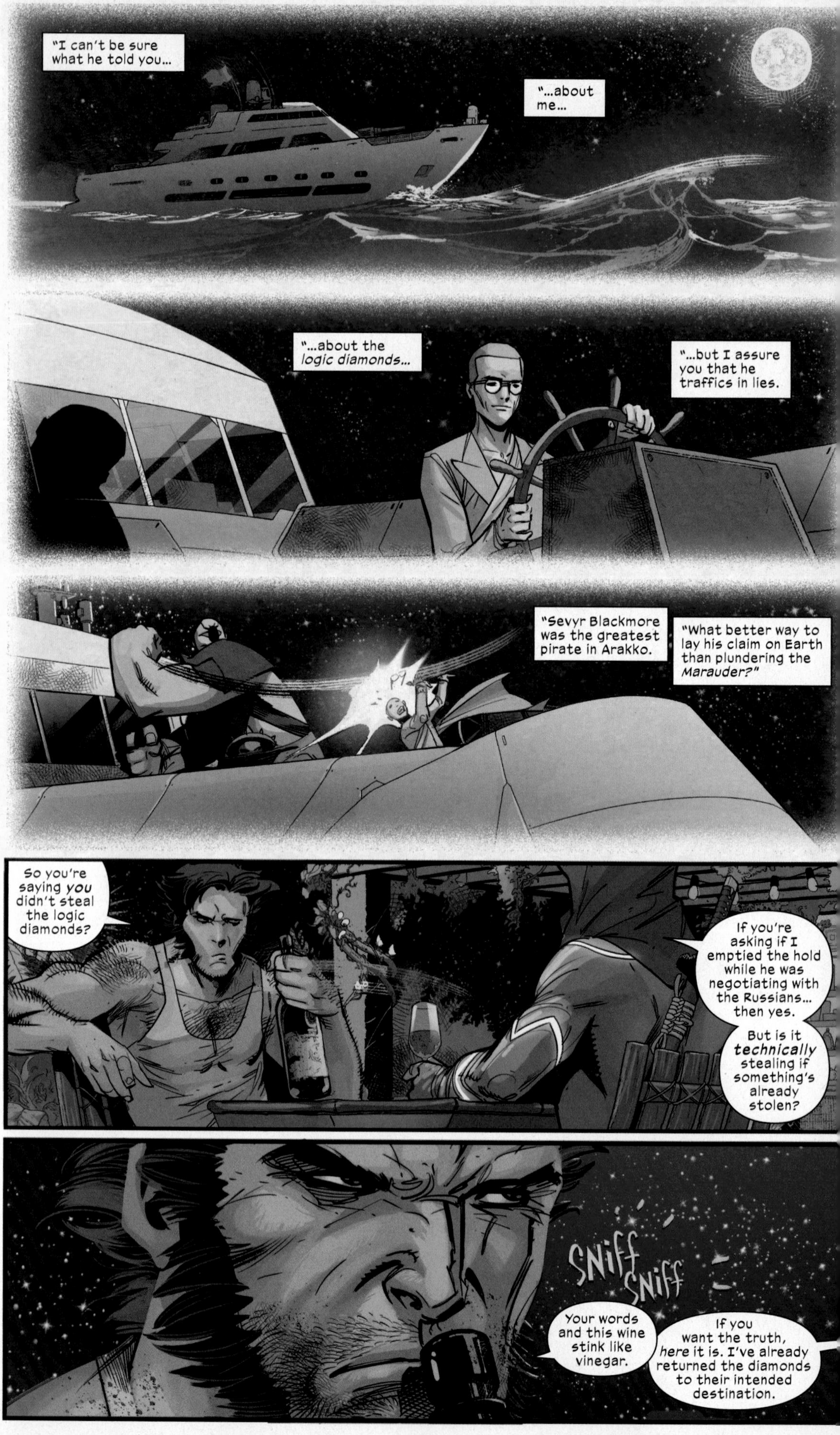
"I can't be sure what he told you...
"...about me...
"...about the *logic diamonds*...
"...but I assure you that he traffics in lies.
"Sevyr Blackmore was the greatest pirate in Arakko.
"What better way to lay his claim on Earth than plundering the *Marauder?*"
So you're saying *you* didn't steal the logic diamonds?
If you're asking if I emptied the hold while he was negotiating with the Russians... then yes.
But is it *technically* stealing if something's already stolen?
SNIFF SNIFF
Your words and this wine stink like vinegar.
If you want the truth, *here* it is. I've already returned the diamonds to their intended destination.

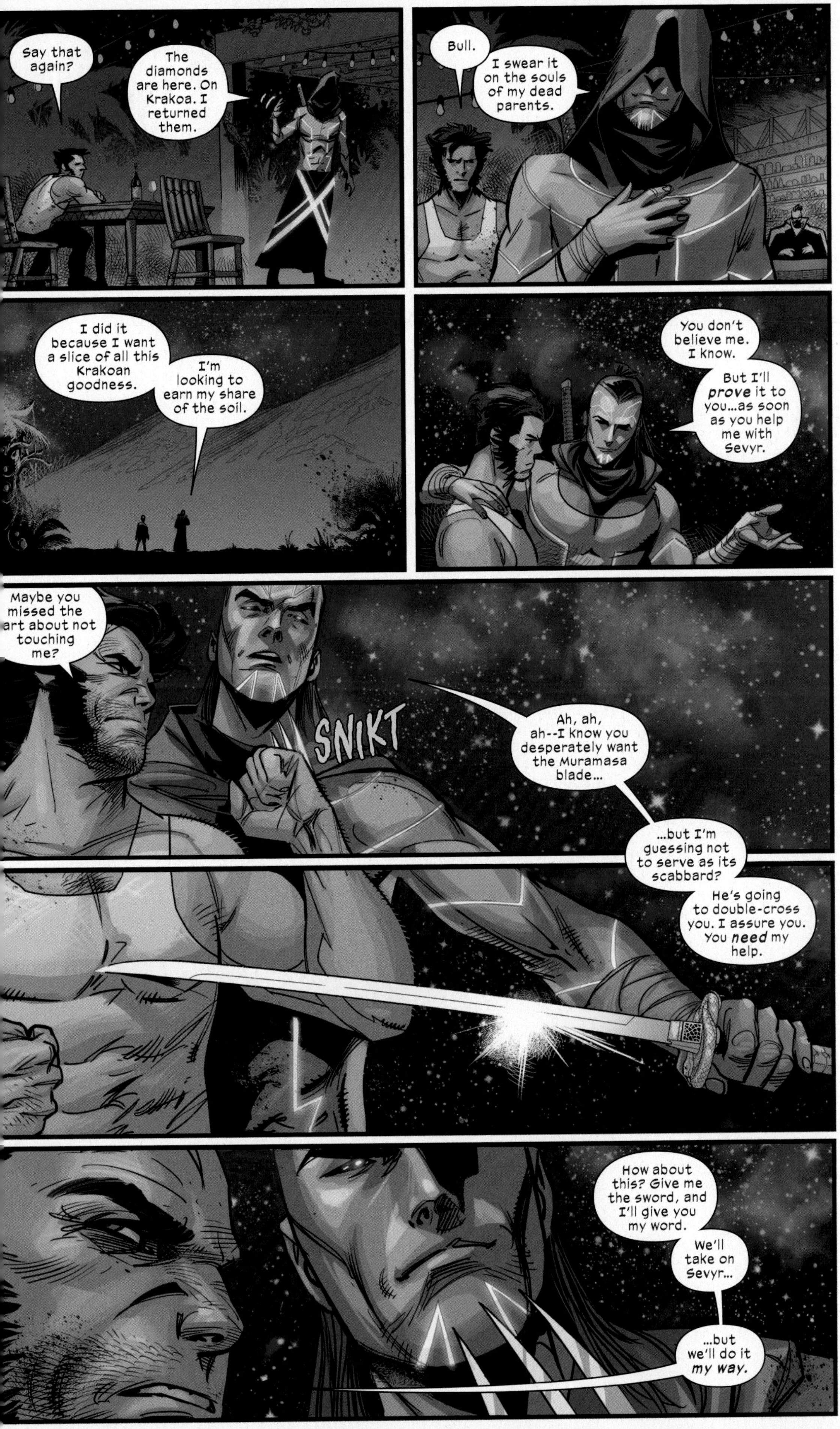

Say that again?
The diamonds are here. On Krakoa. I returned them.
Bull.
I swear it on the souls of my dead parents.
I did it because I want a slice of all this Krakoan goodness.
I'm looking to earn my share of the soil.
You don't believe me. I know.
But I'll *prove* it to you...as soon as you help me with Sevyr.
Maybe you missed the art about not touching me?
SNIKT
Ah, ah, ah--I know you desperately want the Muramasa blade...
...but I'm guessing not to serve as its scabbard?
He's going to double-cross you. I assure you. You *need* my help.
How about this? Give me the sword, and I'll give you my word.
We'll take on Sevyr...
...but we'll do it *my way.*

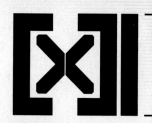

SAGE'S LOGBOOK: MURAMASA BLADES

///Relevant Articles///

:Muramasa:

: Country of origin: Japan
: Arguably the world's greatest swordsmith
: Madman
: Questionable mentor figure for Logan
: Body Status: Deceased
: Soul Status: Entombed

:The Hand:

: Offshoot extremist sect <reborn>
: Midnight Temple/Sacrificial Altar/Portal to Hell
: Muramasa forced into their servitude
: Status: Active

:The Beast:

: Demon
: Offspring: Hell Bride (demonic name unknown)
: Mission: <still collating>
: Status: Active

:Blades:

: Point of Origin: Hell Forge
: Style: Twin katanas
: Ingredients: Tamahagane: tempered with Muramasa's soul
: Status: Masterpieces
: Capabilities: Means of slicing through adamantium
: Origins: Forged as totemic bond in marriage ceremony of Hell Bride
                                        (groom deceased)

:Logan:

: Priority Mission: Acquisition of Muramasa blades
: Intent (practical): Safekeeping of ultimate weapon
: Intent (personal): Union of broken soul

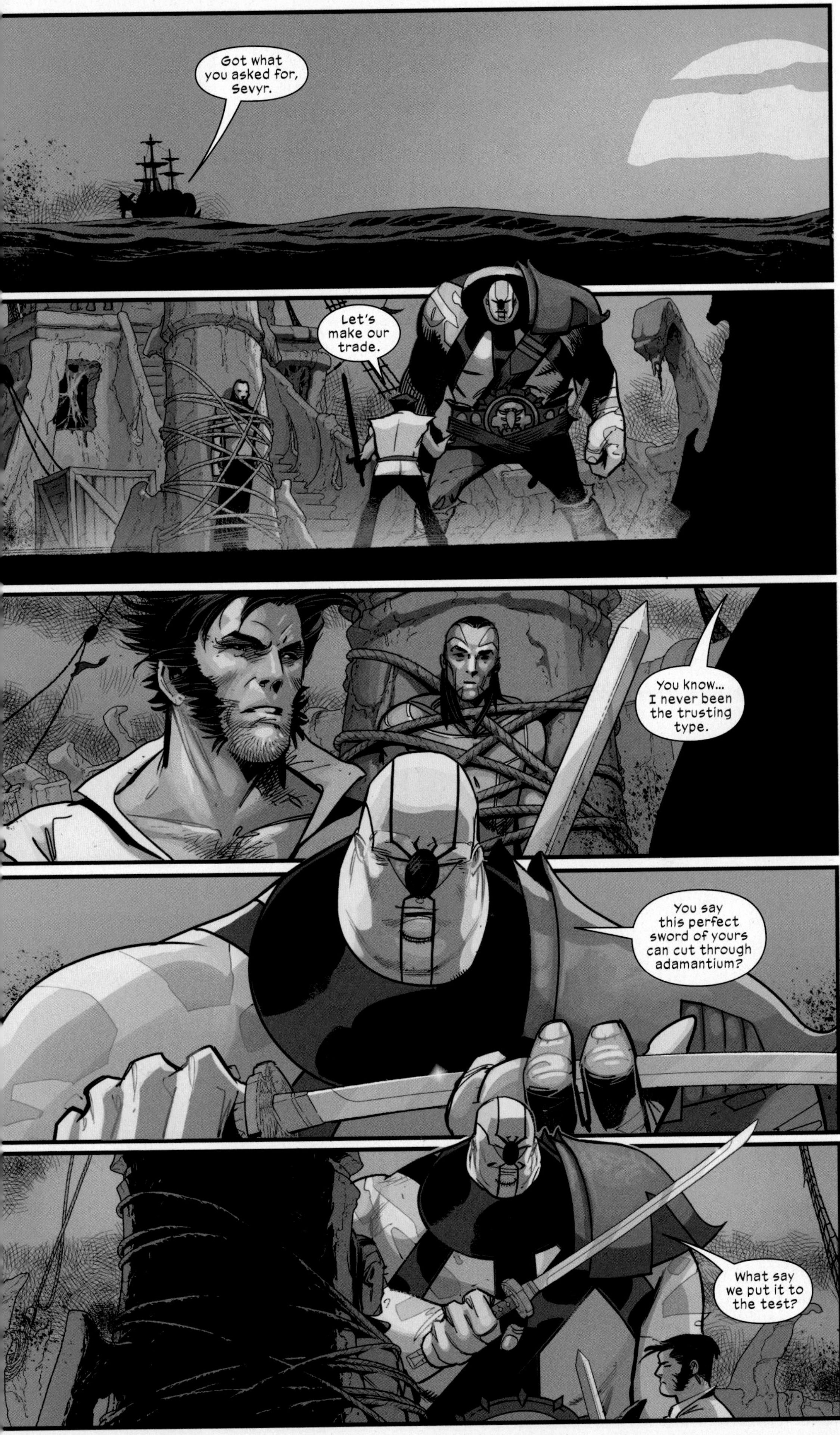

Got what you asked for, Sevyr.
Let's make our trade.
You know... I never been the trusting type.
You say this perfect sword of yours can cut through adamantium?
What say we put it to the test?

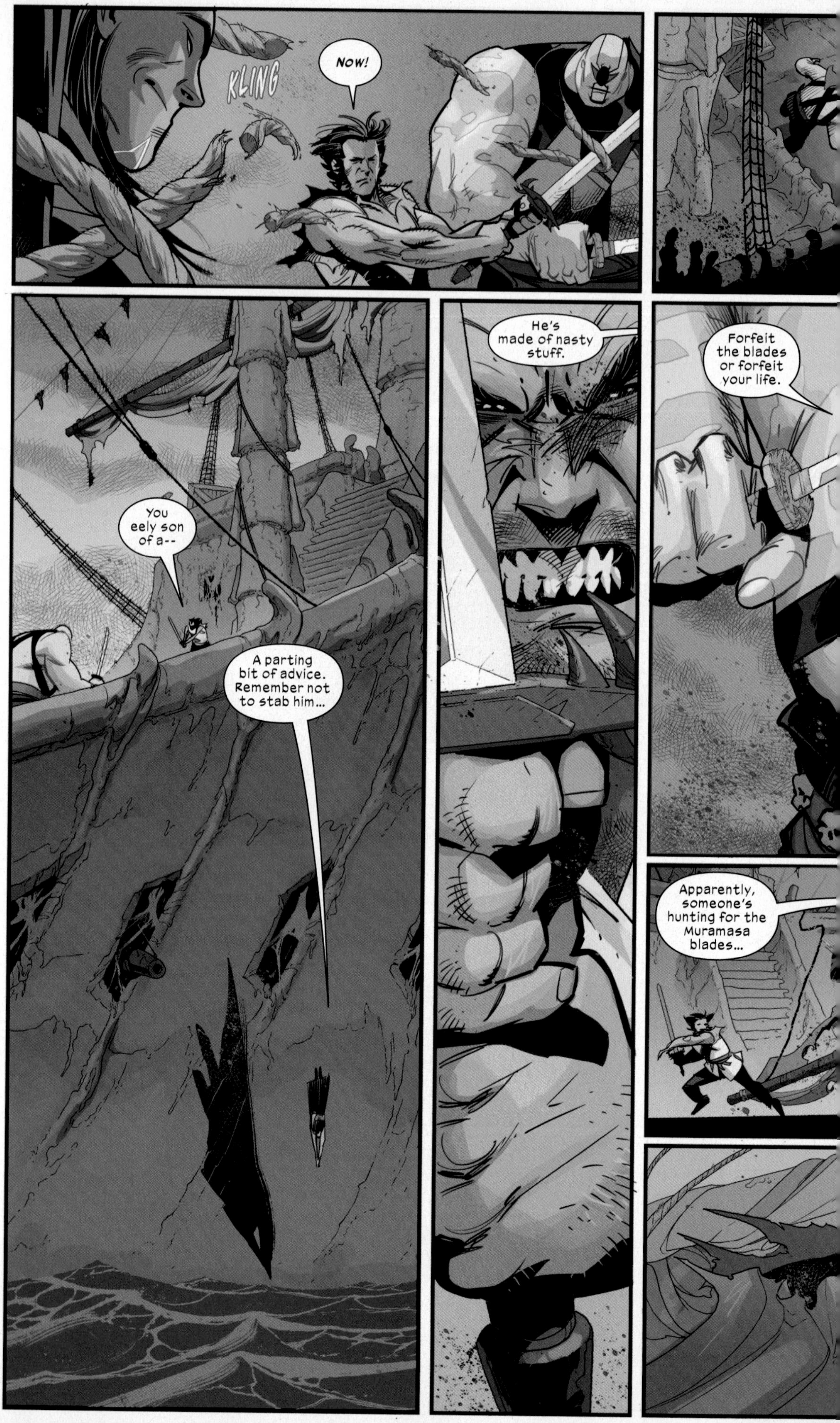
KLING
NOW!
You eely son of a--
A parting bit of advice. Remember not to stab him...
He's made of nasty stuff.
Forfeit the blades or forfeit your life.
Apparently, someone's hunting for the Muramasa blades...

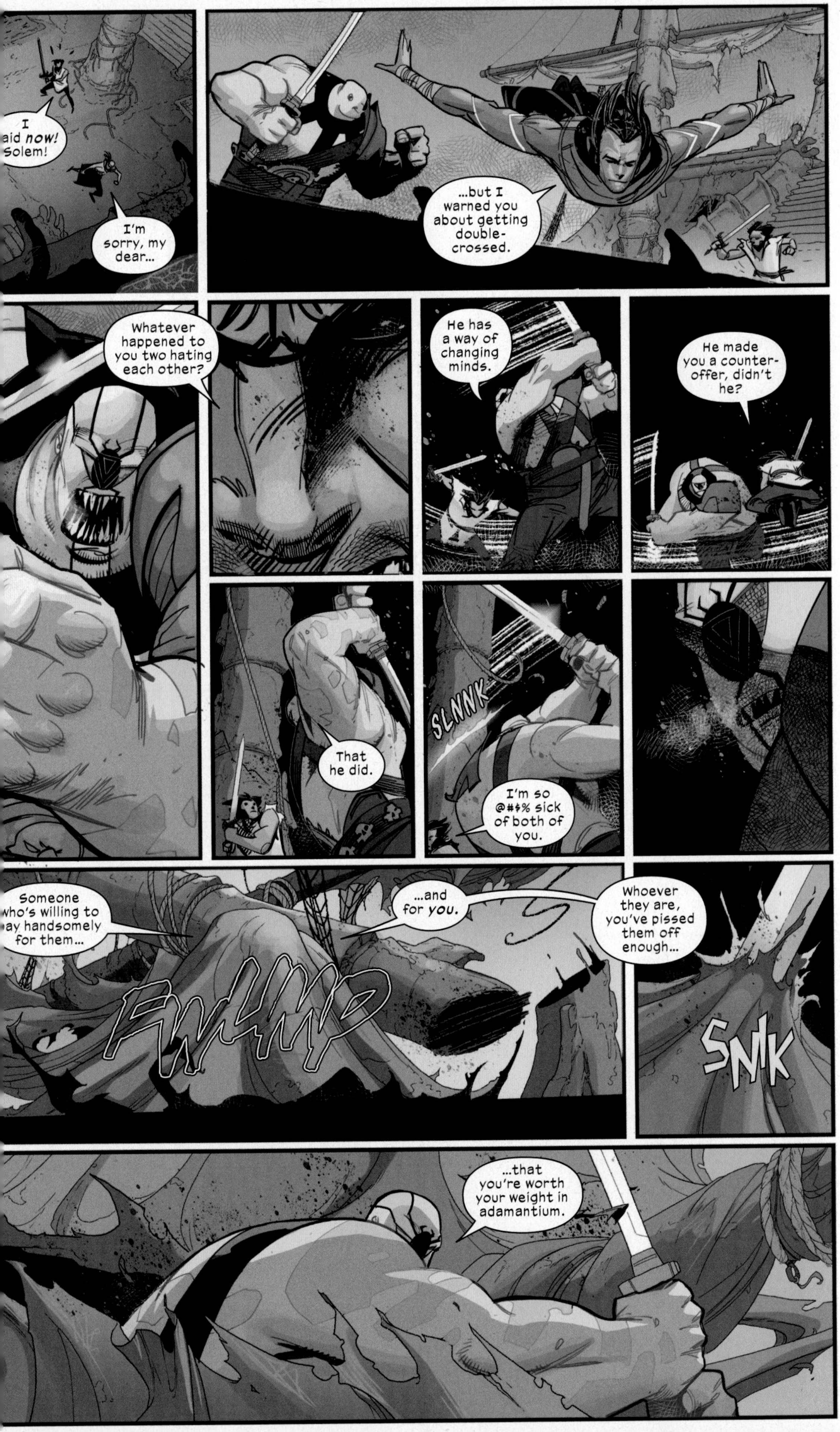
I aid now! Solem!
I'm sorry, my dear...
...but I warned you about getting double-crossed.
Whatever happened to you two hating each other?
He has a way of changing minds.
He made you a counter-offer, didn't he?
That he did.
SLNNK
I'm so @#$% sick of both of you.
Someone who's willing to ay handsomely for them...
FWUMP
...and for you.
Whoever they are, you've pissed them off enough...
SNIK
...that you're worth your weight in adamantium.

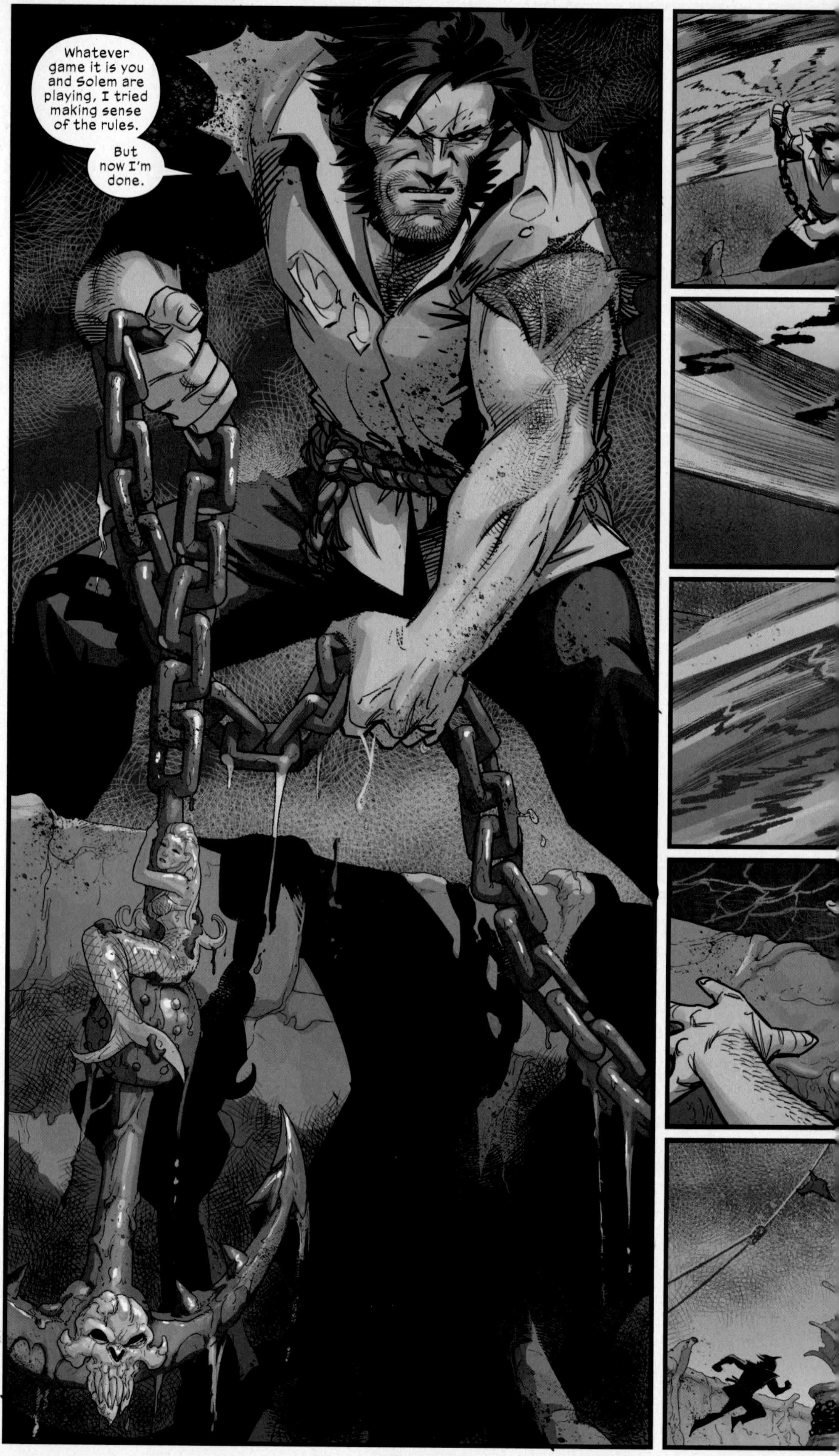
Whatever game it is you and Solem are playing, I tried making sense of the rules.
But now I'm done.

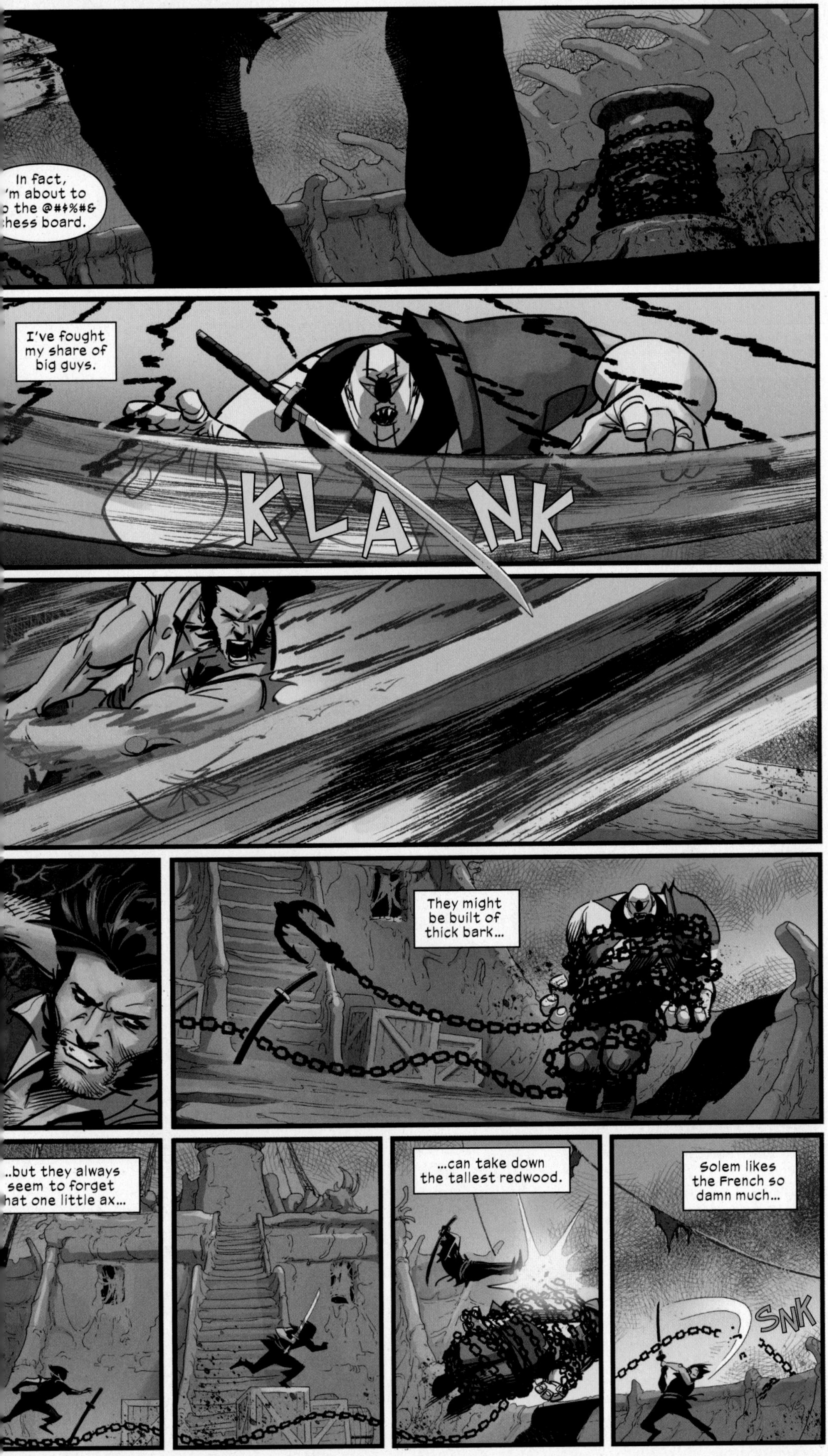
In fact,
'm about to
o the @#$%#&
hess board.
I've fought
my share of
big guys.
KLANK
They might
be built of
thick bark...
..but they always
seem to forget
hat one little ax...
...can take down
the tallest redwood.
Solem likes
the French so
damn much...
SNK

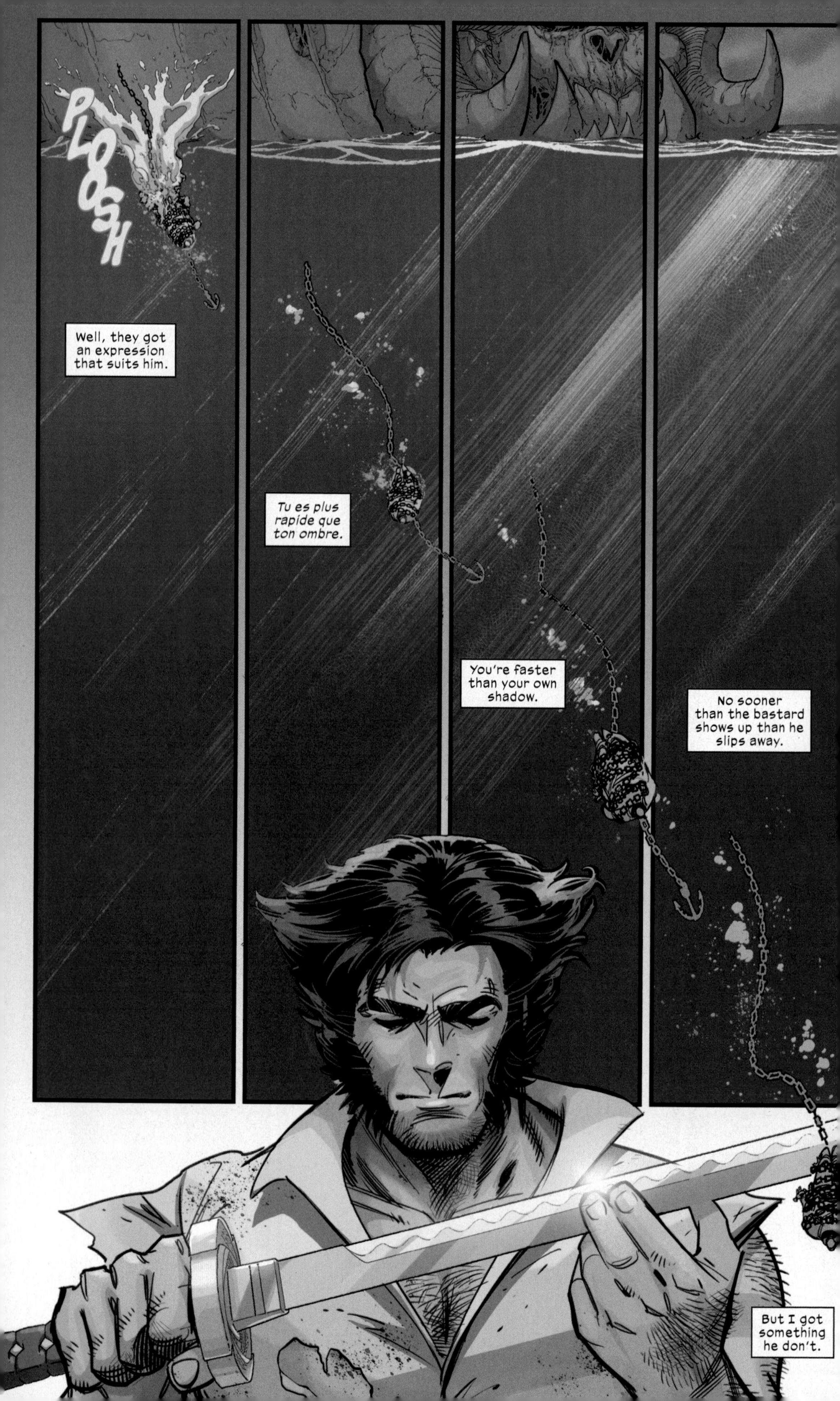
PLOOSH
Well, they got an expression that suits him.
Tu es plus rapide que ton ombre.
You're faster than your own shadow.
No sooner than the bastard shows up than he slips away.
But I got something he don't.

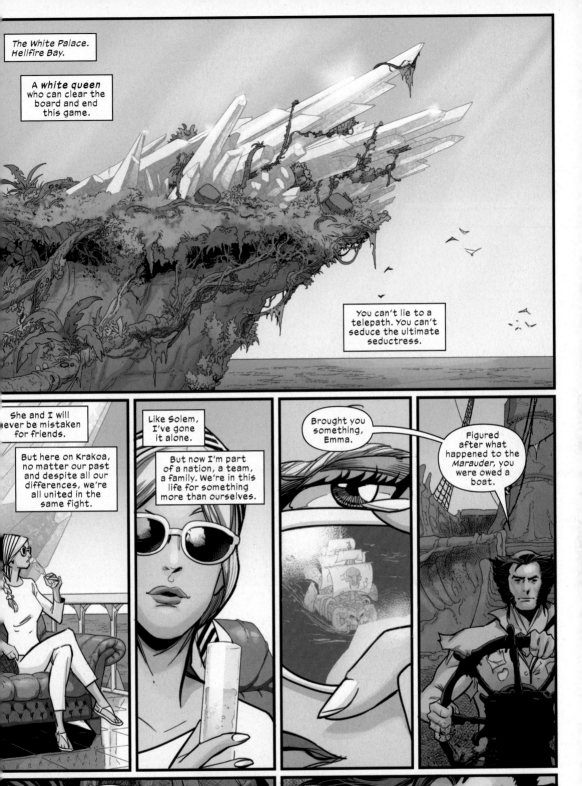

The White Palace. Hellfire Bay.

A *white queen* who can clear the board and end this game.

You can't lie to a telepath. You can't seduce the ultimate seductress.

She and I will never be mistaken for friends.

But here on Krakoa, no matter our past and despite all our differences, we're all united in the same fight.

Like Solem, I've gone it alone.

But now I'm part of a nation, a team, a family. We're in this life for something more than ourselves.

Brought you something, Emma.

Figured after what happened to the *Marauder*, you were owed a boat.

How revolting... I don't suppose it comes with a hold full of diamonds?

About that...

Wondered if I might bum a favor.

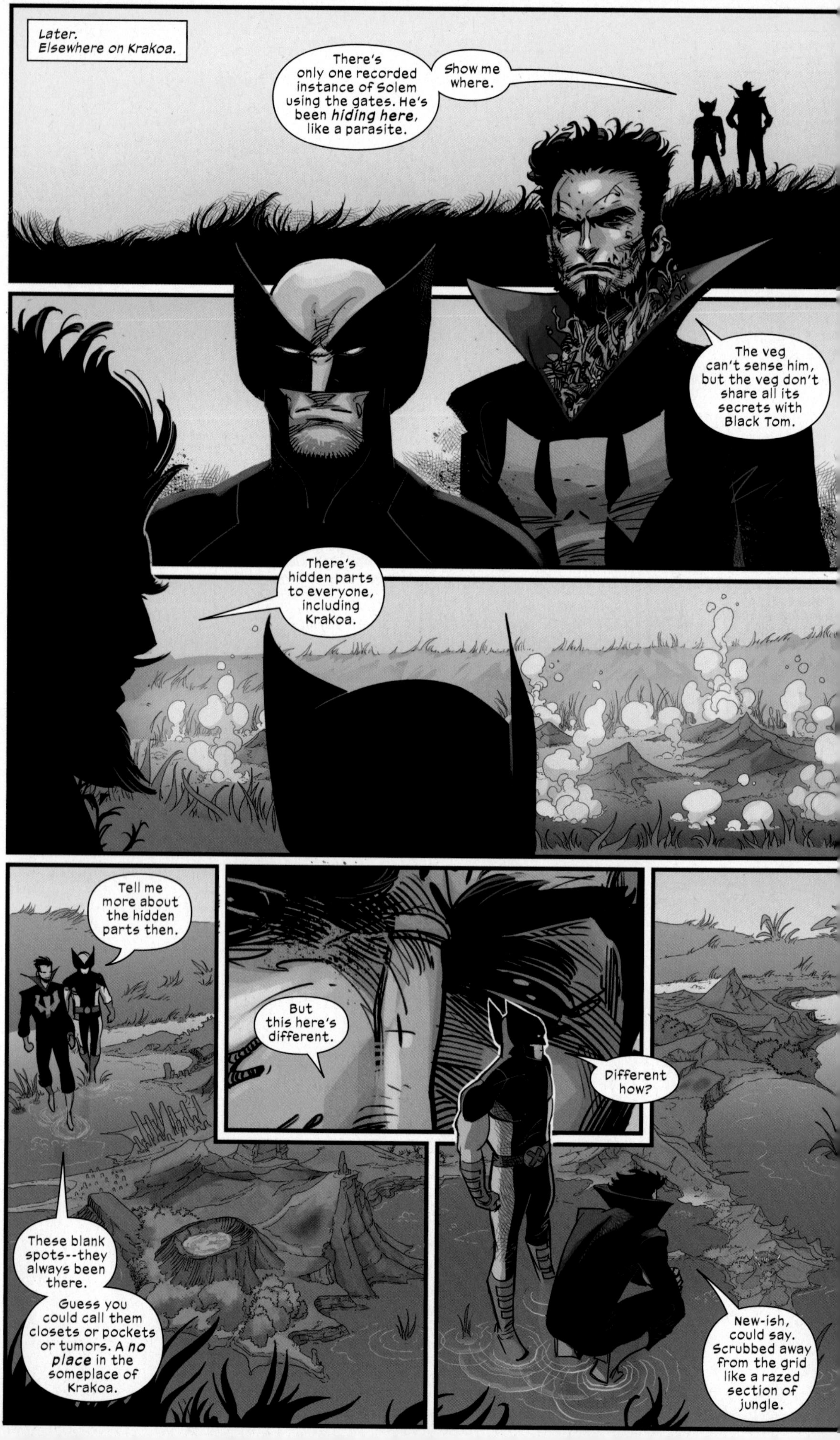
Later.
Elsewhere on Krakoa.
There's only one recorded instance of Solem using the gates. He's been *hiding here*, like a parasite.
Show me where.
The veg can't sense him, but the veg don't share all its secrets with Black Tom.
There's hidden parts to everyone, including Krakoa.
Tell me more about the hidden parts then.
But this here's different.
Different how?
These blank spots--they always been there.
Guess you could call them closets or pockets or tumors. A *no place* in the someplace of Krakoa.
New-ish, could say. Scrubbed away from the grid like a razed section of jungle.

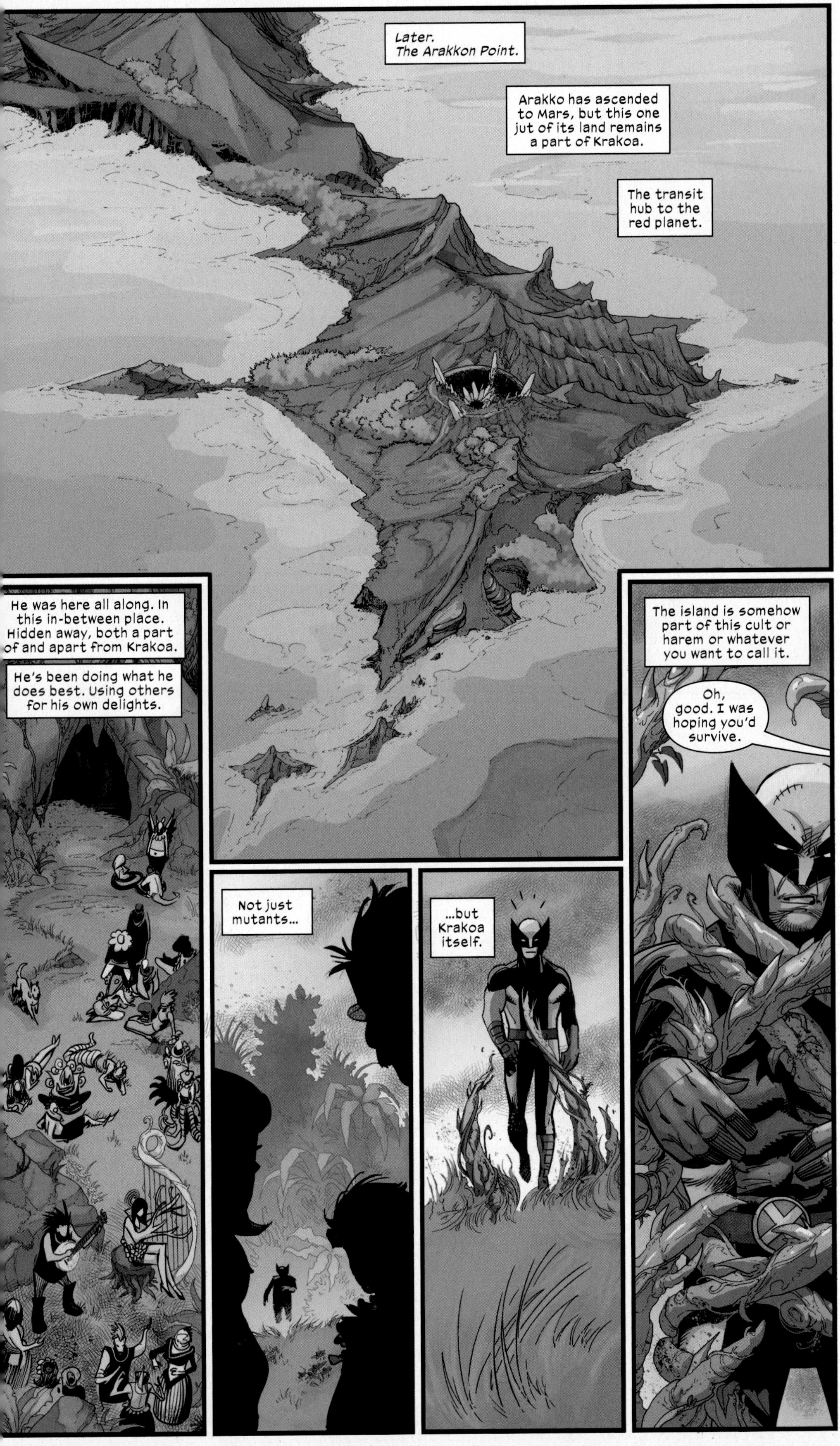
Later.
The Arakkon Point.
Arakko has ascended to Mars, but this one jut of its land remains a part of Krakoa.
The transit hub to the red planet.
He was here all along. In this in-between place. Hidden away, both a part of and apart from Krakoa.
He's been doing what he does best. Using others for his own delights.
Not just mutants...
...but Krakoa itself.
The island is somehow part of this cult or harem or whatever you want to call it.
Oh, good. I was hoping you'd survive.

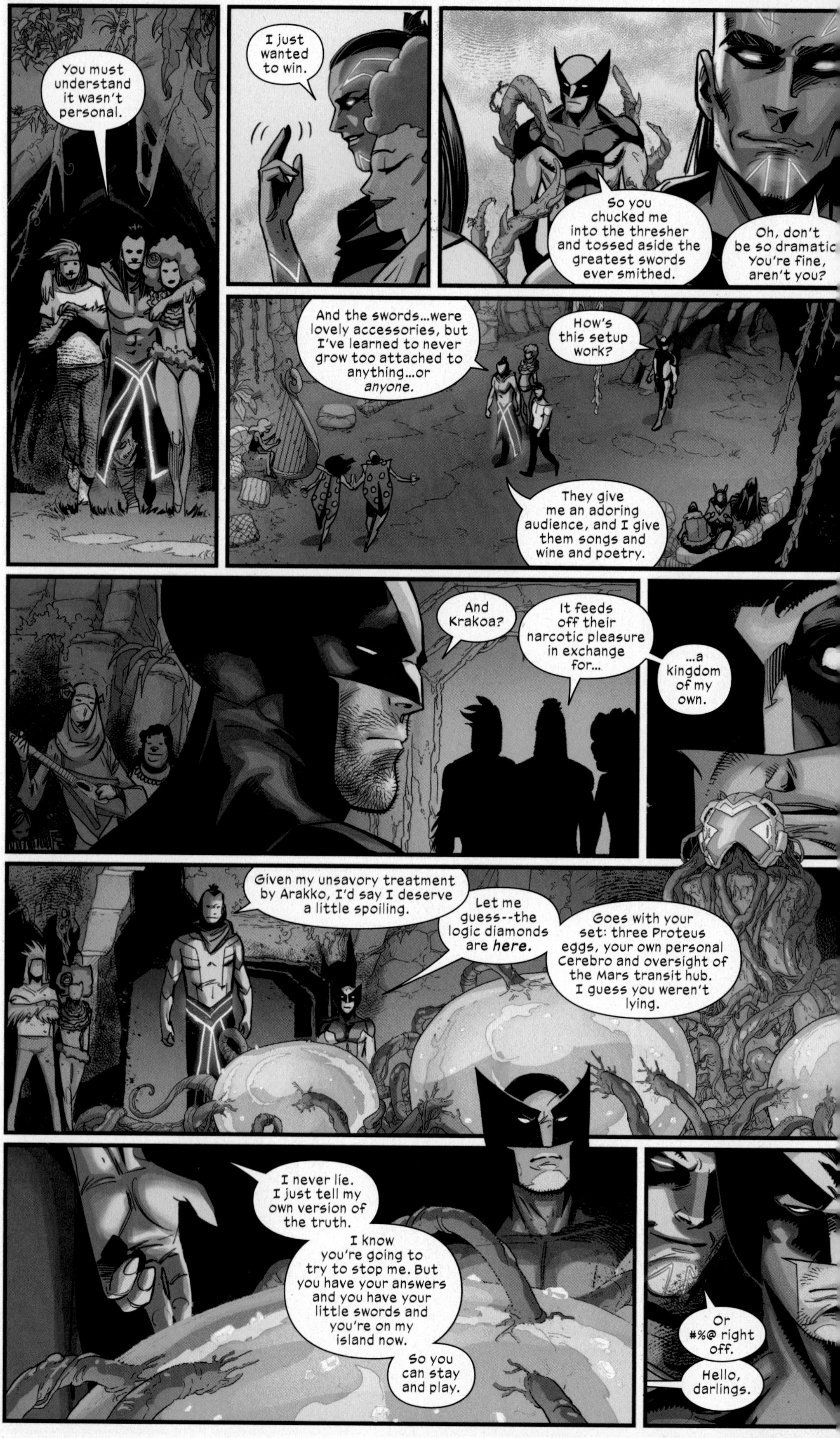
You must understand it wasn't personal.
I just wanted to win.
So you chucked me into the thresher and tossed aside the greatest swords ever smithed.
Oh, don't be so dramatic You're fine, aren't you?
And the swords...were lovely accessories, but I've learned to never grow too attached to anything...or anyone.
How's this setup work?
They give me an adoring audience, and I give them songs and wine and poetry.
And Krakoa?
It feeds off their narcotic pleasure in exchange for...
...a kingdom of my own.
Given my unsavory treatment by Arakko, I'd say I deserve a little spoiling.
Let me guess--the logic diamonds are here.
Goes with your set: three Proteus eggs, your own personal Cerebro and oversight of the Mars transit hub. I guess you weren't lying.
I never lie. I just tell my own version of the truth.
I know you're going to try to stop me. But you have your answers and you have your little swords and you're on my island now.
So you can stay and play.
Or #%@ right off.
Hello, darlings.

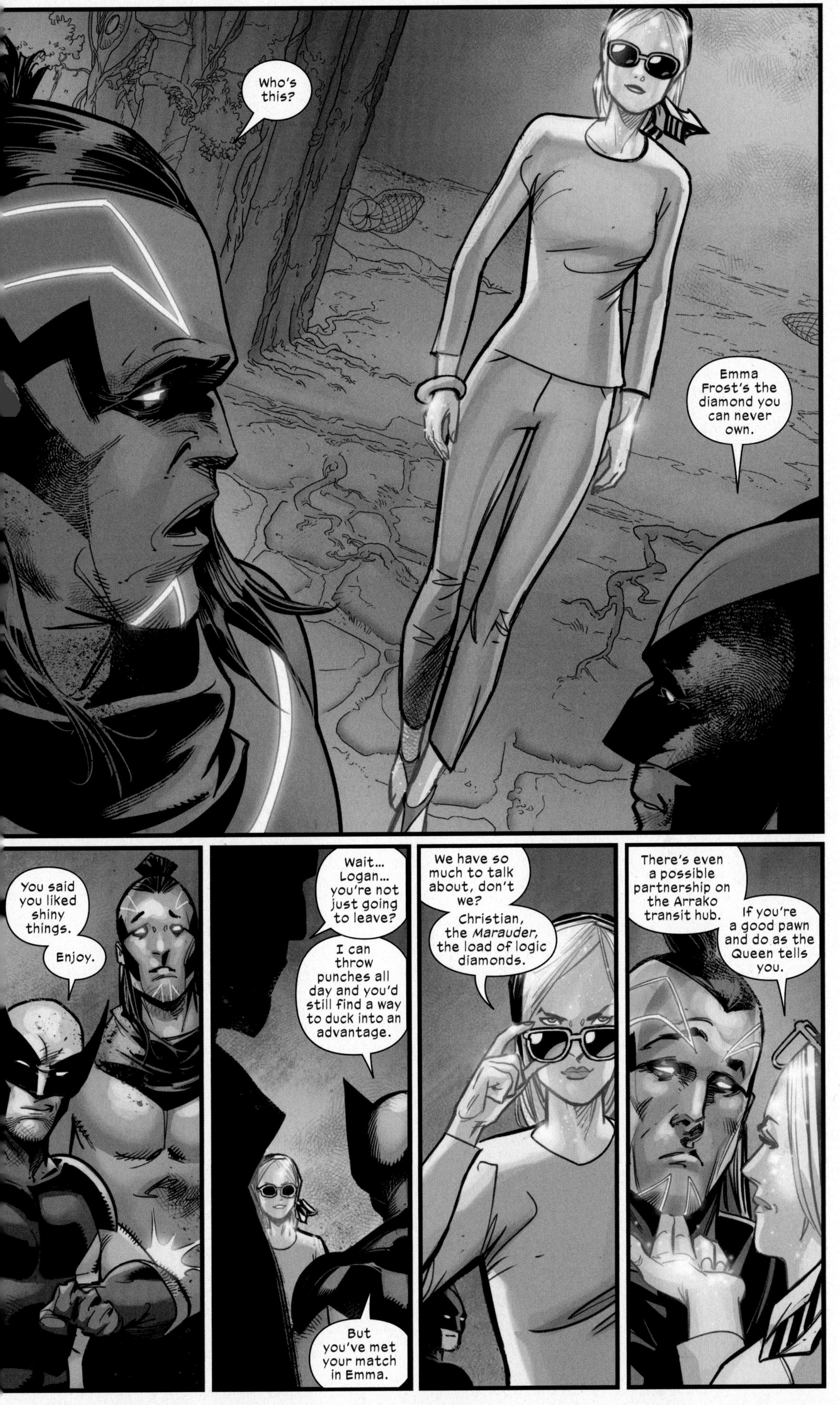
Who's this?
Emma Frost's the diamond you can never own.
You said you liked shiny things.
Enjoy.
Wait... Logan... you're not just going to leave?
I can throw punches all day and you'd still find a way to duck into an advantage.
But you've met your match in Emma.
We have so much to talk about, don't we?
Christian, the *Marauder*, the load of logic diamonds.
There's even a possible partnership on the Arrako transit hub.
If you're a good pawn and do as the Queen tells you.

SAGE'S LOGBOOK

Report from Emma Frost: Solem Interrogation
//Notable Excerpts//

"When you lie long enough, you lose track of the truth, and he has lied a long, long time."

"His primary impulse is one of pleasure. Self pleasure. It overrides any sense of morality. He would cut a throat for a sip of wine."

"His adamantium skin prevents any injury. So he knows no harm except emotional pain, which he has steeled himself against."

"I didn't know you could &%$# Krakoa. But he found a way."

"Curiously he adores dogs for their whorish affection."

"He hasn't faced a psychic interrogation before, but he swiftly developed defensive techniques, including conjuring lewd images."

"My first impulse is to place him in the Hole. Then again...he might be a useful, if unsavory, tool."

"He really, really wants to &%$# Wolverine. Then again, he really, really wants to &%$# everyone and everything."

"Given all the trouble with our Cerebro backups lately, I see a compelling reason to store a helmet in a black hole. A backup of the backup. The latest reason puts the blame as much on Krakoa as Solem.

He somehow convinced the island to insert a slime mold into the helmet, interrupting its circuitry. Forge replaced it, with the old helmet left forgotten on a shelf in the Arsenal. Solem stole it and -- once in his possession -- the slime mold retreated."

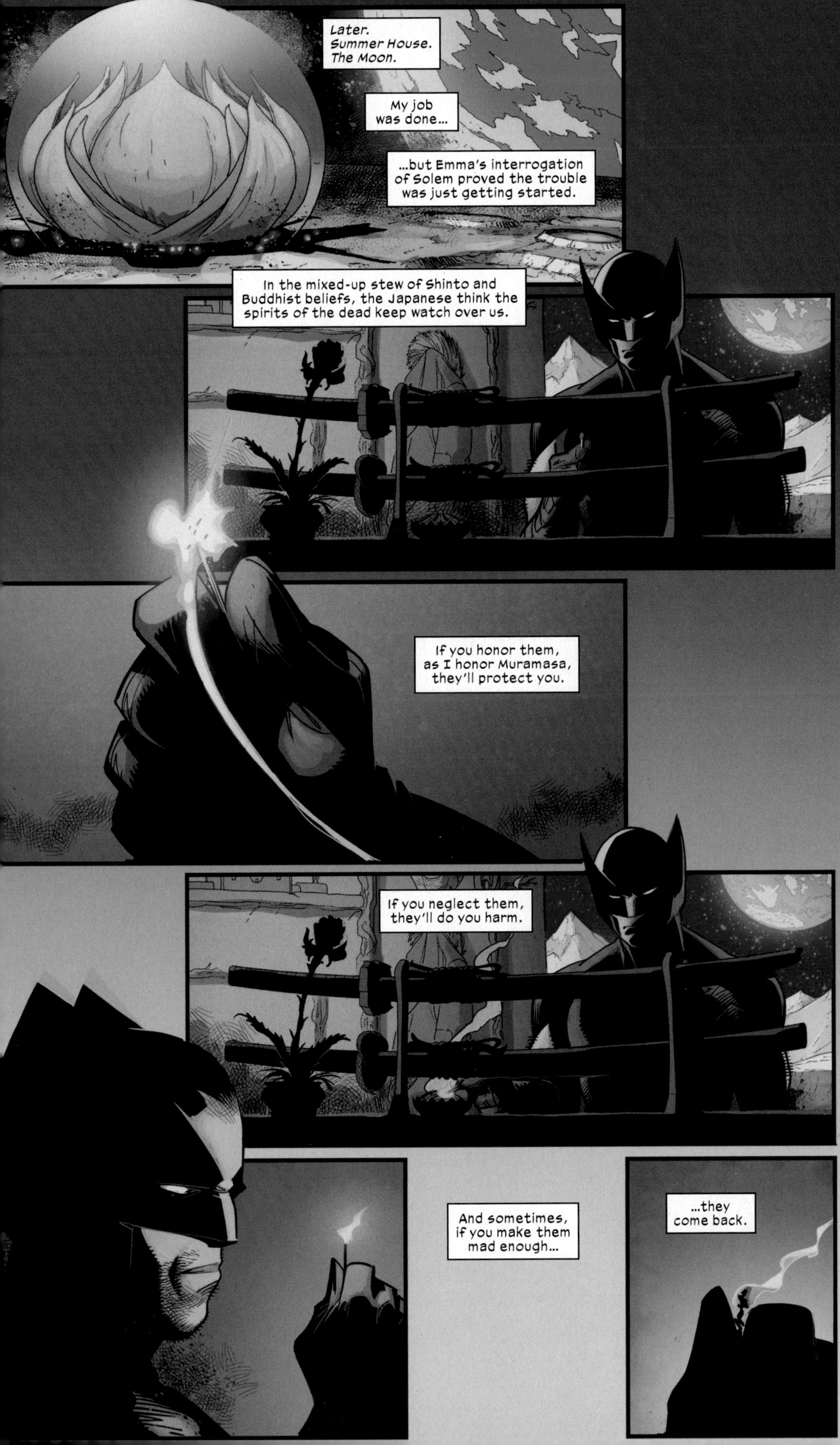

Later.
Summer House.
The Moon.
My job was done...
...but Emma's interrogation of Solem proved the trouble was just getting started.
In the mixed-up stew of Shinto and Buddhist beliefs, the Japanese think the spirits of the dead keep watch over us.
If you honor them, as I honor Muramasa, they'll protect you.
If you neglect them, they'll do you harm.
And sometimes, if you make them mad enough...
...they come back.

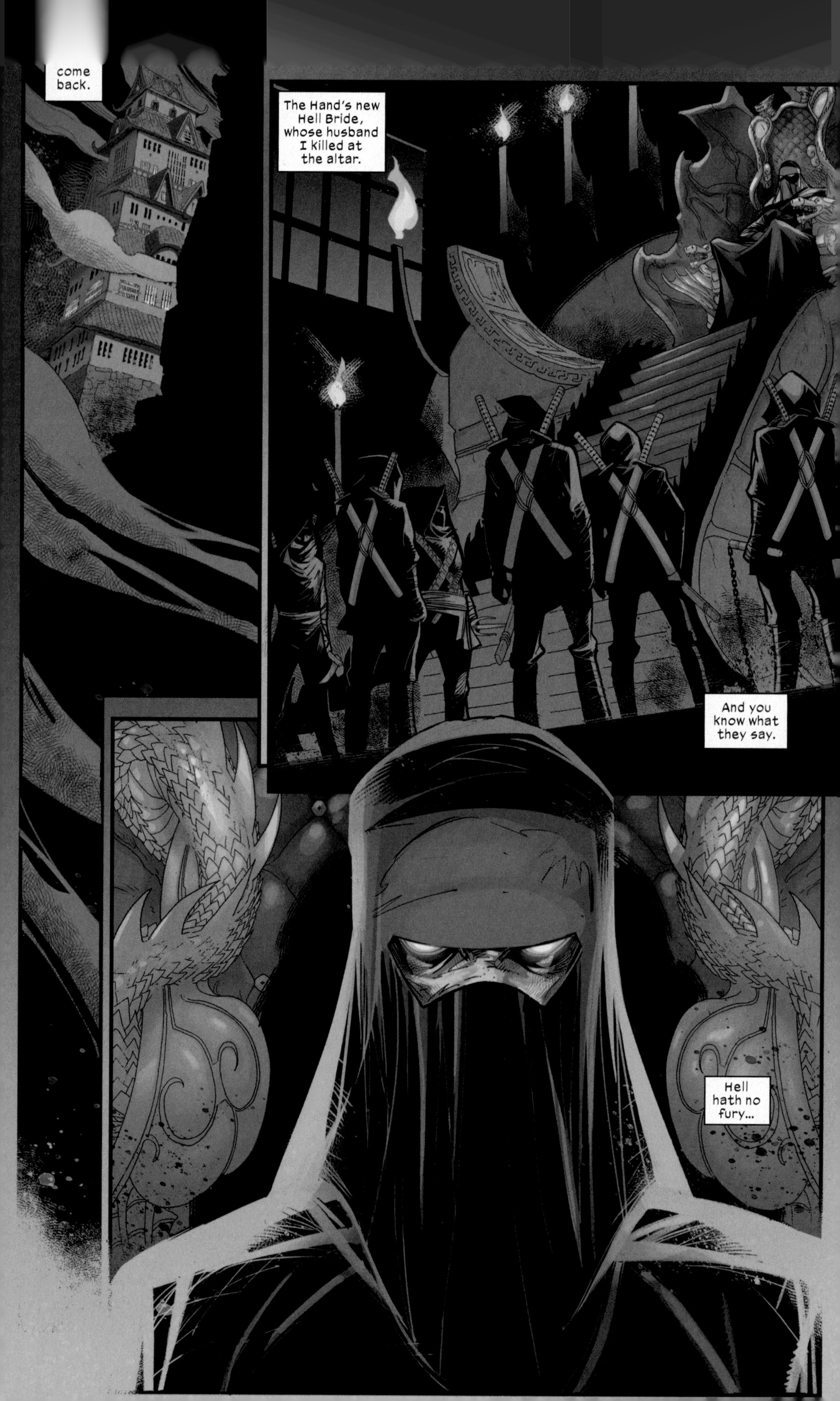
come back.
The Hand's new Hell Bride, whose husband I killed at the altar.
And you know what they say.
Hell hath no fury...

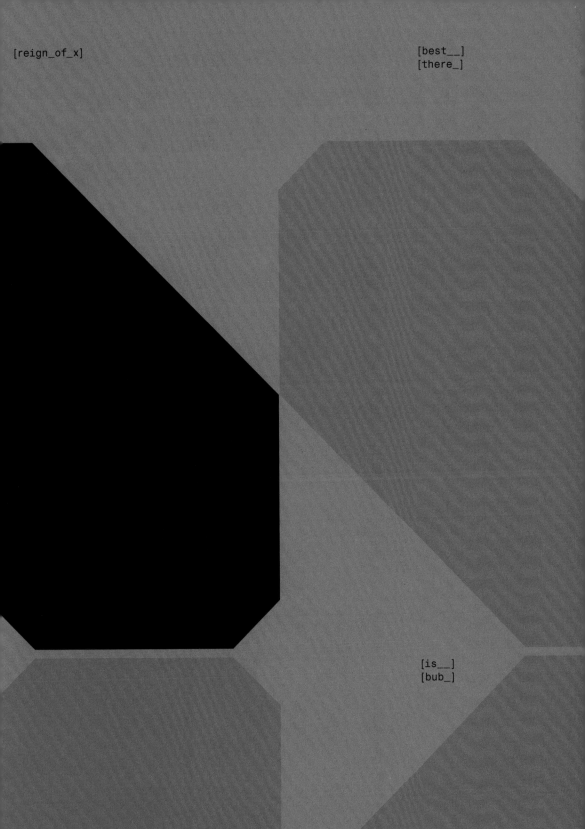

[reign_of_x]

[best__]
[there_]

[is__]
[bub_]

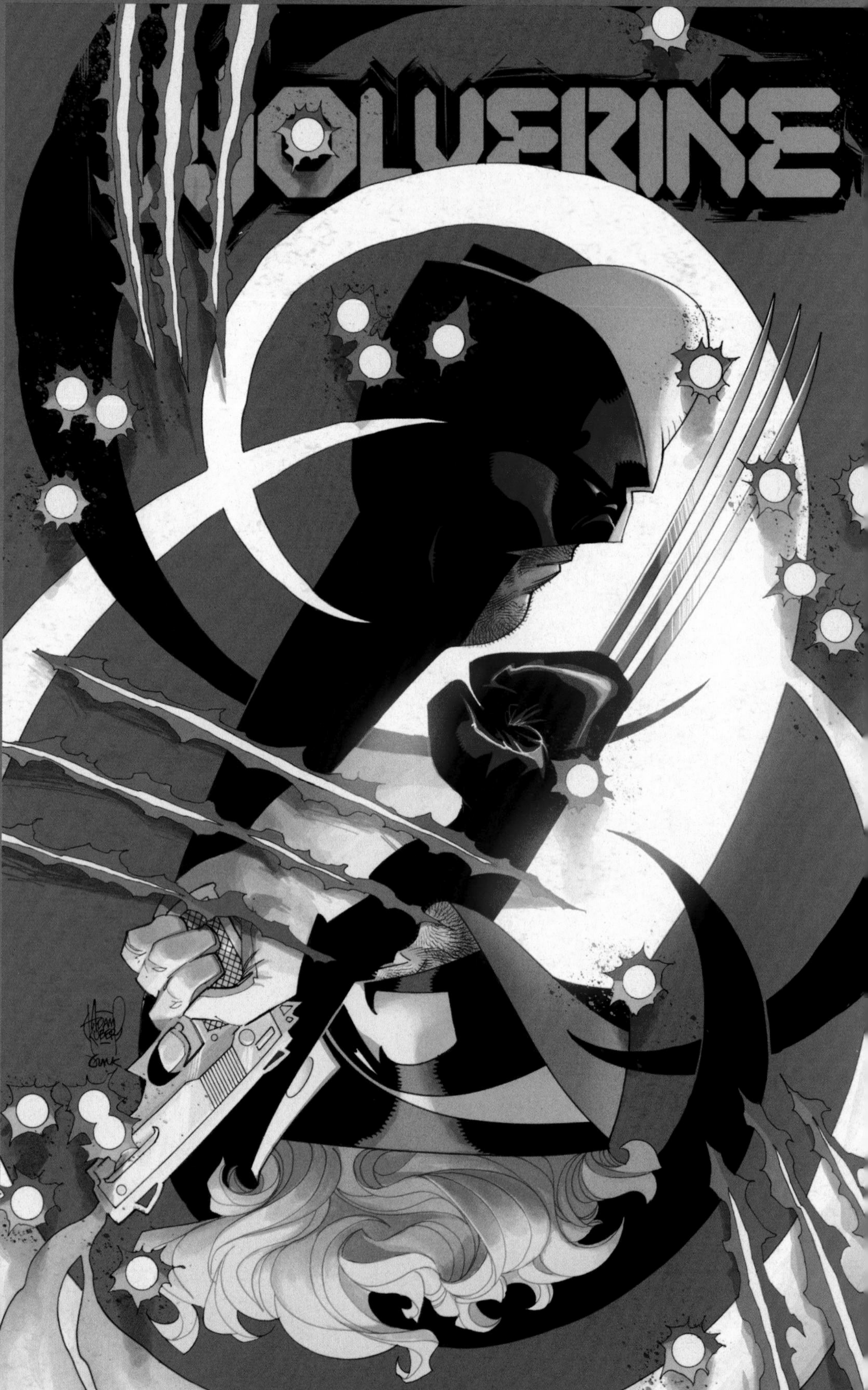
WOLVERINE

Message in a Bottle

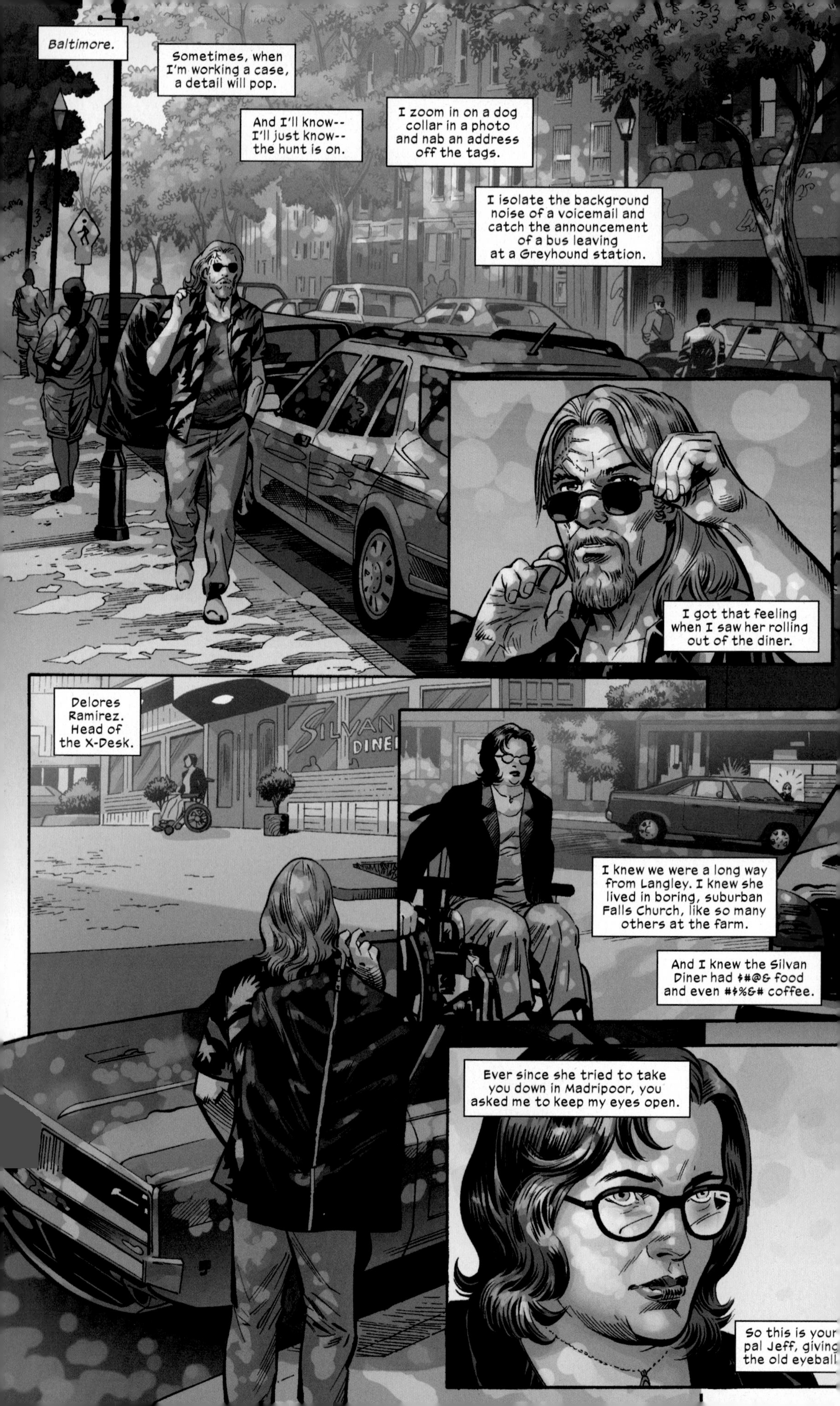
Baltimore.
Sometimes, when I'm working a case, a detail will pop.
And I'll know-- I'll just know-- the hunt is on.
I zoom in on a dog collar in a photo and nab an address off the tags.
I isolate the background noise of a voicemail and catch the announcement of a bus leaving at a Greyhound station.
I got that feeling when I saw her rolling out of the diner.
Delores Ramirez. Head of the X-Desk.
SILVAN DINER
I knew we were a long way from Langley. I knew she lived in boring, suburban Falls Church, like so many others at the farm.
And I knew the Silvan Diner had $#@& food and even #$%&# coffee.
Ever since she tried to take you down in Madripoor, you asked me to keep my eyes open.
So this is your pal Jeff, giving the old eyeball

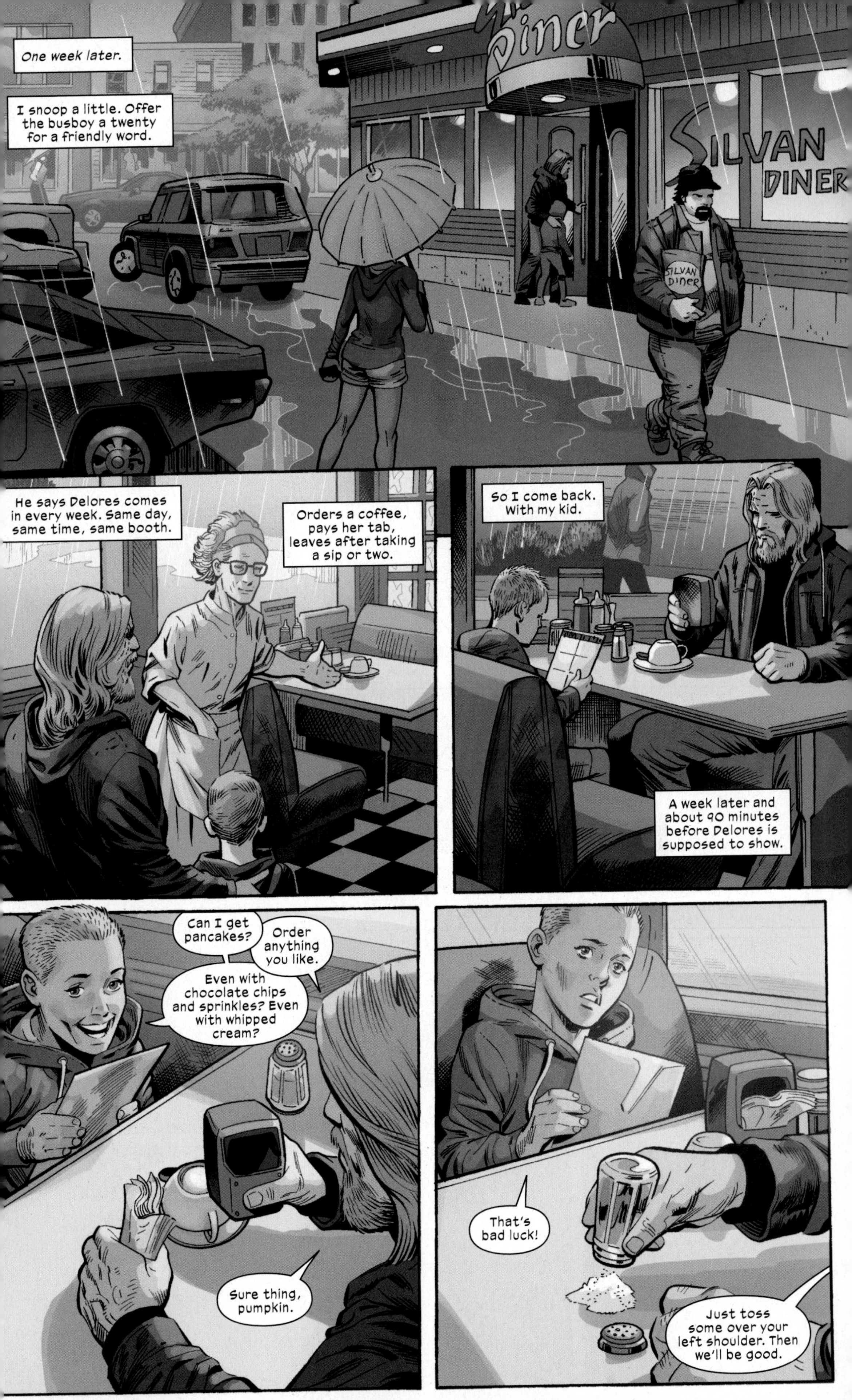

One week later.
I snoop a little. Offer the busboy a twenty for a friendly word.
Diner
SILVAN DINER
SILVAN DINER
He says Delores comes in every week. Same day, same time, same booth.
Orders a coffee, pays her tab, leaves after taking a sip or two.
So I come back. With my kid.
A week later and about 90 minutes before Delores is supposed to show.
Can I get pancakes?
Order anything you like.
Even with chocolate chips and sprinkles? Even with whipped cream?
Sure thing, pumpkin.
That's bad luck!
Just toss some over your left shoulder. Then we'll be good.

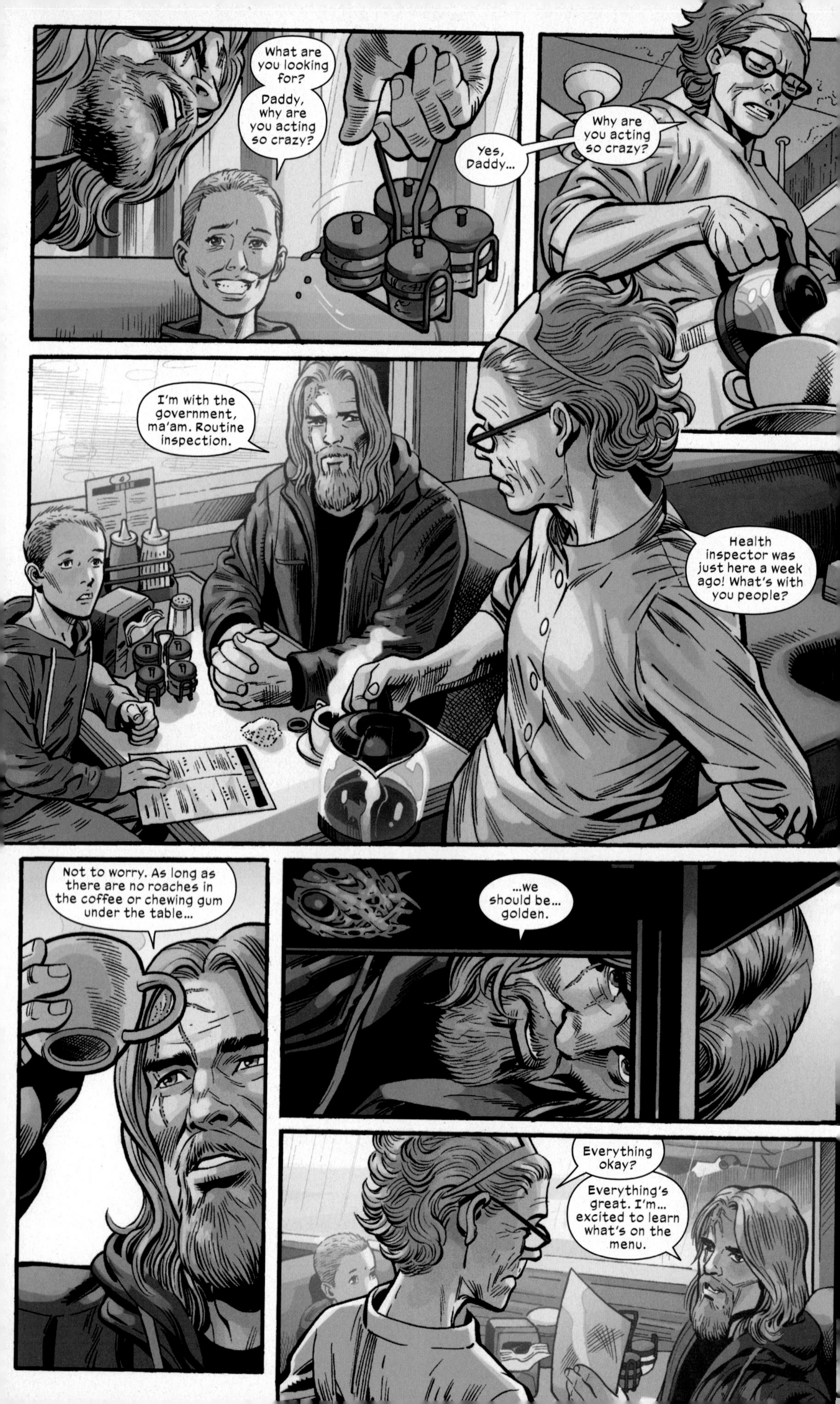
What are you looking for?
Daddy, why are you acting so crazy?
Yes, Daddy...
Why are you acting so crazy?
I'm with the government, ma'am. Routine inspection.
Health inspector was just here a week ago! What's with you people?
Not to worry. As long as there are no roaches in the coffee or chewing gum under the table...
...we should be... golden.
Everything okay?
Everything's great. I'm... excited to learn what's on the menu.

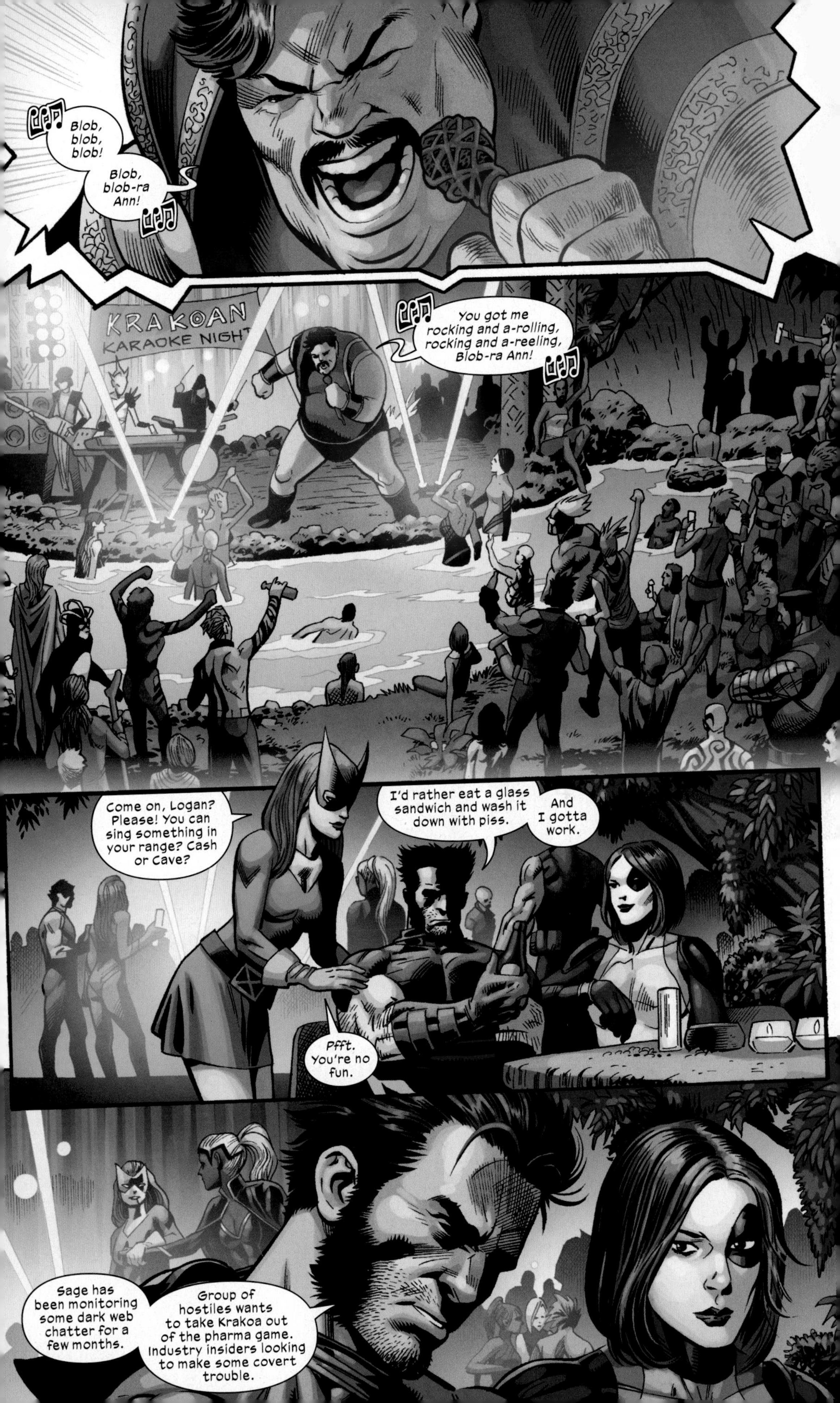

Blob, blob, blob!
Blob, blob-ra Ann!
KRAKOAN KARAOKE NIGHT
You got me rocking and a-rolling, rocking and a-reeling, Blob-ra Ann!
Come on, Logan? Please! You can sing something in your range? Cash or Cave?
I'd rather eat a glass sandwich and wash it down with piss.
And I gotta work.
Pfft. You're no fun.
Sage has been monitoring some dark web chatter for a few months.
Group of hostiles wants to take Krakoa out of the pharma game. Industry insiders looking to make some covert trouble.

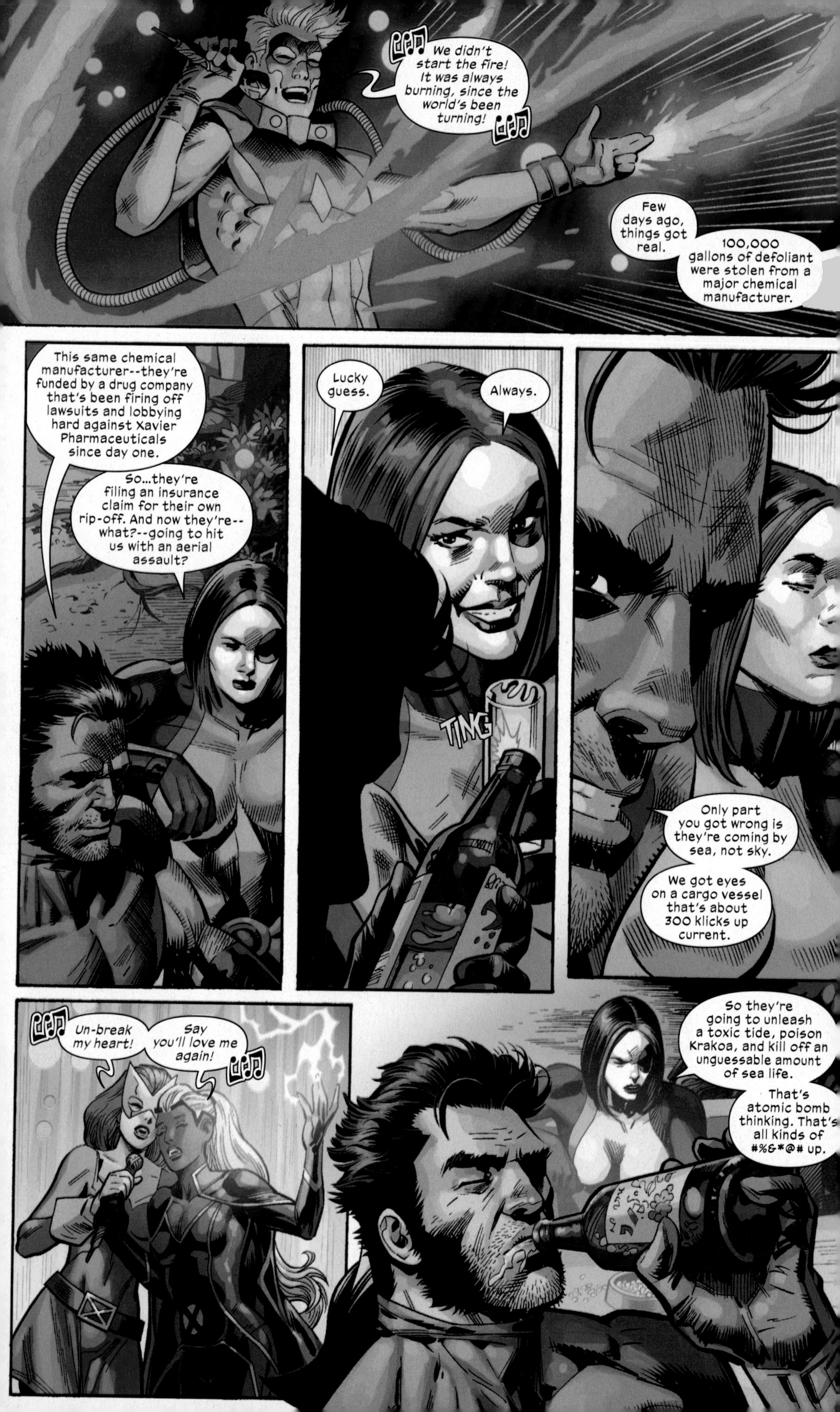
We didn't start the fire! It was always burning, since the world's been turning!
Few days ago, things got real.
100,000 gallons of defoliant were stolen from a major chemical manufacturer.
This same chemical manufacturer--they're funded by a drug company that's been firing off lawsuits and lobbying hard against Xavier Pharmaceuticals since day one.
So...they're filing an insurance claim for their own rip-off. And now they're--what?--going to hit us with an aerial assault?
Lucky guess.
Always.
TING
Only part you got wrong is they're coming by sea, not sky.
We got eyes on a cargo vessel that's about 300 klicks up current.
Un-break my heart!
Say you'll love me again!
So they're going to unleash a toxic tide, poison Krakoa, and kill off an unguessable amount of sea life.
That's atomic bomb thinking. That's all kinds of #%&*@# up.

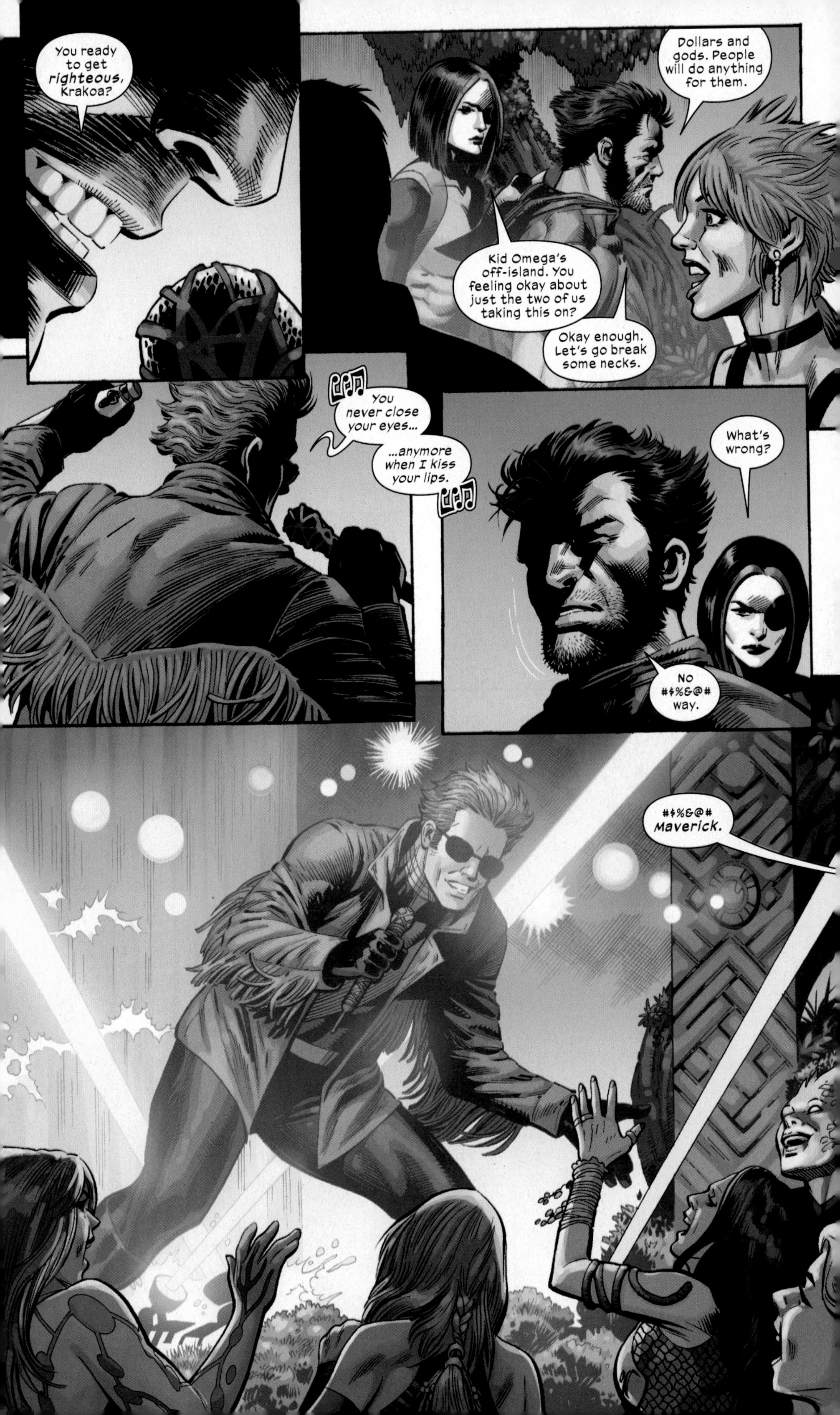
You ready to get righteous, Krakoa?
Dollars and gods. People will do anything for them.
Kid Omega's off-island. You feeling okay about just the two of us taking this on?
Okay enough. Let's go break some necks.
You never close your eyes...
...anymore when I kiss your lips.
What's wrong?
No #$%&@# way.
#$%&@# Maverick.

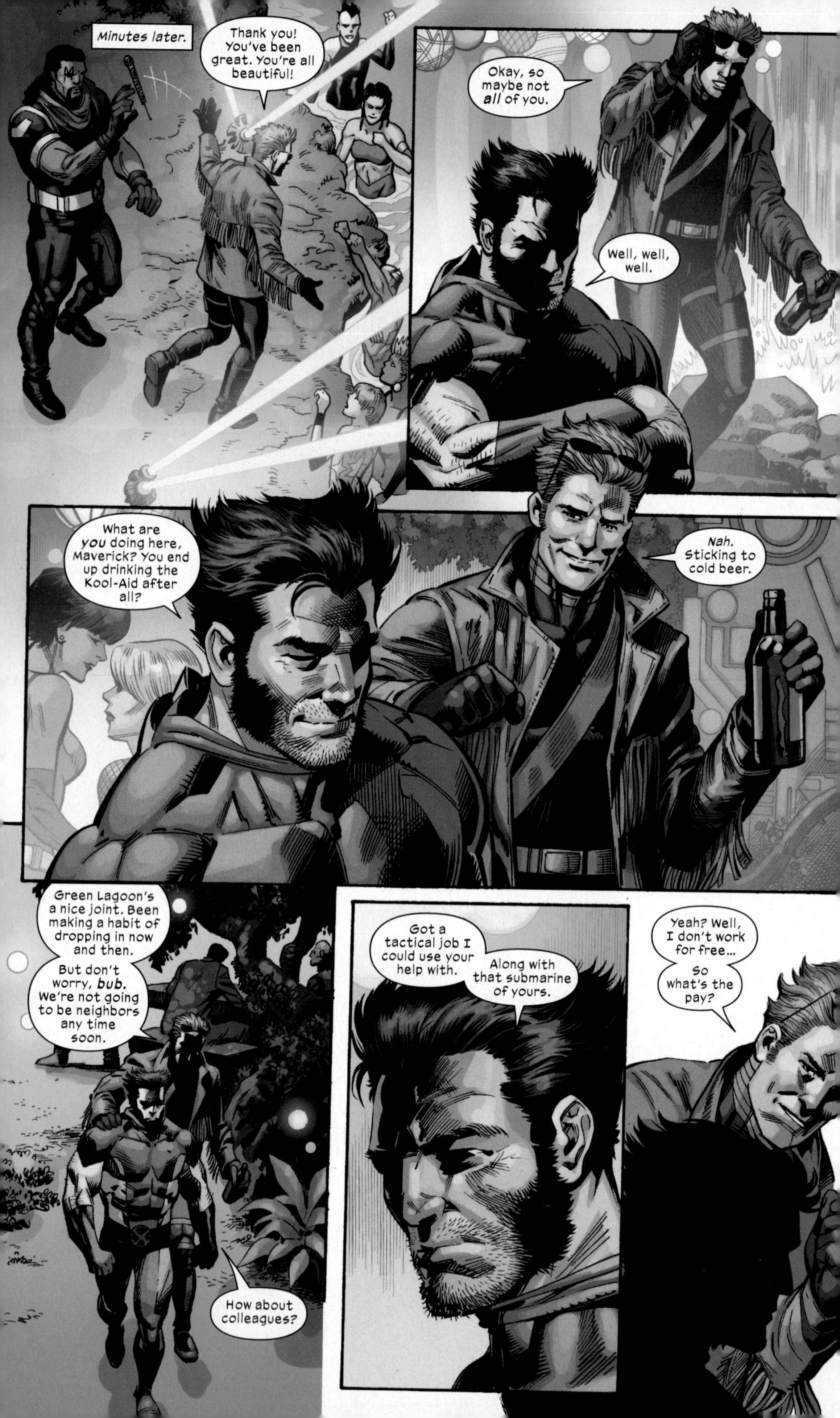

Minutes later.
Thank you! You've been great. You're all beautiful!
Okay, so maybe not *all* of you.
Well, well, well.
What are *you* doing here, Maverick? You end up drinking the Kool-Aid after all?
Nah. Sticking to cold beer.
Green Lagoon's a nice joint. Been making a habit of dropping in now and then.
But don't worry, *bub.* We're not going to be neighbors any time soon.
How about colleagues?
Got a tactical job I could use your help with.
Along with that submarine of yours.
Yeah? Well, I don't work for free...
So what's the pay?

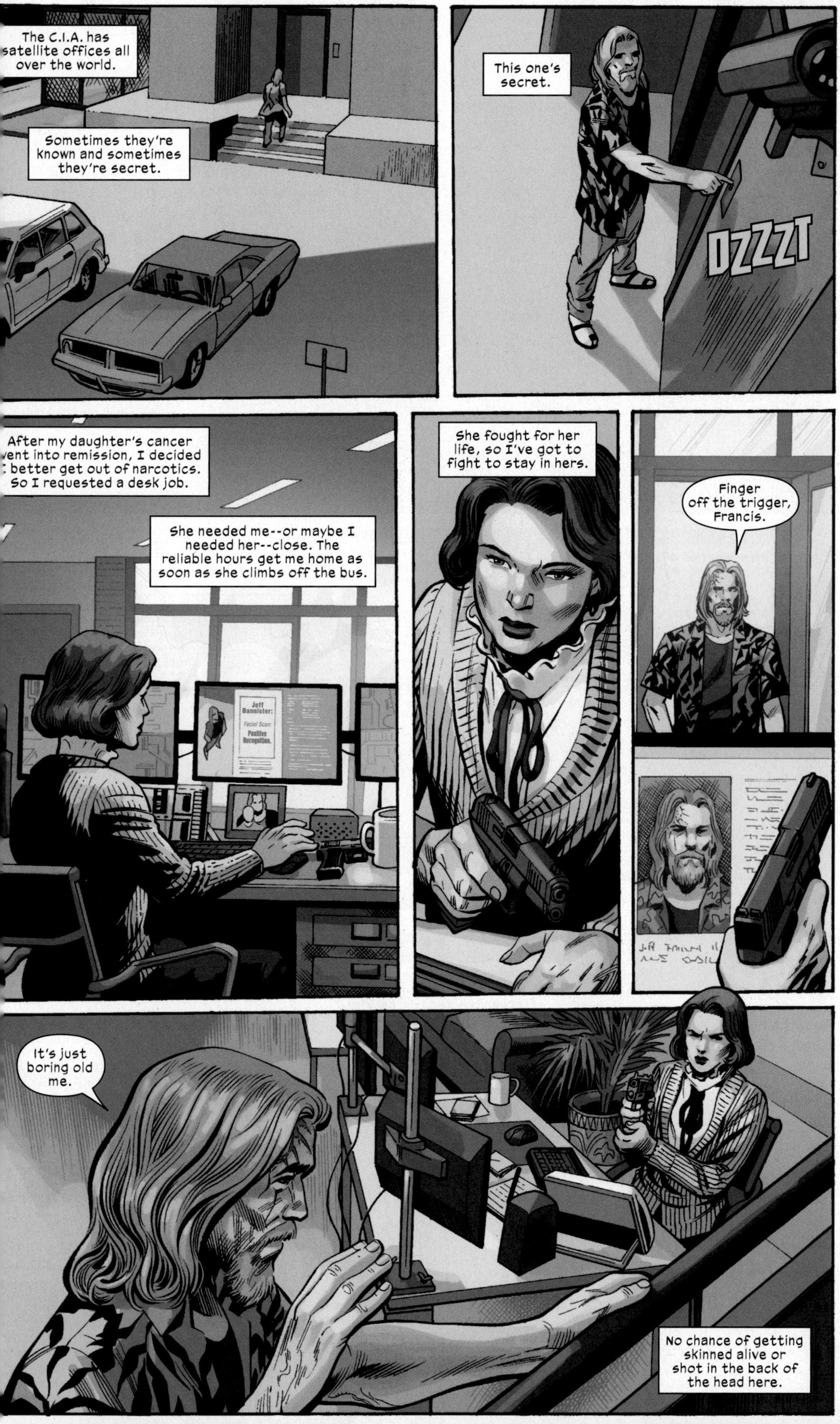

The C.I.A. has satellite offices all over the world.
Sometimes they're known and sometimes they're secret.
This one's secret.
DZZZT
After my daughter's cancer vent into remission, I decided better get out of narcotics. So I requested a desk job.
She needed me--or maybe I needed her--close. The reliable hours get me home as soon as she climbs off the bus.
Jeff Bannister: Facial Scan: Positive Recognition.
She fought for her life, so I've got to fight to stay in hers.
Finger off the trigger, Francis.
It's just boring old me.
No chance of getting skinned alive or shot in the back of the head here.

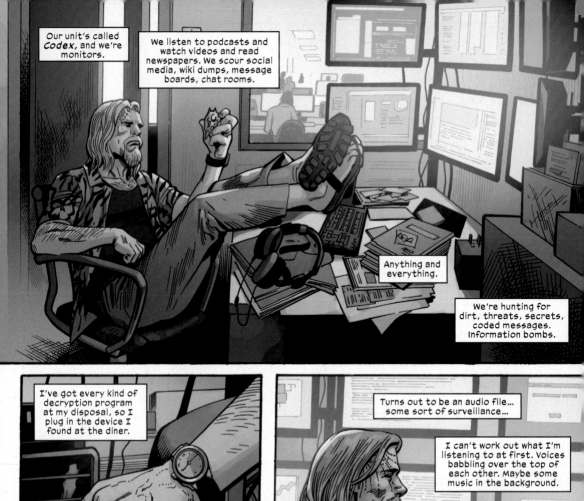

Our unit's called *Codex,* and we're monitors.

We listen to podcasts and watch videos and read newspapers. We scour social media, wiki dumps, message boards, chat rooms.

Anything and everything.

We're hunting for dirt, threats, secrets, coded messages. Information bombs.

I've got every kind of decryption program at my disposal, so I plug in the device I found at the diner.

Organic tech. So that means Krakoan or Terra Verdean.

Turns out to be an audio file... some sort of surveillance...

I can't work out what I'm listening to at first. Voices babbling over the top of each other. Maybe some music in the background.

So I filter out the background noise and isolate some of the frequencies and realize I'm listening to conversations.

More than a hundred of them altogether. Different conversations, different tracks. Each a clean, discernible file.

This thing's go serious rang and sensitivity

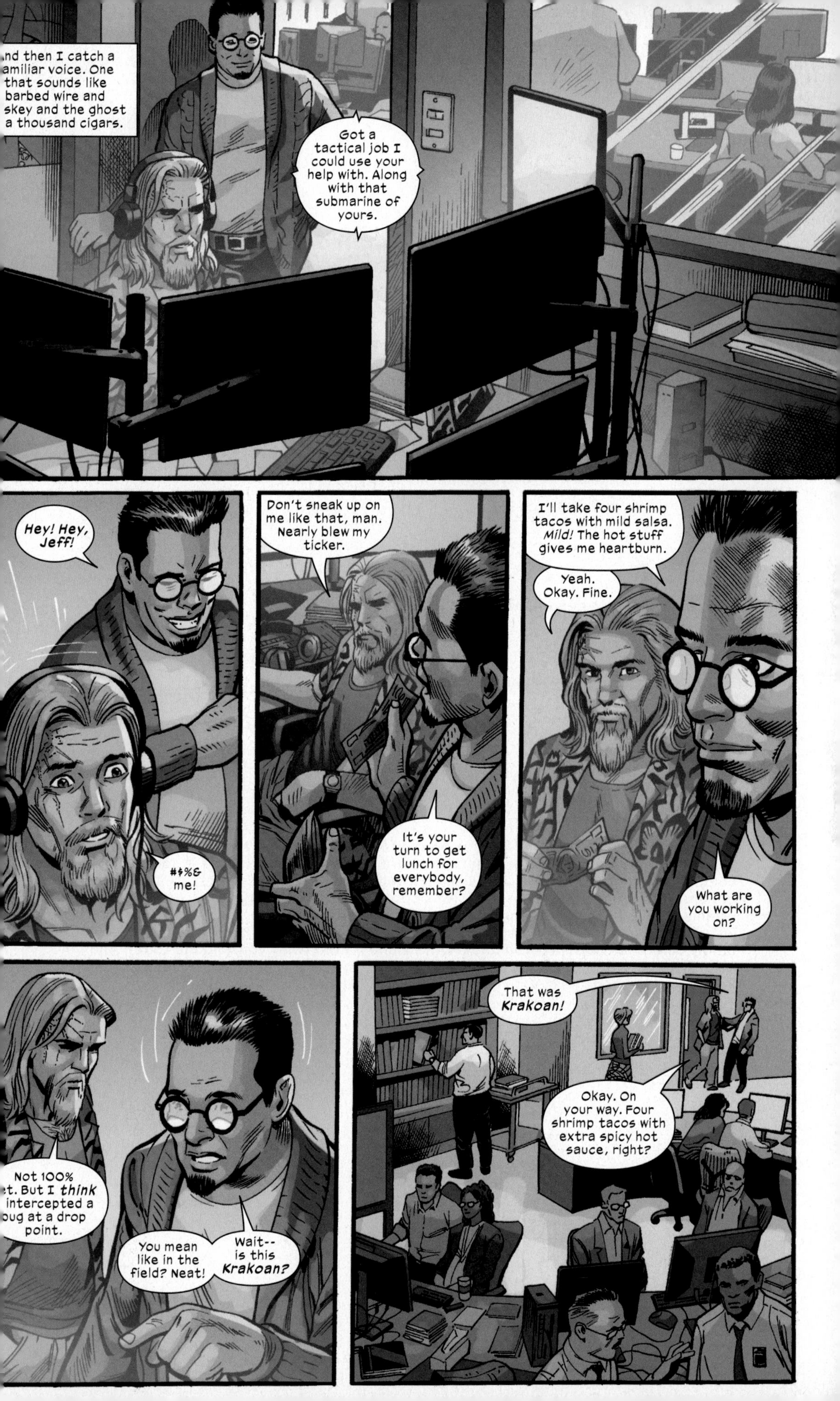

nd then I catch a amiliar voice. One that sounds like barbed wire and skey and the ghost a thousand cigars.
Got a tactical job I could use your help with. Along with that submarine of yours.
Hey! Hey, Jeff!
#$%& me!
Don't sneak up on me like that, man. Nearly blew my ticker.
It's your turn to get lunch for everybody, remember?
I'll take four shrimp tacos with mild salsa. Mild! The hot stuff gives me heartburn.
Yeah. Okay. Fine.
What are you working on?
Not 100% t. But I think intercepted a bug at a drop point.
You mean like in the field? Neat!
Wait-- is this Krakoan?
That was Krakoan!
Okay. On your way. Four shrimp tacos with extra spicy hot sauce, right?

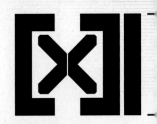

SAGE'S LOGBOOK: TRANSMISSION ALERT

///collating all mentions of "Krakoa"///

<<sources>>
messaging apps
social media
print media
cellular transmissions
digital radio
email
chat rooms
...
...
...

///cross analysis to determine threat level///

Flagged: File C22V57X111
--Cellular transmission--
Tower ping: eNode B ID: Baltimore, MD.

Transcript:

"Yes, um, hello. It's me. But I guess you...probably know that? I'm using the burner phone. You told me to call and leave a message here if anything showed up in the office. Anything compromising about Krakoa. And I think...well...I don't want to overstate things, but one of our analysts found something, and...this could be a jackpot? Again, I don't want to make any promises. But it looks hot. And if it is -- if it's good and valuable, if you're happy about it -- I'm wondering...well, we had an agreement? You said you'd forget about the pictures you found on my computer. You said you'd leave me alone if I did what you told me to do. And now I've done what you told me to do. So...yeah. Okay. I'm going to go now. I guess I...I don't really know what happens next. Do you call me back? Call me back. Bye-bye."

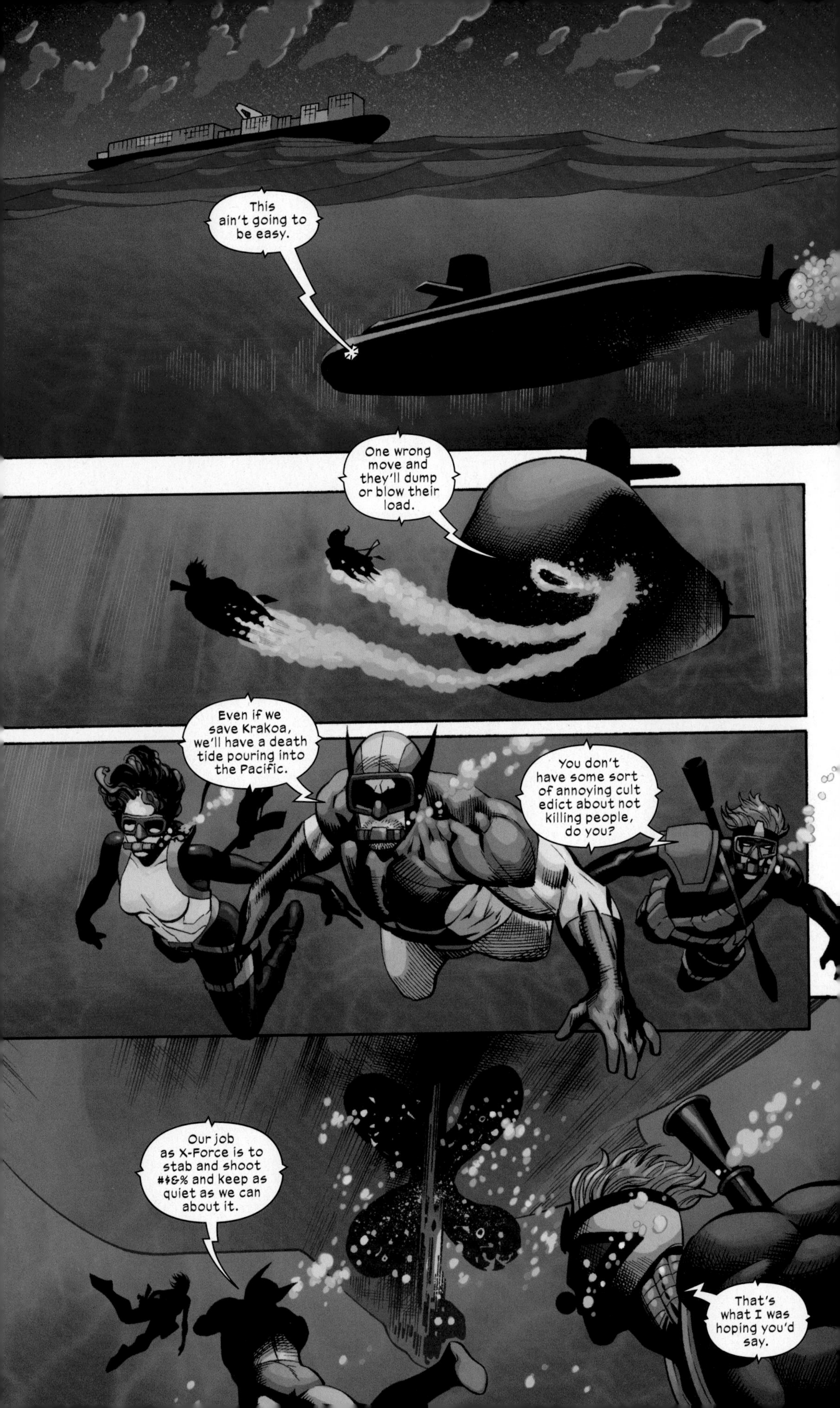
This ain't going to be easy.
One wrong move and they'll dump or blow their load.
Even if we save Krakoa, we'll have a death tide pouring into the Pacific.
You don't have some sort of annoying cult edict about not killing people, do you?
Our job as X-Force is to stab and shoot #$&% and keep as quiet as we can about it.
That's what I was hoping you'd say.

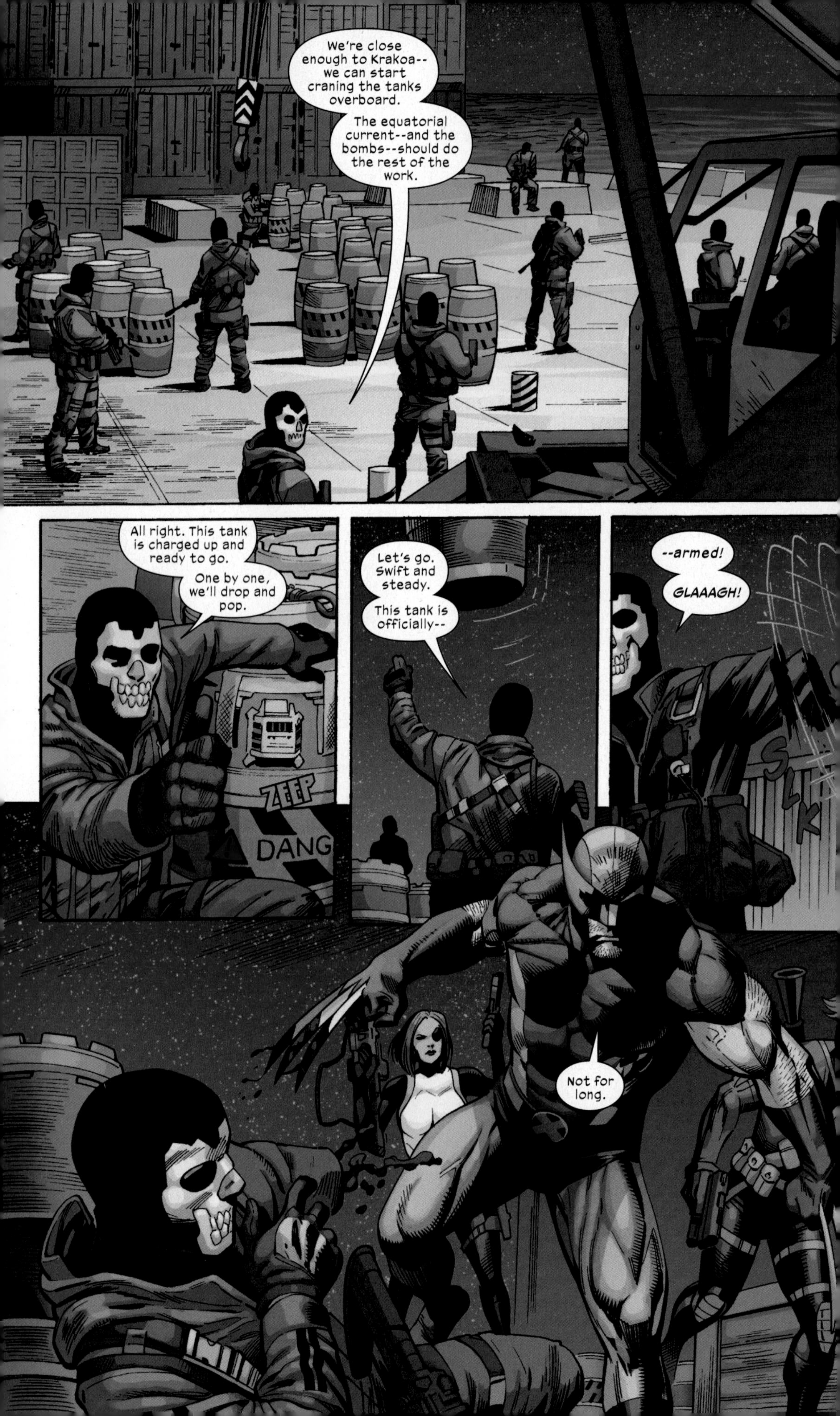
We're close enough to Krakoa-- we can start craning the tanks overboard.
The equatorial current--and the bombs--should do the rest of the work.
All right. This tank is charged up and ready to go.
One by one, we'll drop and pop.
ZEEP
DANG
Let's go. Swift and steady.
This tank is officially--
--armed!
GLAAAGH!
SLK
Not for long.

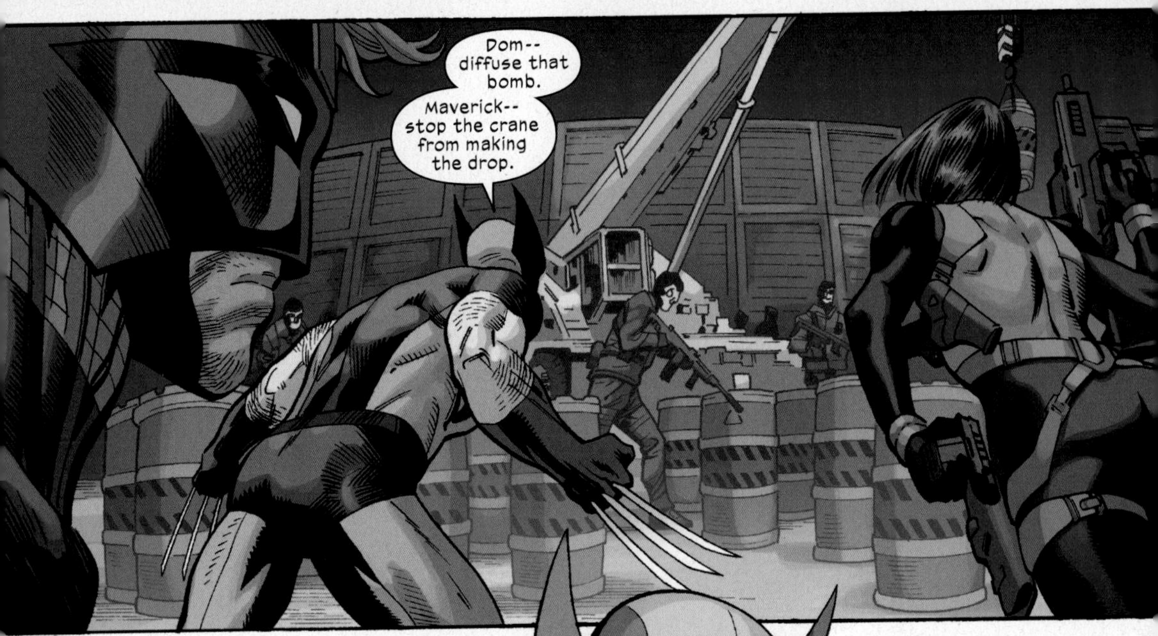
Dom--
diffuse that
bomb.
Maverick--
stop the crane
from making
the drop.

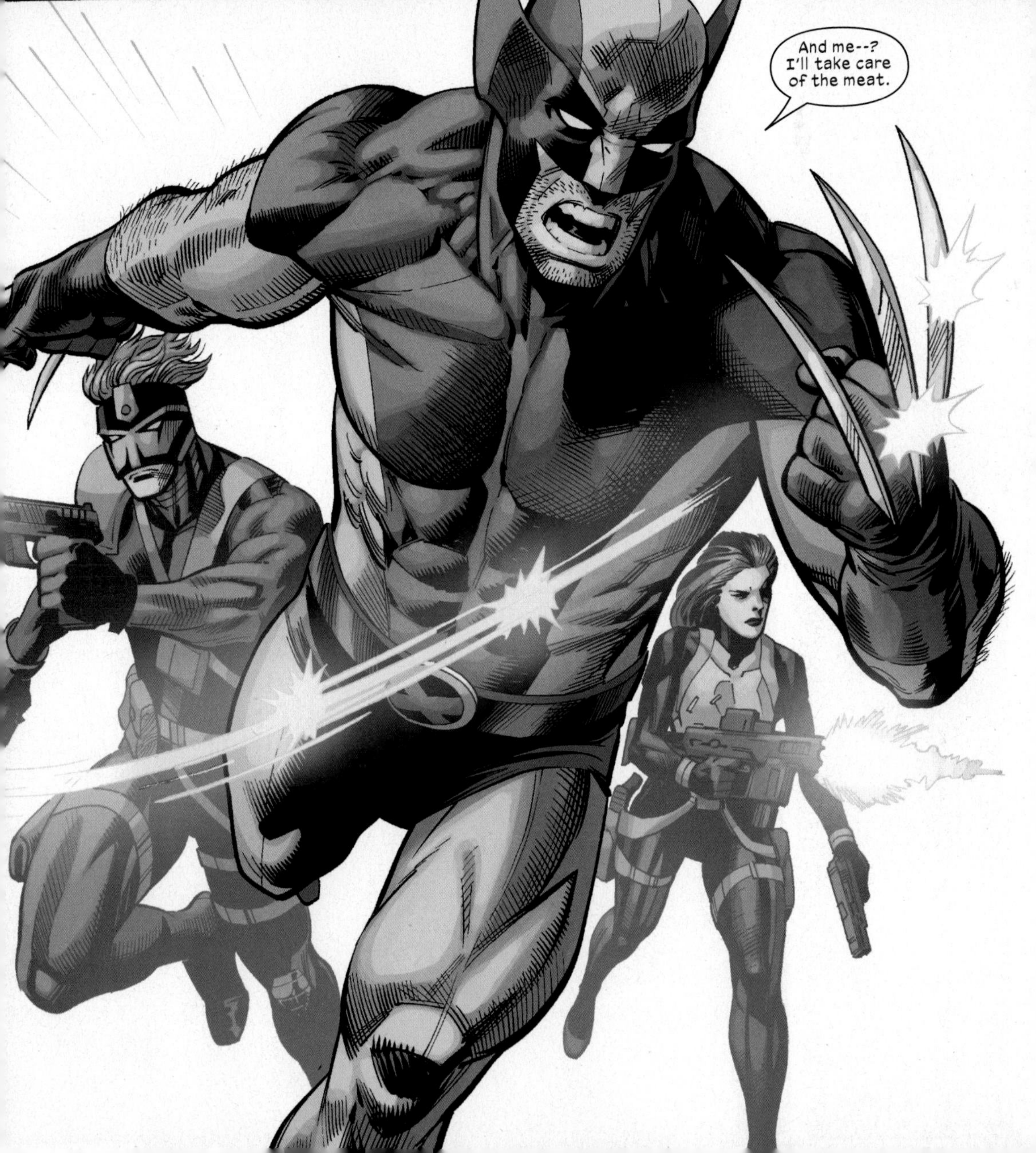
And me--?
I'll take care
of the meat.

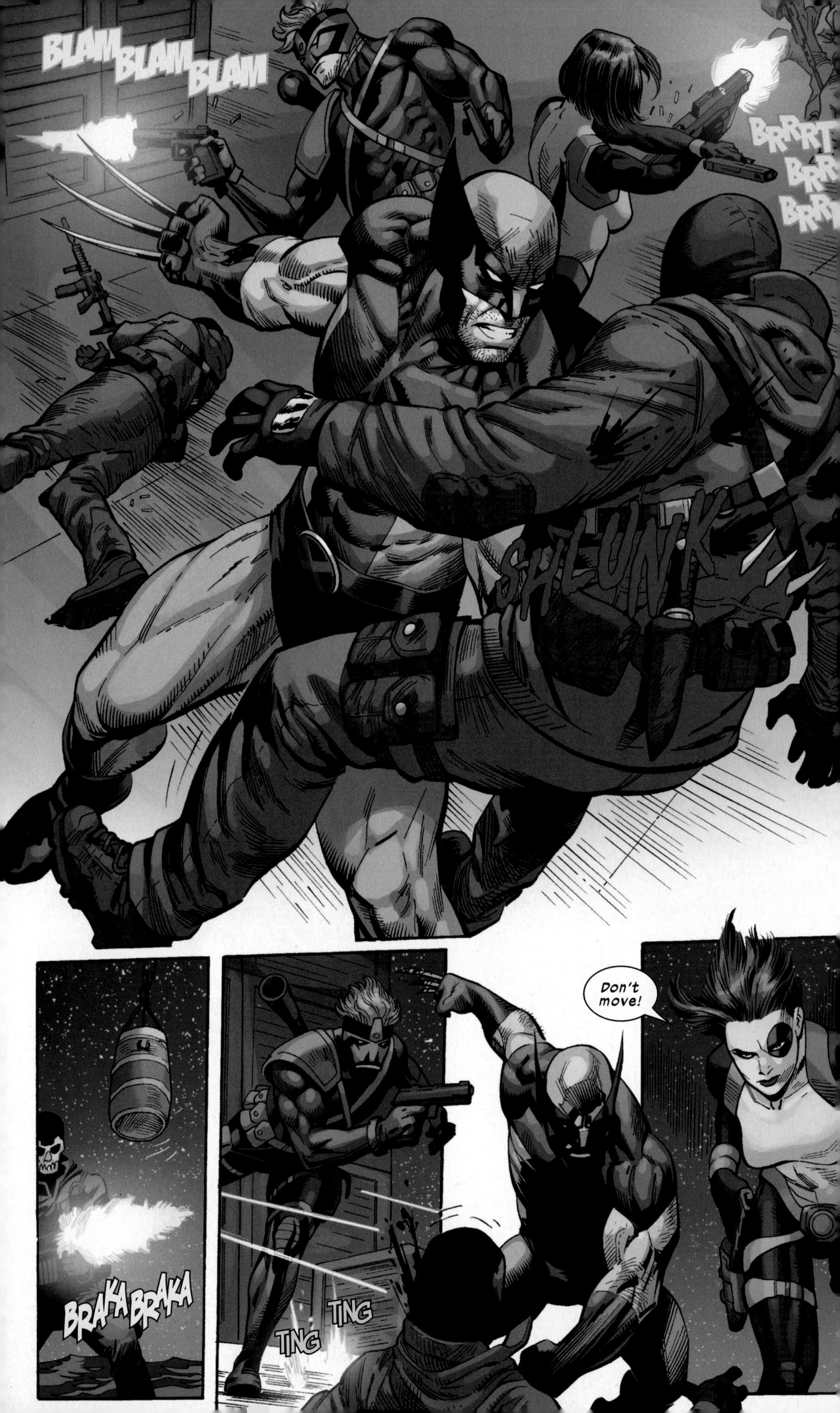
BLAM BLAM BLAM
BRRRT BRRR BRRR
SHLUNK
BRAKA BRAKA
TING TING
Don't move!

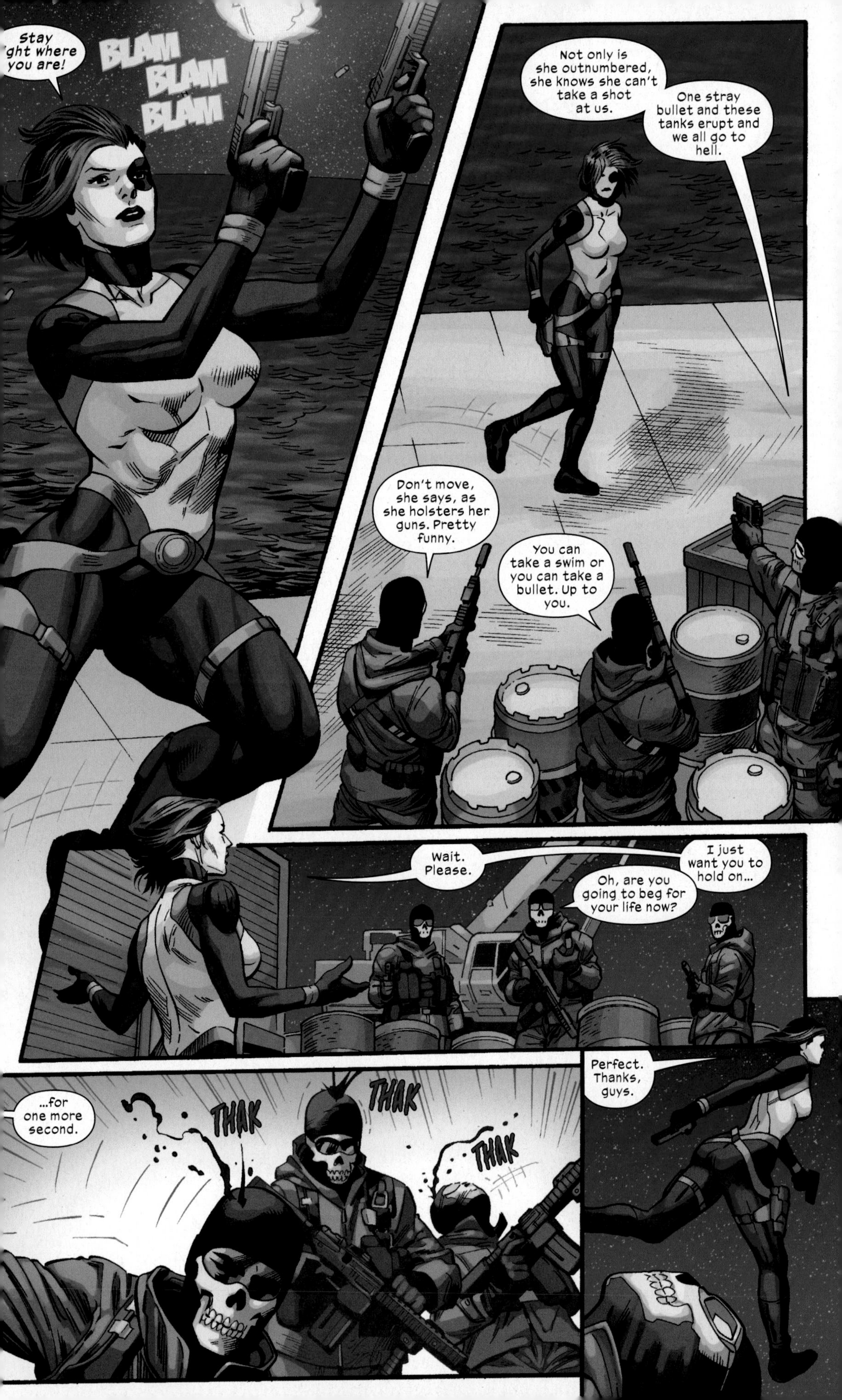

Stay
'ght where you are!
BLAM BLAM BLAM
Not only is she outnumbered, she knows she can't take a shot at us.
One stray bullet and these tanks erupt and we all go to hell.
Don't move, she says, as she holsters her guns. Pretty funny.
You can take a swim or you can take a bullet. Up to you.
Wait. Please.
I just want you to hold on...
Oh, are you going to beg for your life now?
...for one more second.
THAK
THAK
THAK
Perfect. Thanks, guys.

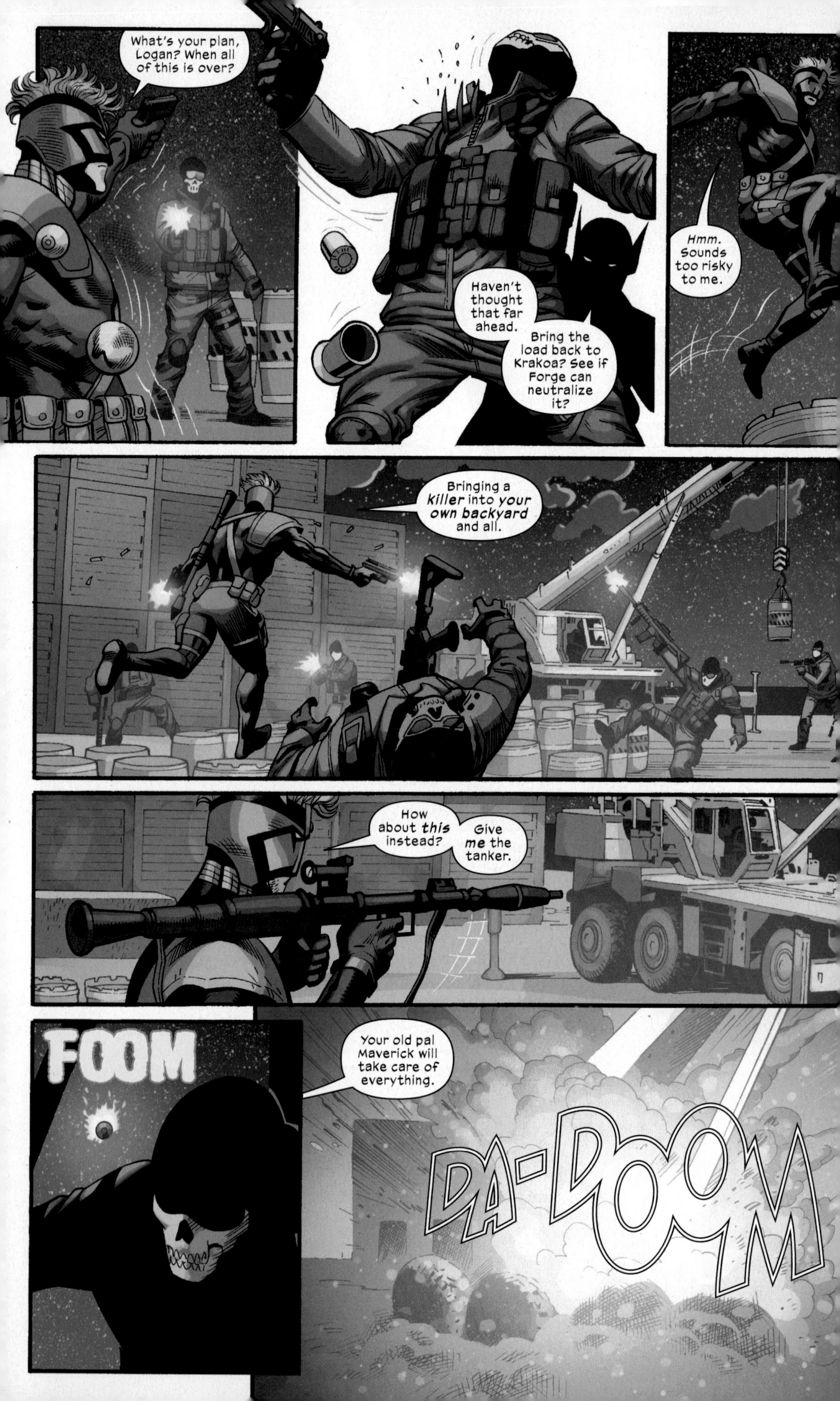
What's your plan, Logan? When all of this is over?
Haven't thought that far ahead.
Bring the load back to Krakoa? See if Forge can neutralize it?
Hmm. Sounds too risky to me.
Bringing a *killer* into *your own backyard* and all.
How about *this* instead?
Give *me* the tanker.
FOOM
Your old pal Maverick will take care of everything.
DA-DOOM

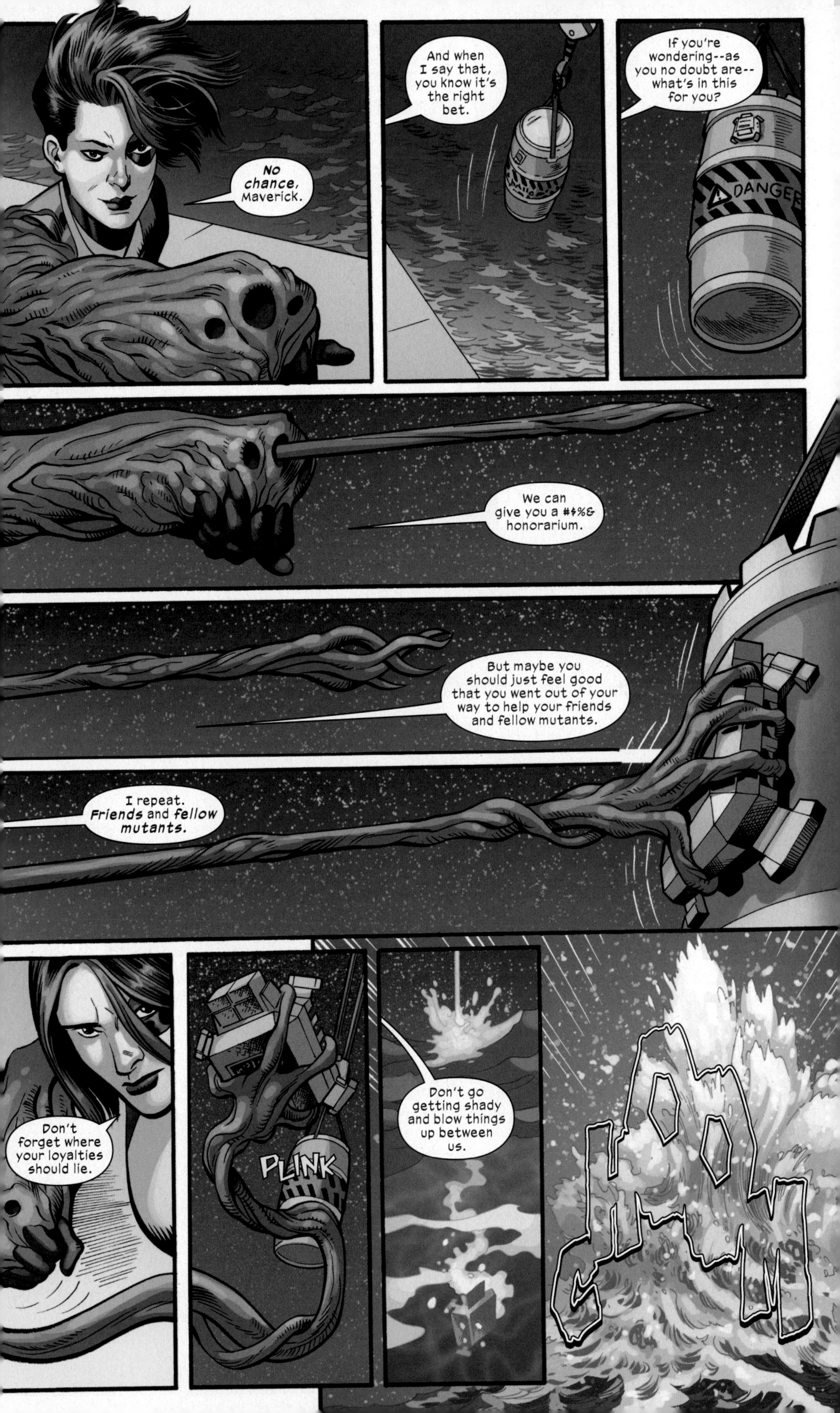
No chance, Maverick.
And when I say that, you know it's the right bet.
If you're wondering--as you no doubt are--what's in this for you?
DANGER
We can give you a #$%& honorarium.
But maybe you should just feel good that you went out of your way to help your friends and fellow mutants.
I repeat. Friends and fellow mutants.
Don't forget where your loyalties should lie.
PLINK
Don't go getting shady and blow things up between us.

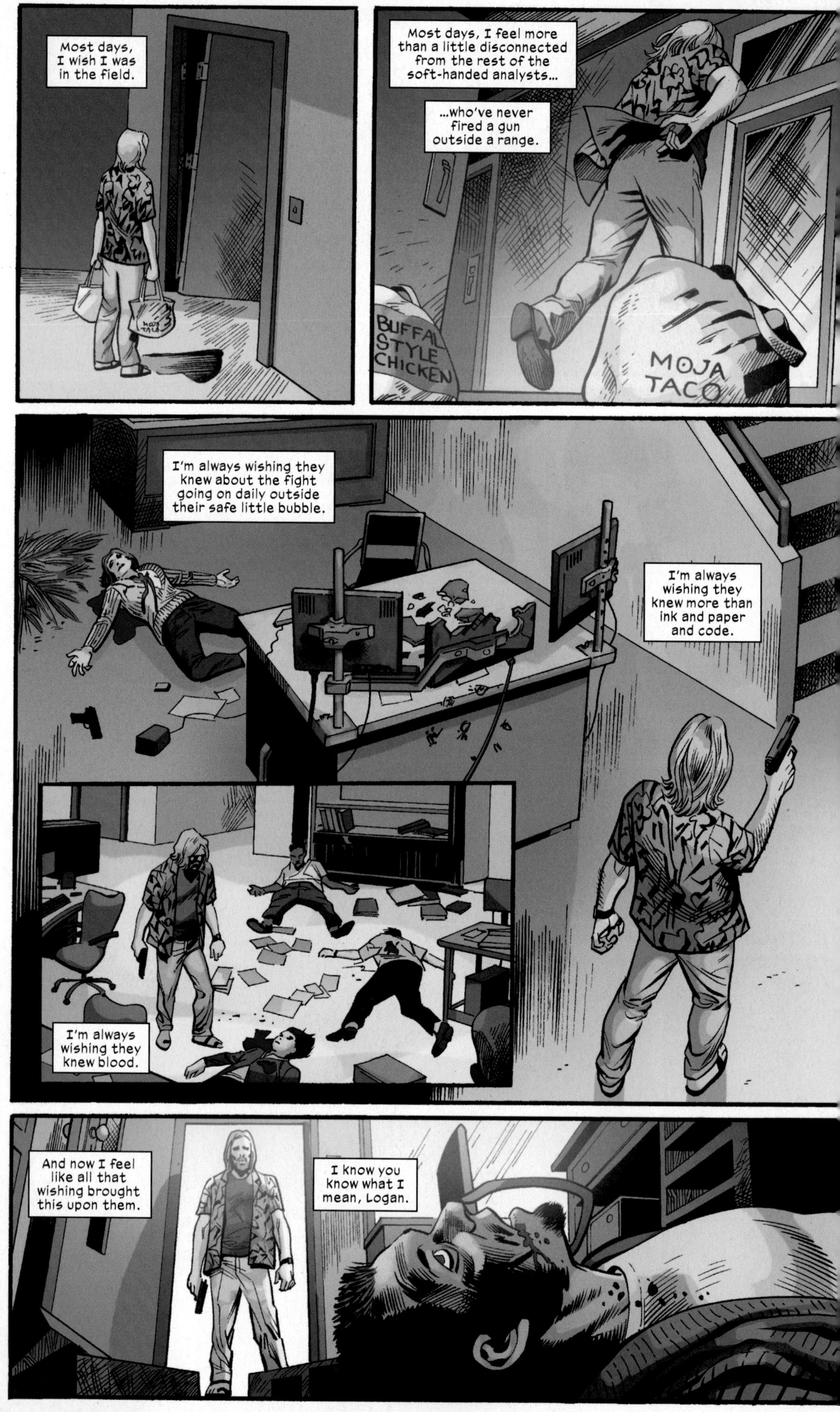
Most days, I wish I was in the field.
Most days, I feel more than a little disconnected from the rest of the soft-handed analysts...
...who've never fired a gun outside a range.
BUFFALO STYLE CHICKEN
MOJA TACO
I'm always wishing they knew about the fight going on daily outside their safe little bubble.
I'm always wishing they knew more than ink and paper and code.
I'm always wishing they knew blood.
And now I feel like all that wishing brought this upon them.
I know you know what I mean, Logan.

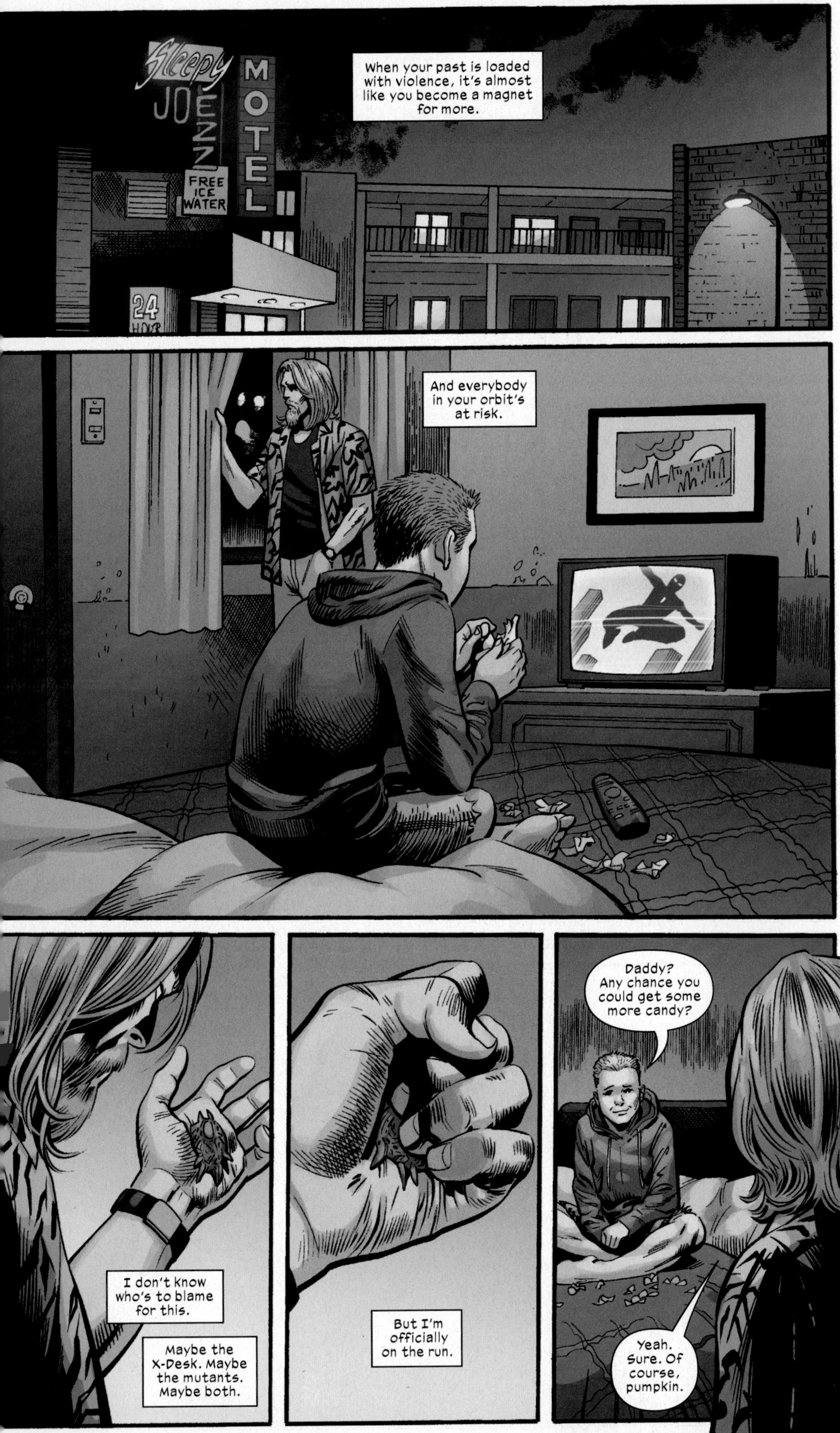
Sleepy JOE ZZZ
MOTEL
FREE ICE WATER
24 HOUR
When your past is loaded with violence, it's almost like you become a magnet for more.
And everybody in your orbit's at risk.
I don't know who's to blame for this.
Maybe the X-Desk. Maybe the mutants. Maybe both.
But I'm officially on the run.
Daddy? Any chance you could get some more candy?
Yeah. Sure. Of course, pumpkin.

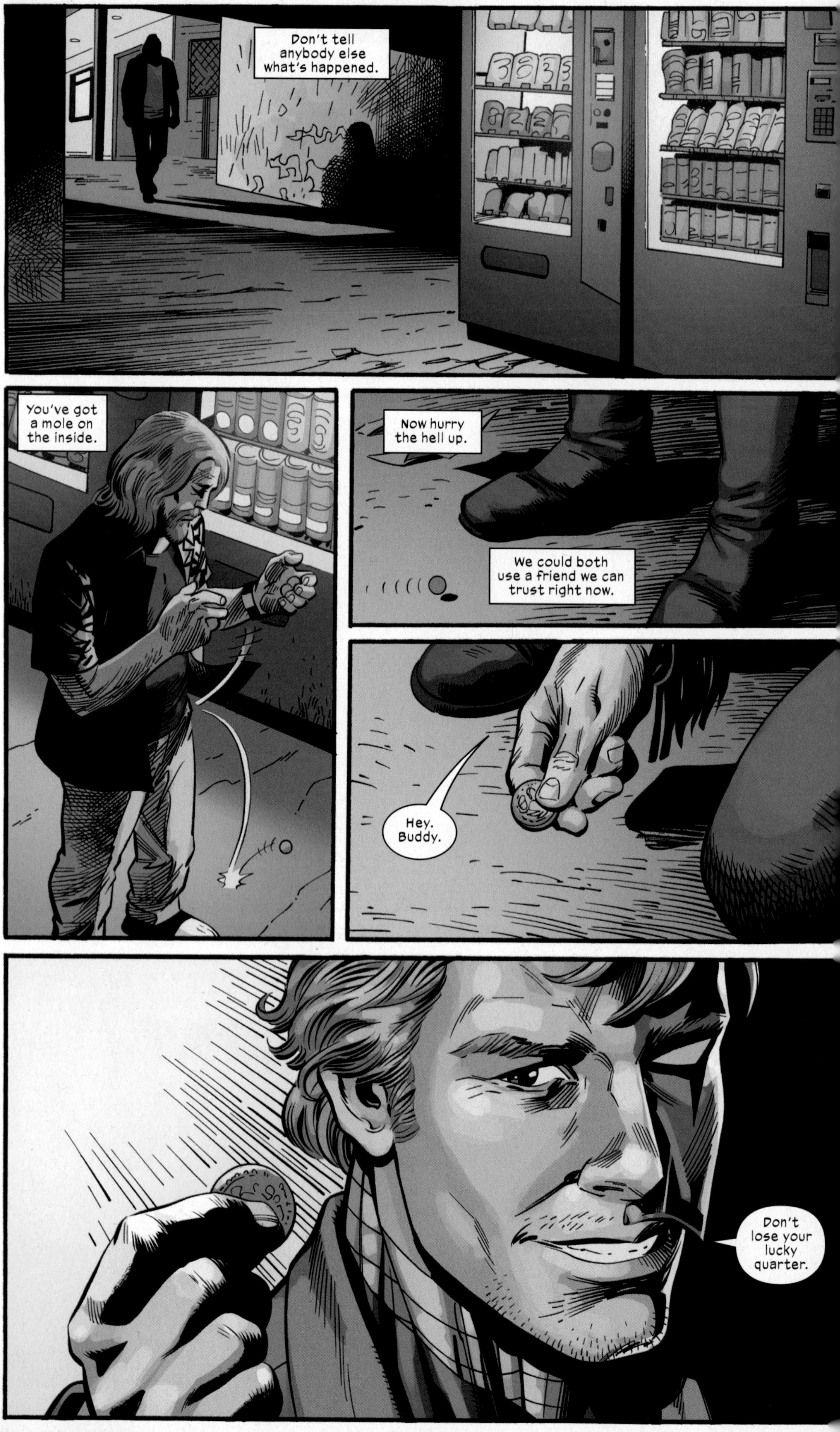
Don't tell anybody else what's happened.
You've got a mole on the inside.
Now hurry the hell up.
We could both use a friend we can trust right now.
Hey. Buddy.
Don't lose your lucky quarter.

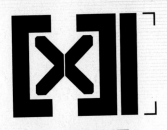

SAGE'S LOGBOOK: FIELD REPORT: WOLVERINE

Transcript:

Me and Jeff, we got a system. I planted a Krakoan gate in his backyard. We meet up there maybe once a week for some beer and bull.

He changed up his gig at Langley, so he's working regular hours now. He's always home in the evenings -- always. Farting around with his lawn, watching a movie with his kid. Always.

But not tonight.

Tonight, the lights were on, but the back door hung on a hinge. Twenty yards away, I could see the open cupboards in the kitchen, an overturned mattress in a bedroom.

I stepped over a beer bottle in the grass on my way to the house. The stink of men lingered inside. Aftershave and armpits. Every drawer was ripped open. Couch cushions and pillows were slit, the stuffing pulled out. Paintings torn down, carpet ripped up, heating vents yanked and tossed aside.

Somebody had been looking for something.

That's when I remembered the beer bottle in the grass. Right in front of the gate. Nobody keeps a neater yard than Bannister. There's not so much as a single dandelion yellowing that clean green.

I picked it up, shook it, heard the flutter. I smashed the glass against my temple, and sure enough, a note fell out. Addressed to me. Written in sloppy script.

And it began with the line, "Sometimes, when I'm working a case, a detail will pop."

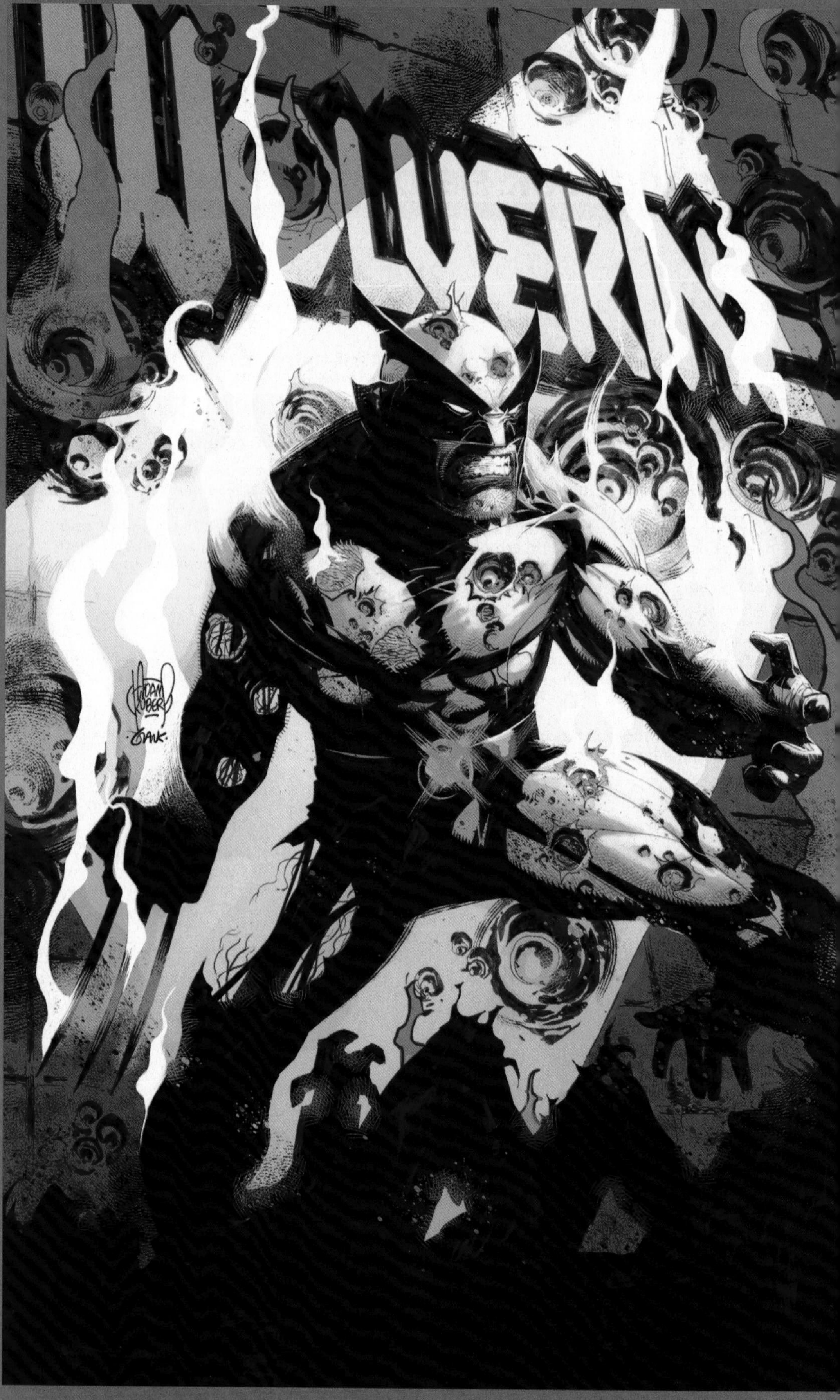

Auction of Secrets

18

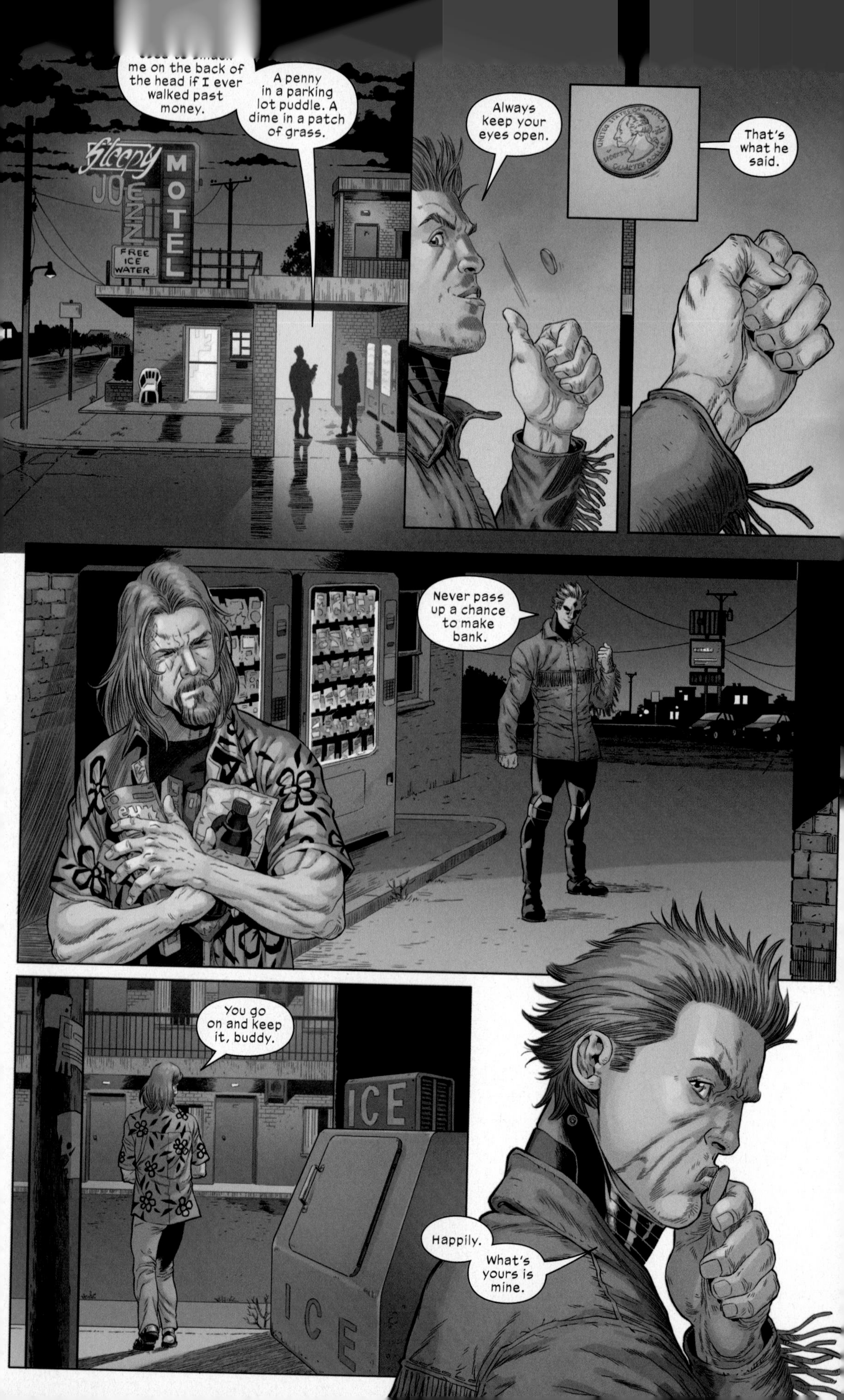

me on the back of the head if I ever walked past money.
A penny in a parking lot puddle. A dime in a patch of grass.
Sleepy
JOE
ZZZ
MOTEL
FREE ICE WATER
Always keep your eyes open.
That's what he said.
Never pass up a chance to make bank.
You go on and keep it, buddy.
ICE
ICE
Happily.
What's yours is mine.

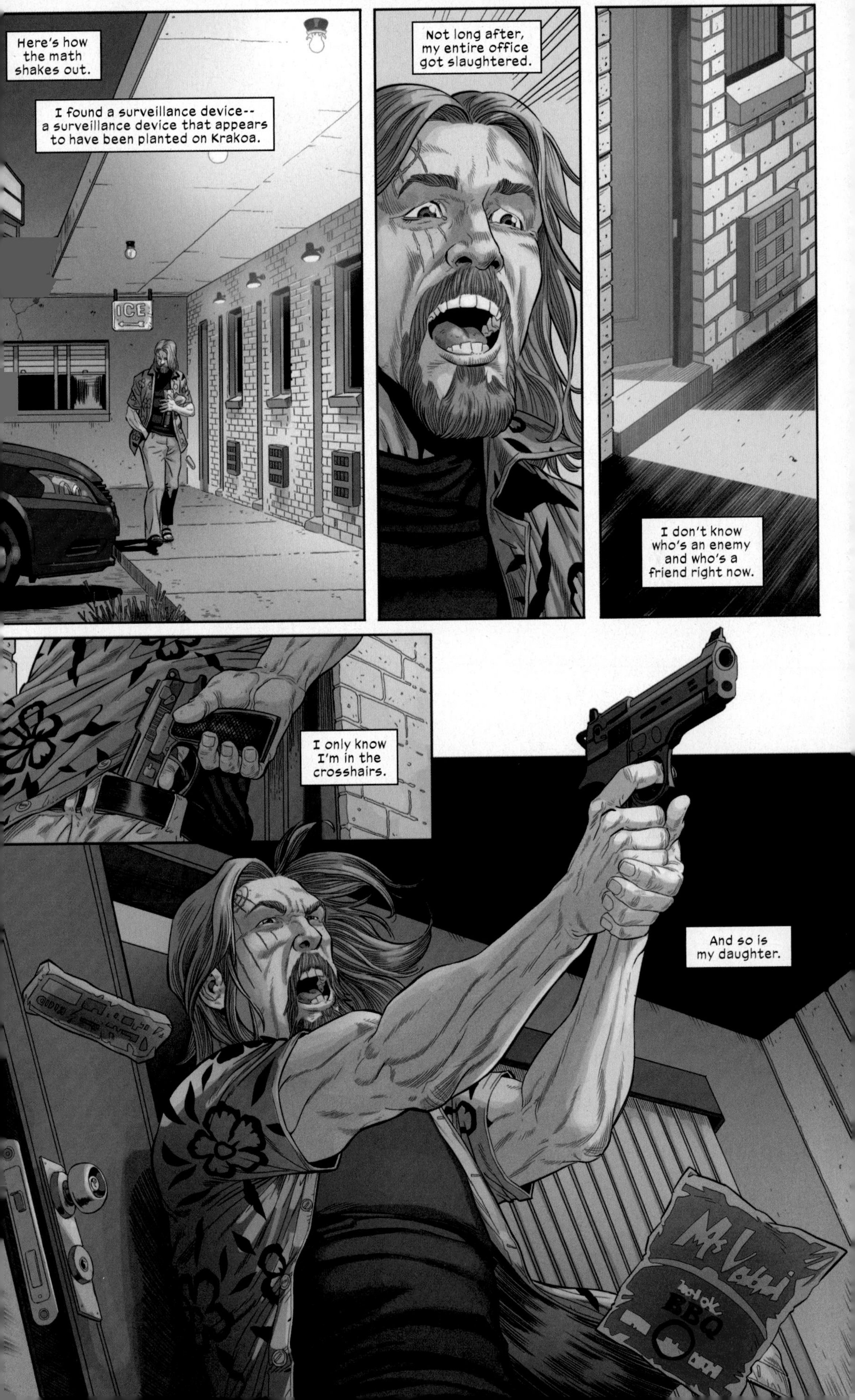
Here's how the math shakes out.
I found a surveillance device-- a surveillance device that appears to have been planted on Krakoa.
ICE
Not long after, my entire office got slaughtered.
I don't know who's an enemy and who's a friend right now.
I only know I'm in the crosshairs.
And so is my daughter.
BBQ

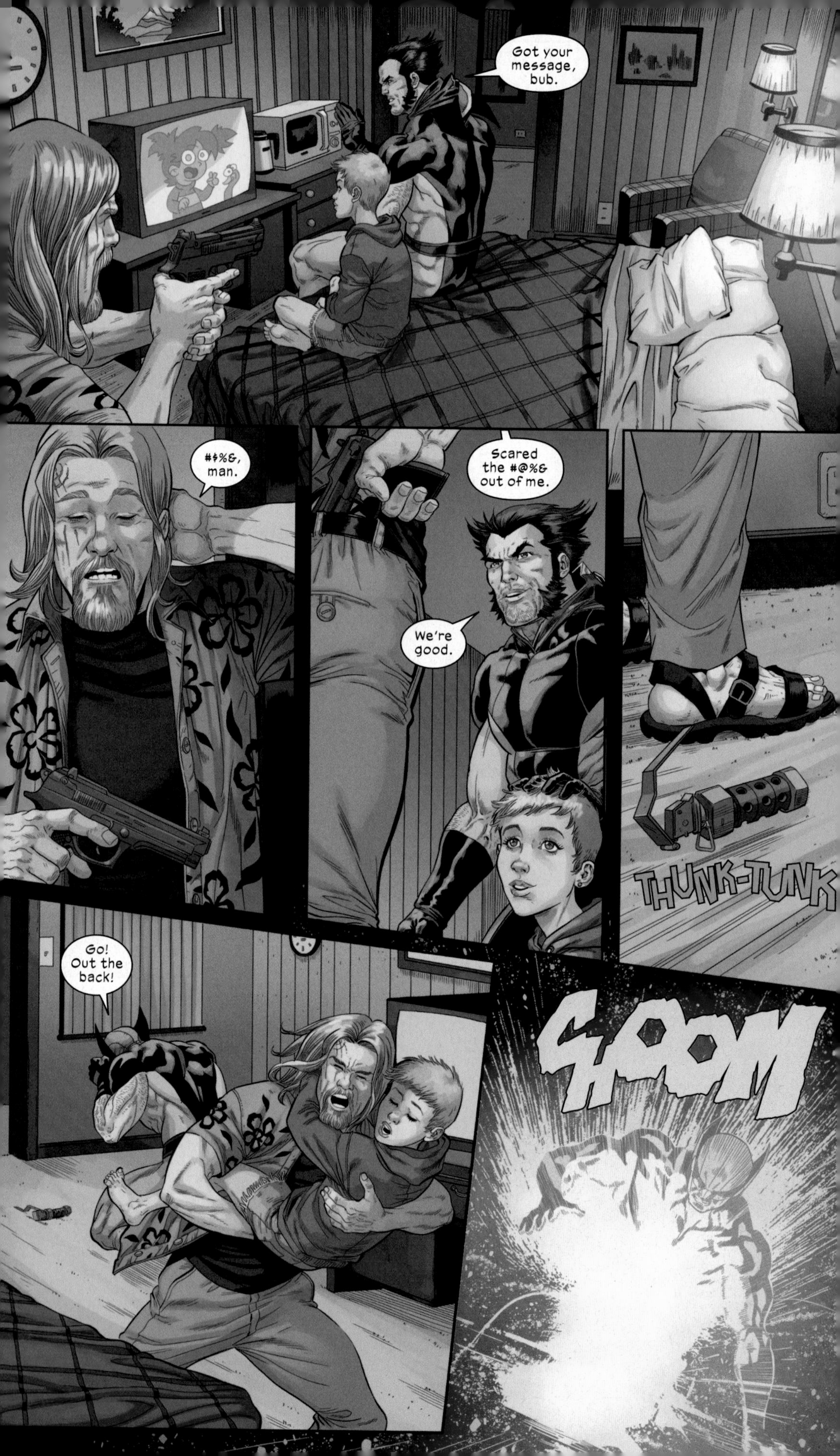
Got your message, bub.
#$%&, man.
Scared the #@%& out of me.
We're good.
THUNK-TUNK
Go! Out the back!
SHOOM

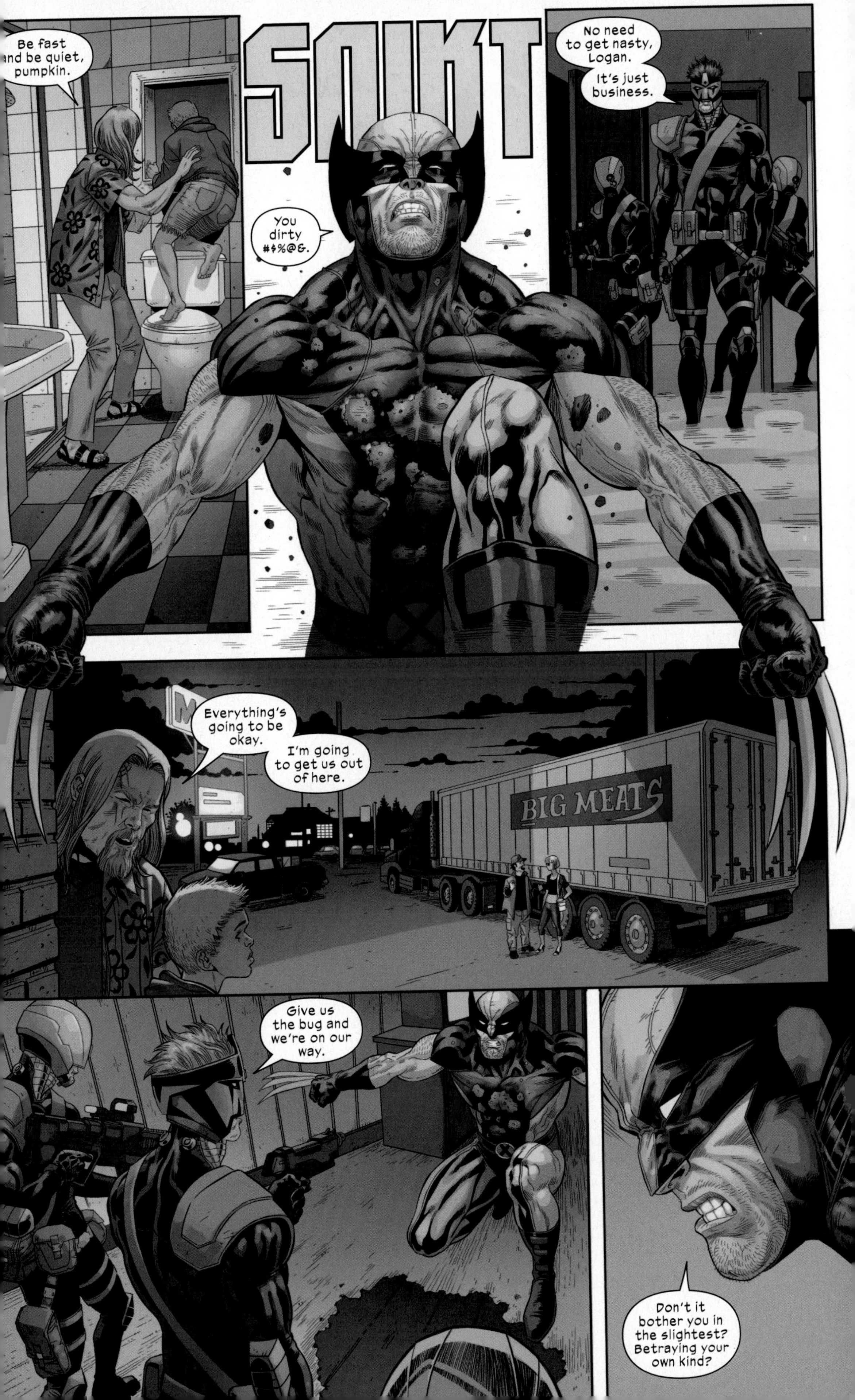
Be fast and be quiet, pumpkin.
SNIKT
You dirty #$%@&.
No need to get nasty, Logan.
It's just business.
Everything's going to be okay.
I'm going to get us out of here.
BIG MEATS
Give us the bug and we're on our way.
Don't it bother you in the slightest? Betraying your own kind?

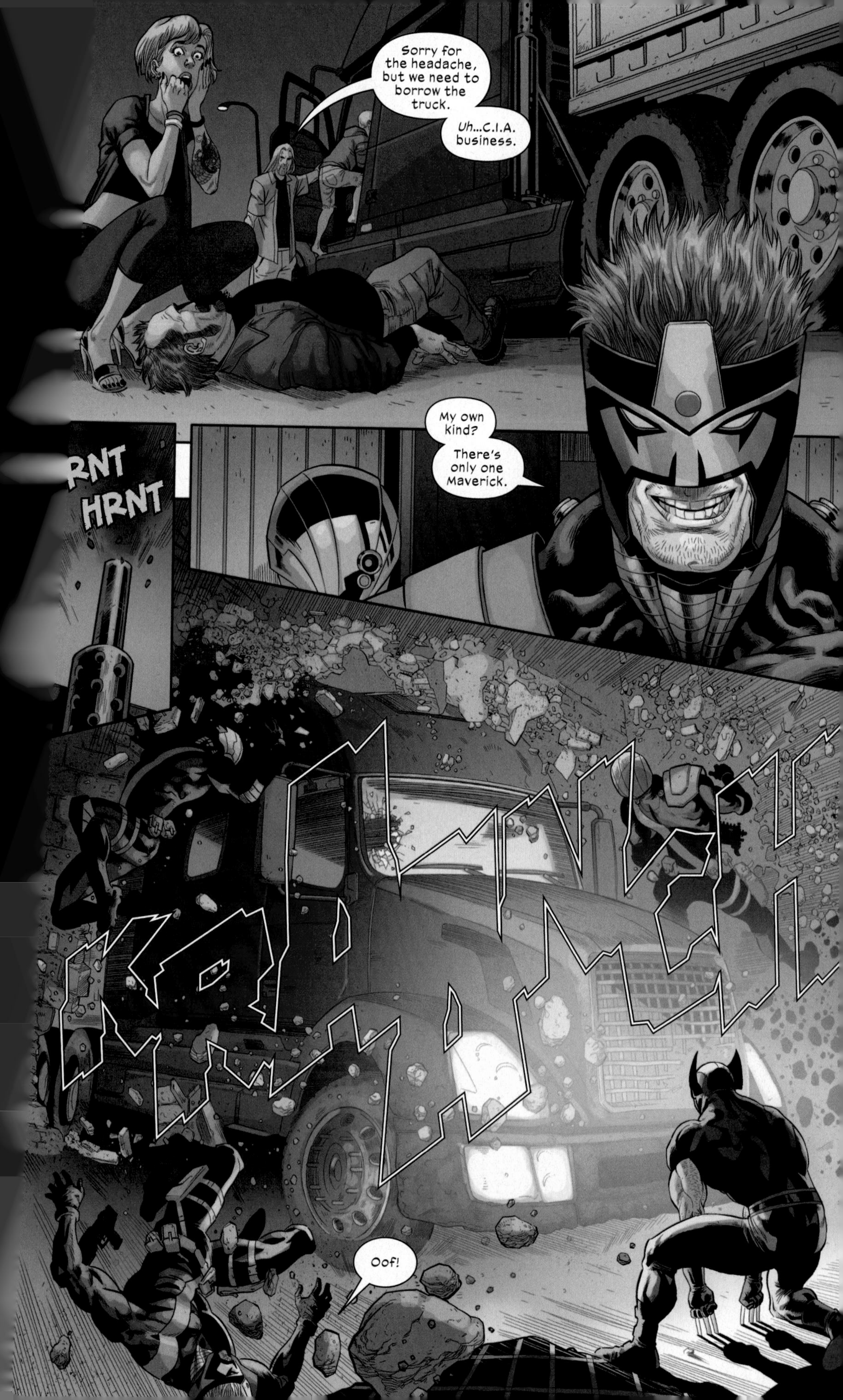

Sorry for the headache, but we need to borrow the truck.
Uh...C.I.A. business.
RNT
HRNT
My own kind?
There's only one Maverick.
Oof!

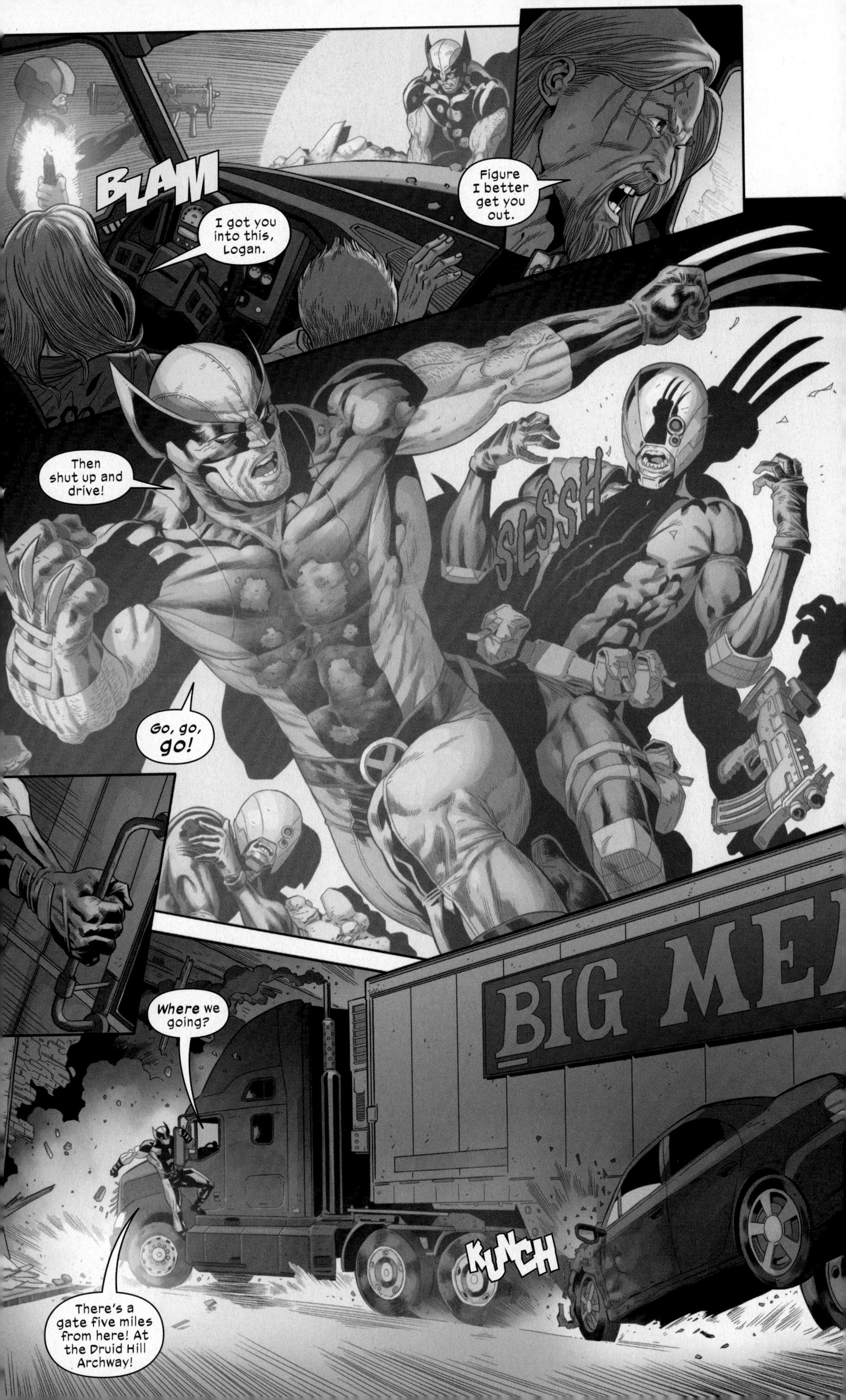
BLAM
Figure I better get you out.
I got you into this, Logan.
Then shut up and drive!
SLSSH
Go, go, go!
BIG ME
Where we going?
KUNCH
There's a gate five miles from here! At the Druid Hill Archway!

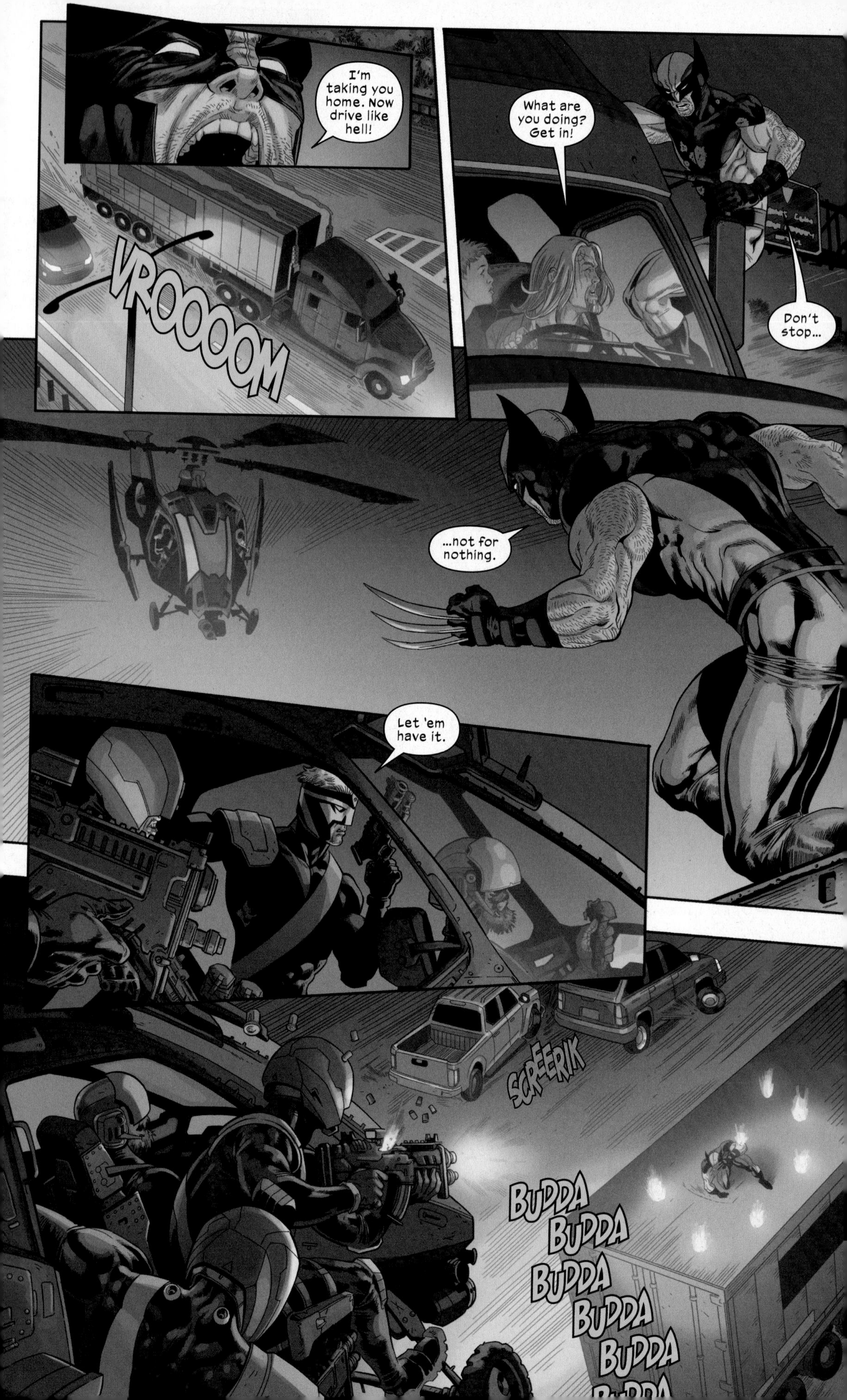

I'm taking you home. Now drive like hell!
VROOOOOM
What are you doing? Get in!
Don't stop...
...not for nothing.
Let 'em have it.
SCREERIK
BUDDA
BUDDA
BUDDA
BUDDA
BUDDA

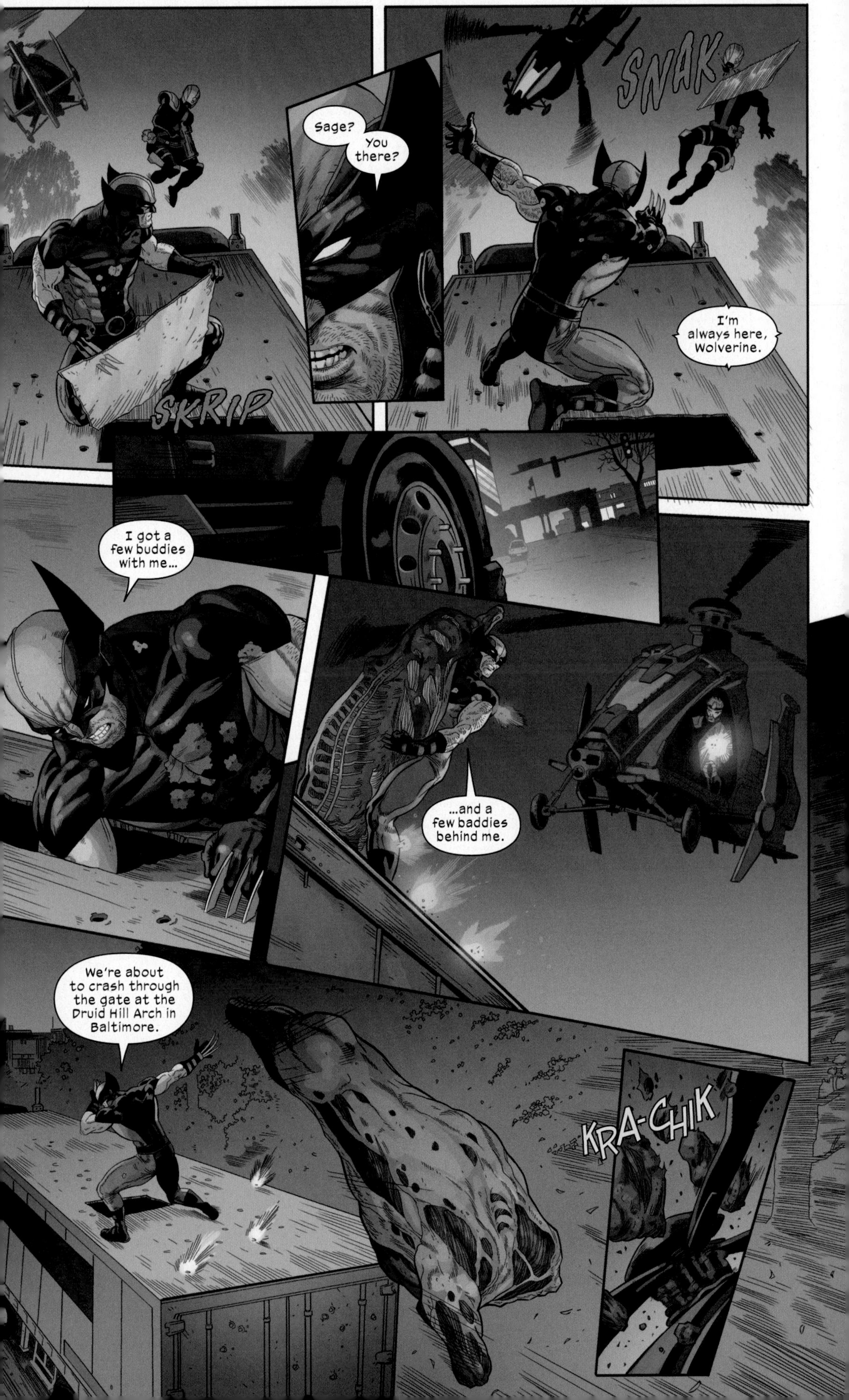
SKRIP
Sage?
You there?
SNAK
I'm always here, Wolverine.
I got a few buddies with me...
...and a few baddies behind me.
We're about to crash through the gate at the Druid Hill Arch in Baltimore.
KRA-CHIK

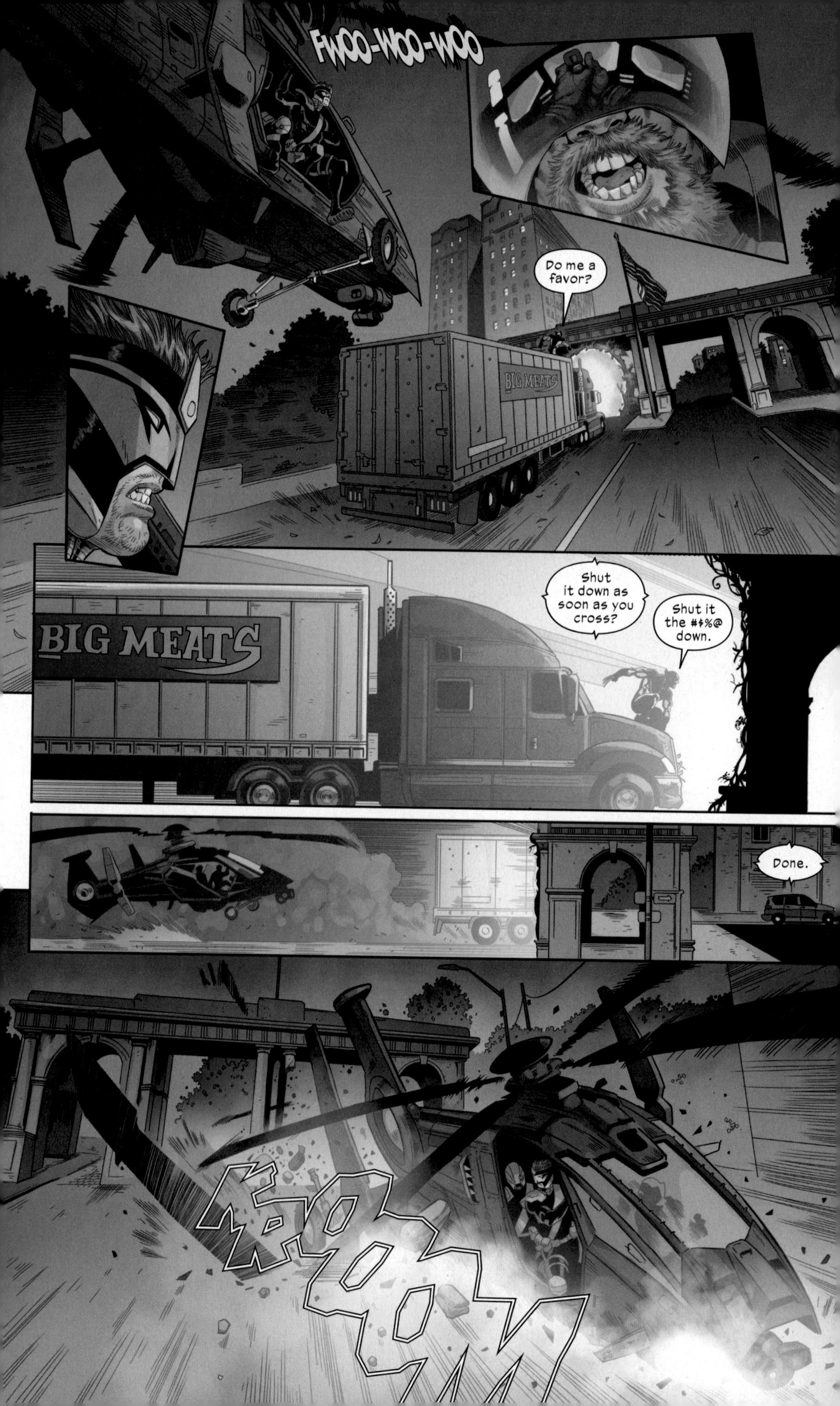
FWOO-WOO-WOO
Do me a favor?
BIG MEATS
BIG MEATS
Shut it down as soon as you cross?
Shut it the #$%@ down.
Done.
KRA-KOOM

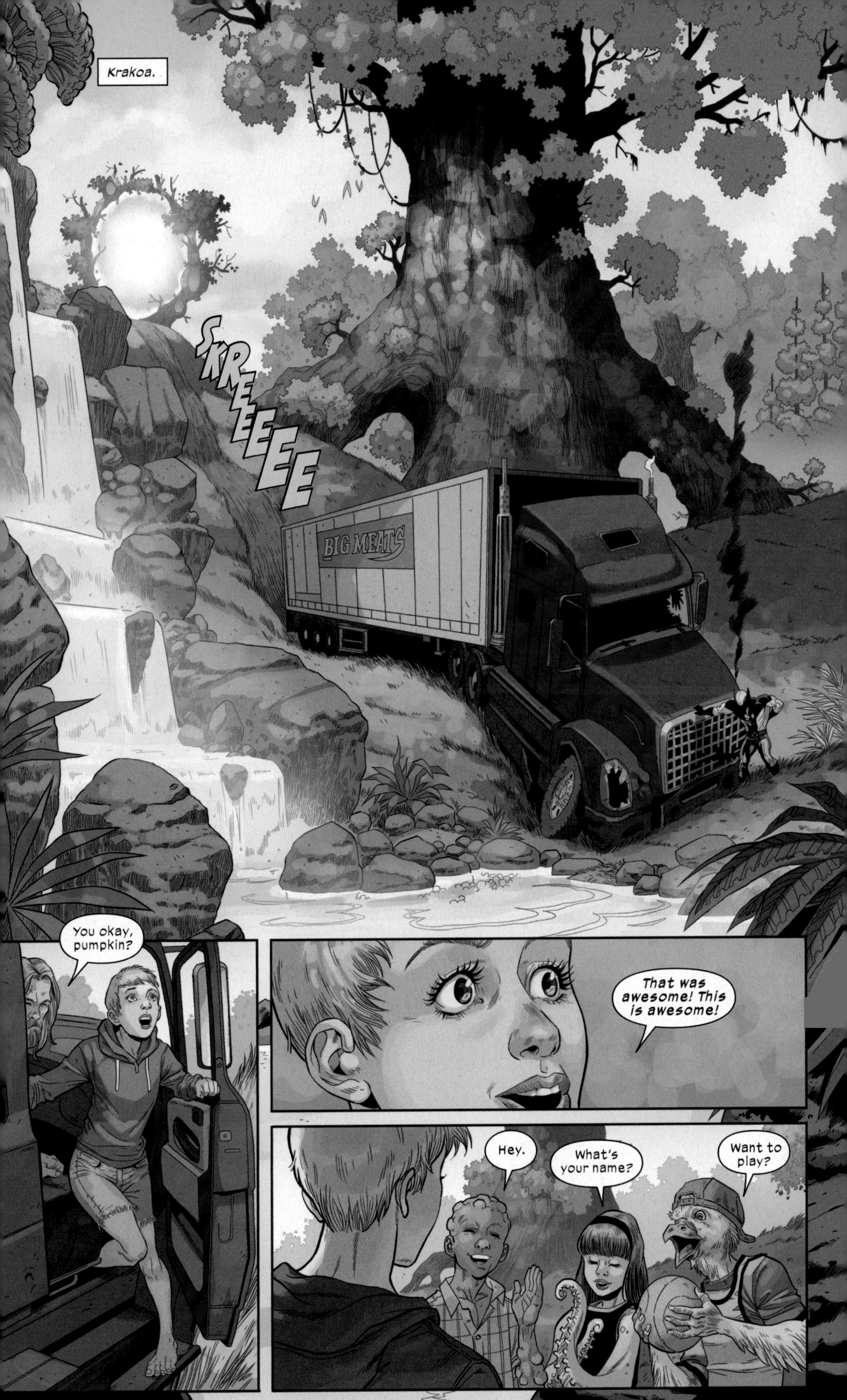

Krakoa.
SKREEEEEE
BIG MEATS
You okay, pumpkin?
That was awesome! This is awesome!
Hey.
What's your name?
Want to play?

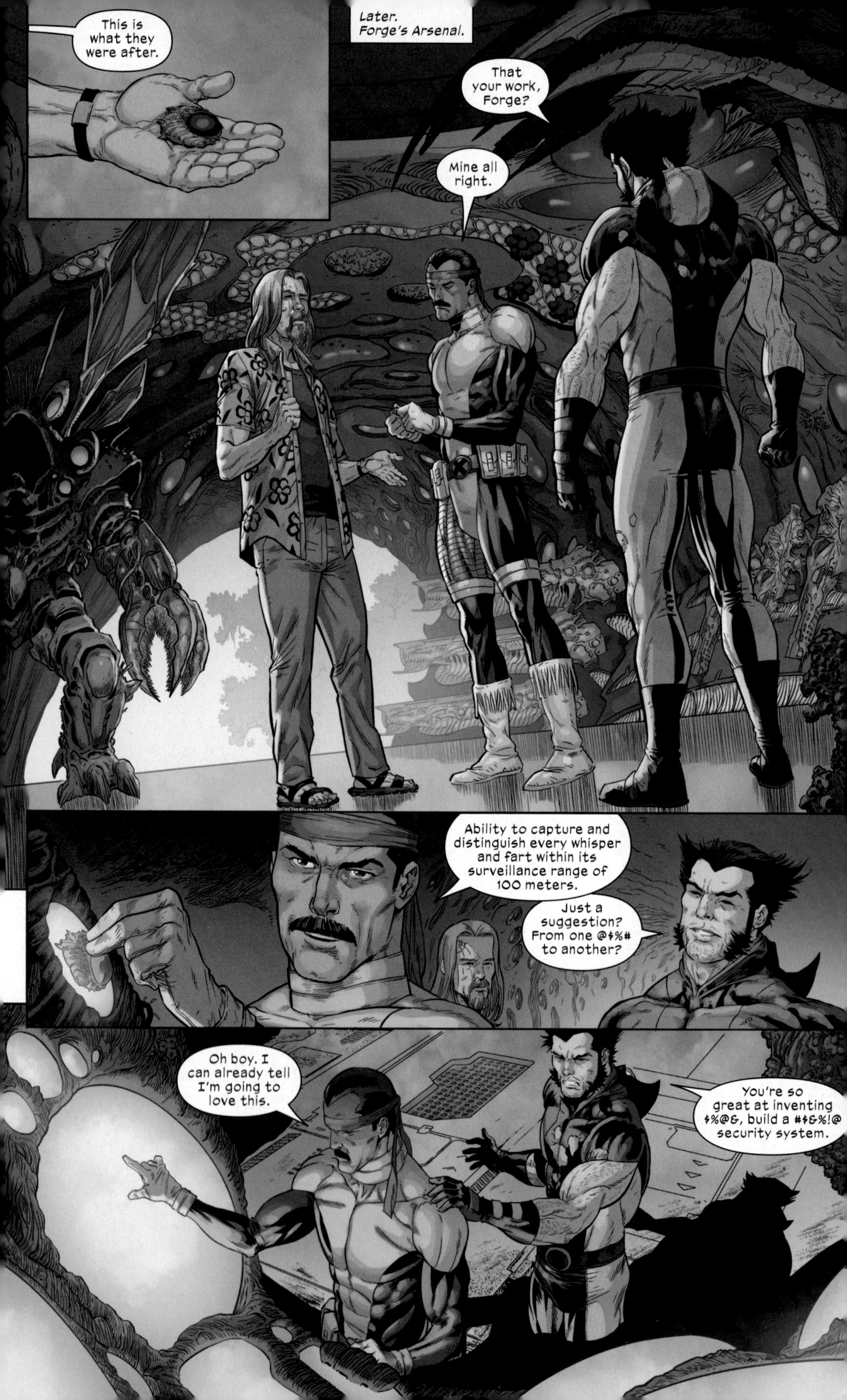
This is what they were after.
Later. Forge's Arsenal.
That your work, Forge?
Mine all right.
Ability to capture and distinguish every whisper and fart within its surveillance range of 100 meters.
Just a suggestion? From one @$%# to another?
Oh boy. I can already tell I'm going to love this.
You're so great at inventing $%@&, build a #$&%!@ security system.

FORGE'S LOGBOOK: SURVEILLANCE DEVICE

Status:

<<stolen -- recovered>>
<<compromised data>>

Suspect:

Maverick

Theories:

: Maverick stole and employed the device because
  he knew about the daily E.M.P. blast
  (only organic tech would have been viable).

: Maverick in league with X-Desk of the C.I.A.

Length of current recording:

164 hours:35 minutes:17 seconds

Unknowns:

: Number of times the device has been used.

: Consistency of Green Lagoon as surveillance site.

: Especially worrisome given that sensitive and
  compromising information is more likely to
  be shared when under the influence.

Follow-up with Sage:

: Cross-check gate traffic with duration of recording.

: Develop short list based on entrances and exits to
  ensure Maverick was working alone.

: Program gates to deny Maverick further entrance.

Ancillary notes:

: Do 100 squats and 100 burpees
  before coffee every morning.

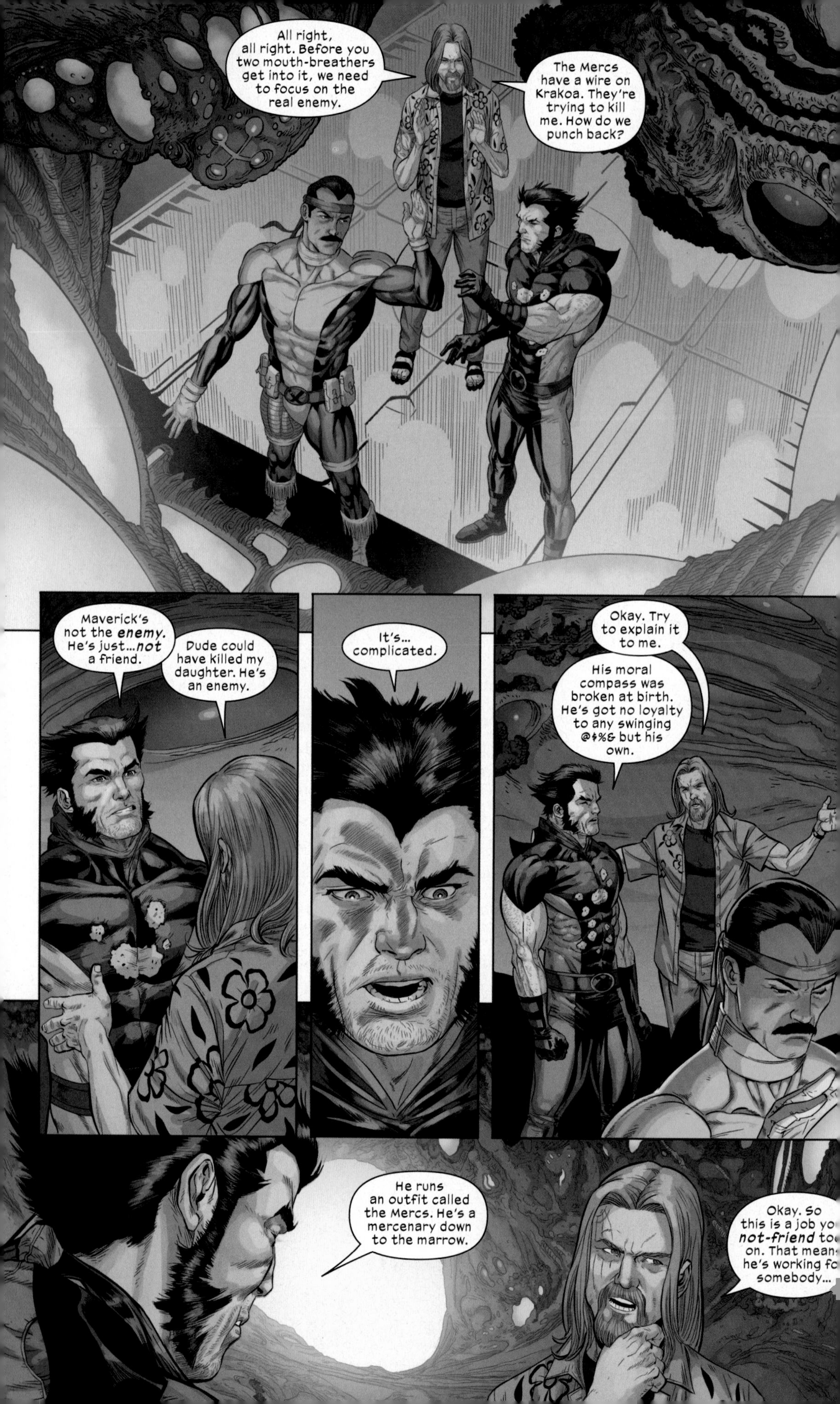

All right, all right. Before you two mouth-breathers get into it, we need to focus on the real enemy.
The Mercs have a wire on Krakoa. They're trying to kill me. How do we punch back?
Maverick's not the *enemy.* He's just...*not* a friend.
Dude could have killed my daughter. He's an enemy.
It's... complicated.
Okay. Try to explain it to me.
His moral compass was broken at birth. He's got no loyalty to any swinging @$%& but his own.
He runs an outfit called the Mercs. He's a mercenary down to the marrow.
Okay. So this is a job yo
not-friend to
on. That mean
he's working fo
somebody...

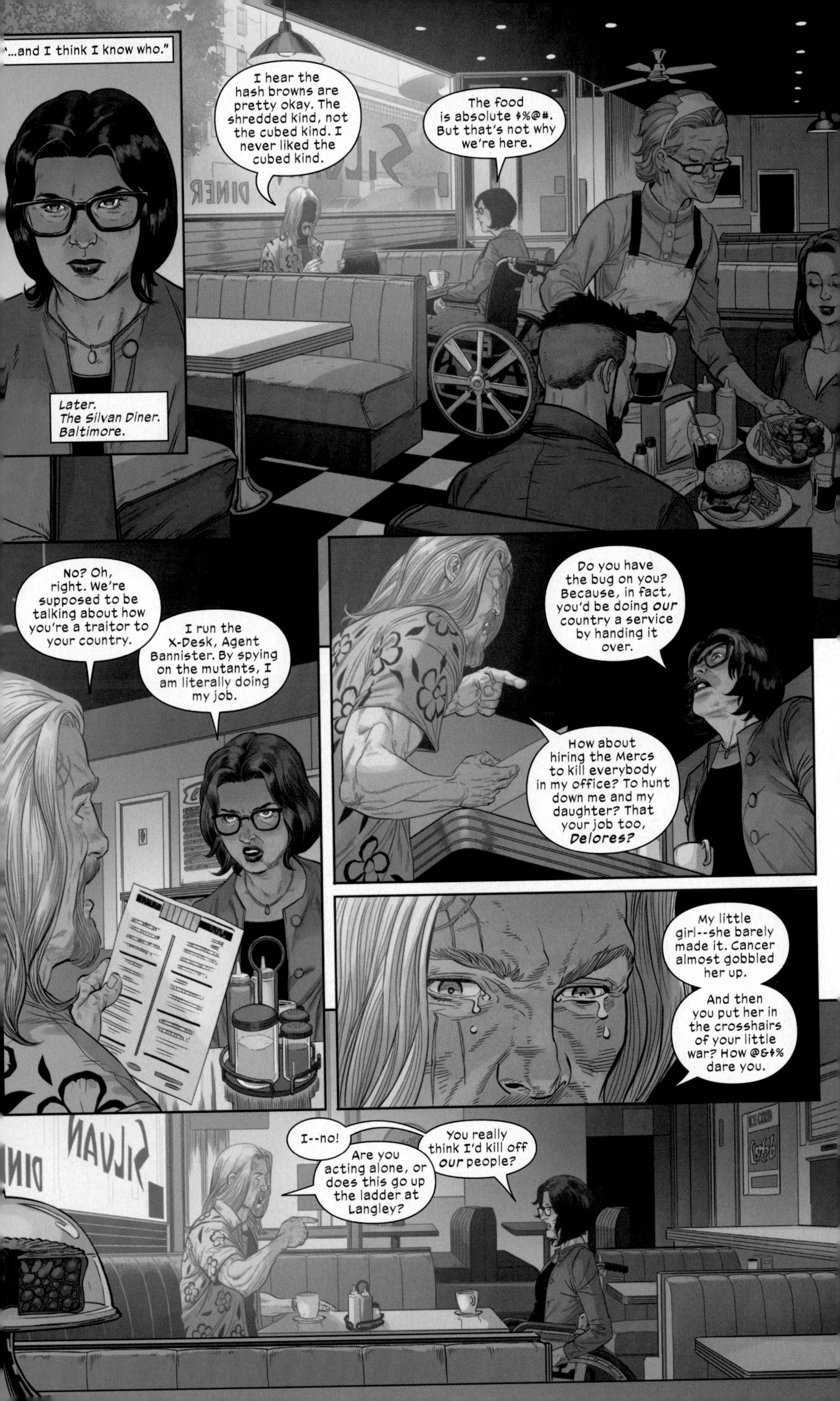
"...and I think I know who."
Later. The Silvan Diner. Baltimore.
I hear the hash browns are pretty okay. The shredded kind, not the cubed kind. I never liked the cubed kind.
The food is absolute $%@#. But that's not why we're here.
No? Oh, right. We're supposed to be talking about how you're a traitor to your country.
I run the X-Desk, Agent Bannister. By spying on the mutants, I am literally doing my job.
Do you have the bug on you? Because, in fact, you'd be doing our country a service by handing it over.
How about hiring the Mercs to kill everybody in my office? To hunt down me and my daughter? That your job too, Delores?
My little girl--she barely made it. Cancer almost gobbled her up.
And then you put her in the crosshairs of your little war? How @&$% dare you.
I--no!
You really think I'd kill off our people?
Are you acting alone, or does this go up the ladder at Langley?

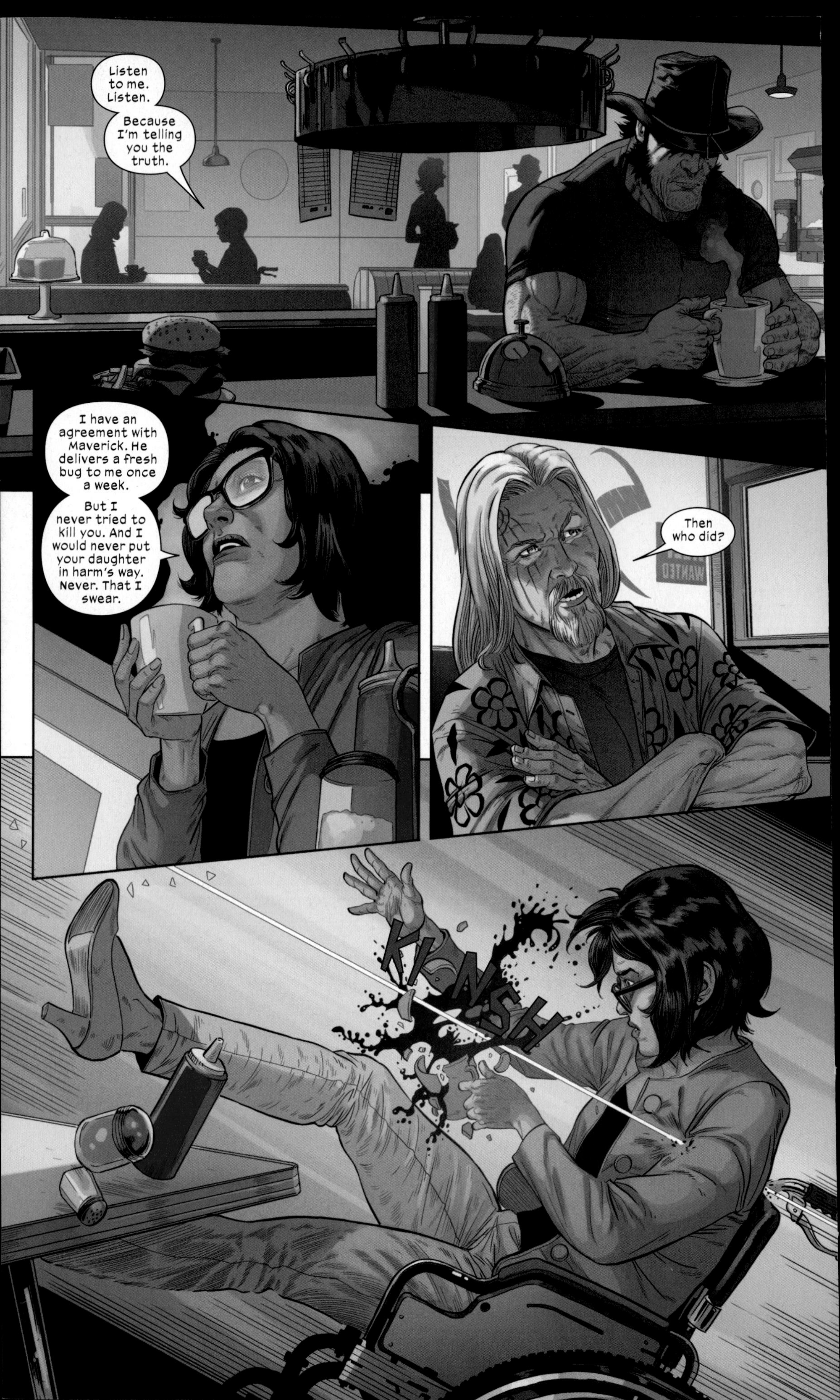

Listen to me. Listen.
Because I'm telling you the truth.
I have an agreement with Maverick. He delivers a fresh bug to me once a week.
But I never tried to kill you. And I would never put your daughter in harm's way. Never. That I swear.
Then who did?
WANTED
KINSH

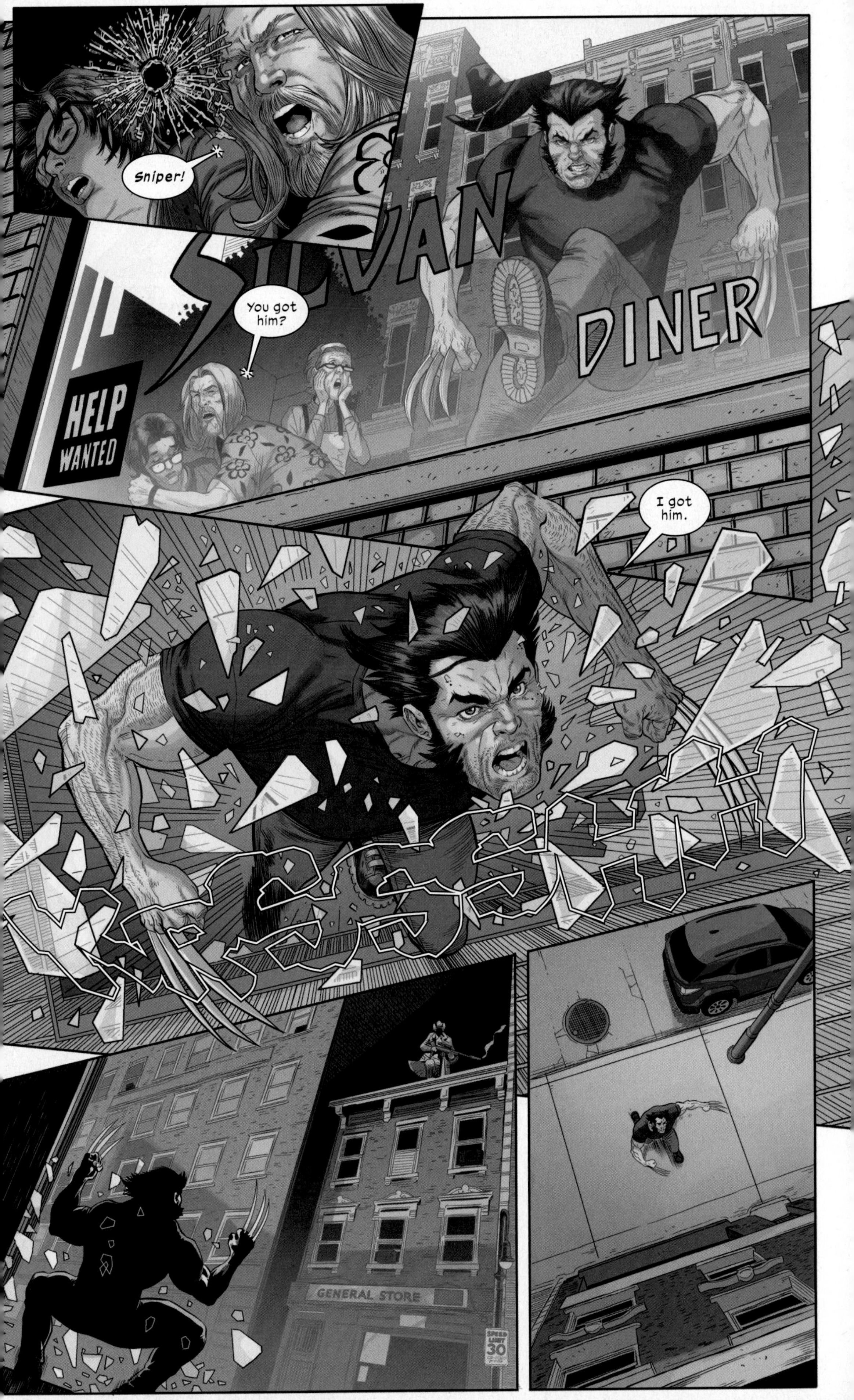
Sniper!
SILVAN
DINER
HELP WANTED
You got him?
I got him.
GENERAL STORE
SPEED LIMIT 30

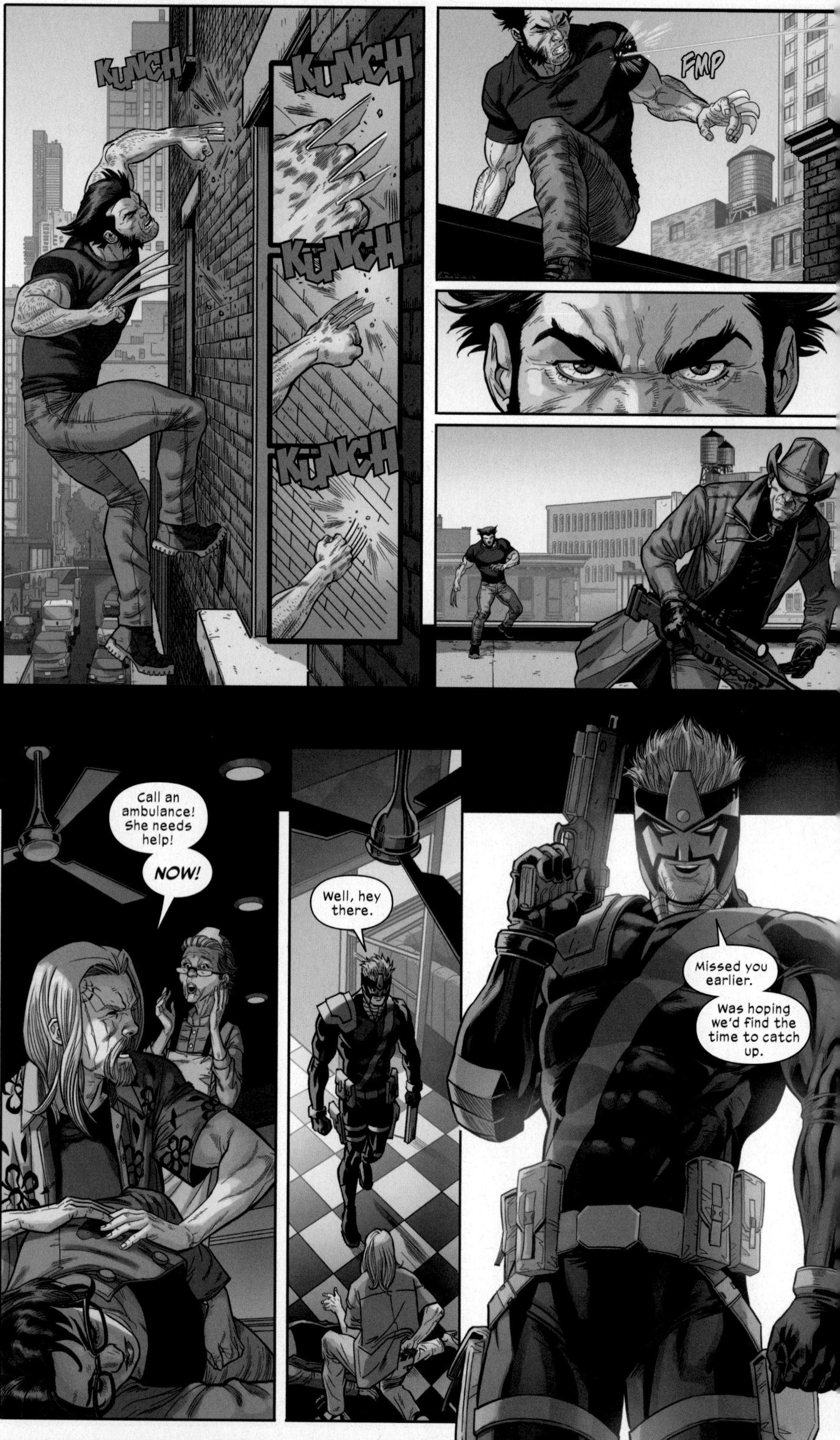
KUNCH
KUNCH
KUNCH
KUNCH
FMP
Call an ambulance! She needs help!
NOW!
Well, hey there.
Missed you earlier.
Was hoping we'd find the time to catch up.

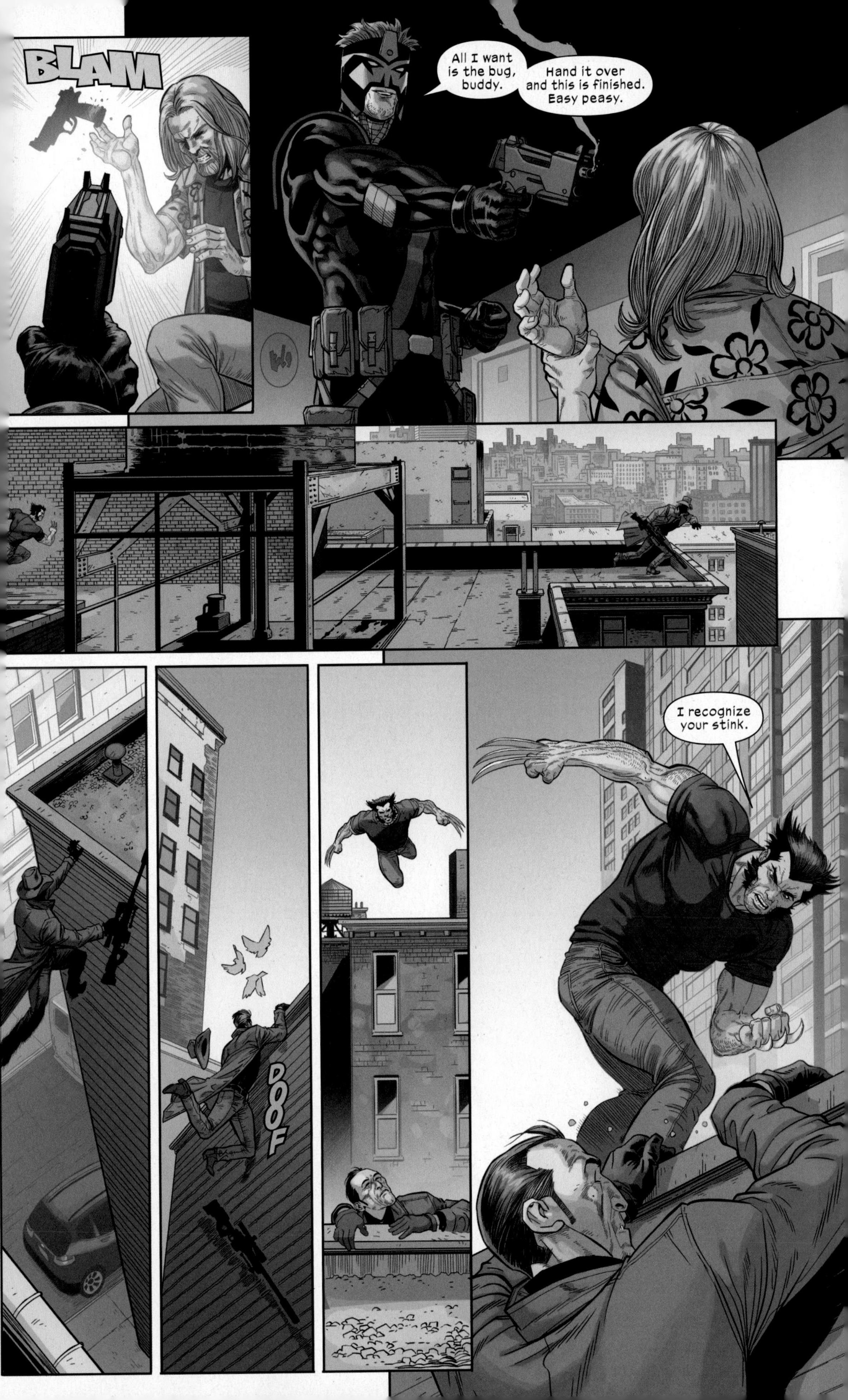
BLAM
All I want is the bug, buddy.
Hand it over and this is finished. Easy peasy.
DOOF
I recognize your stink.

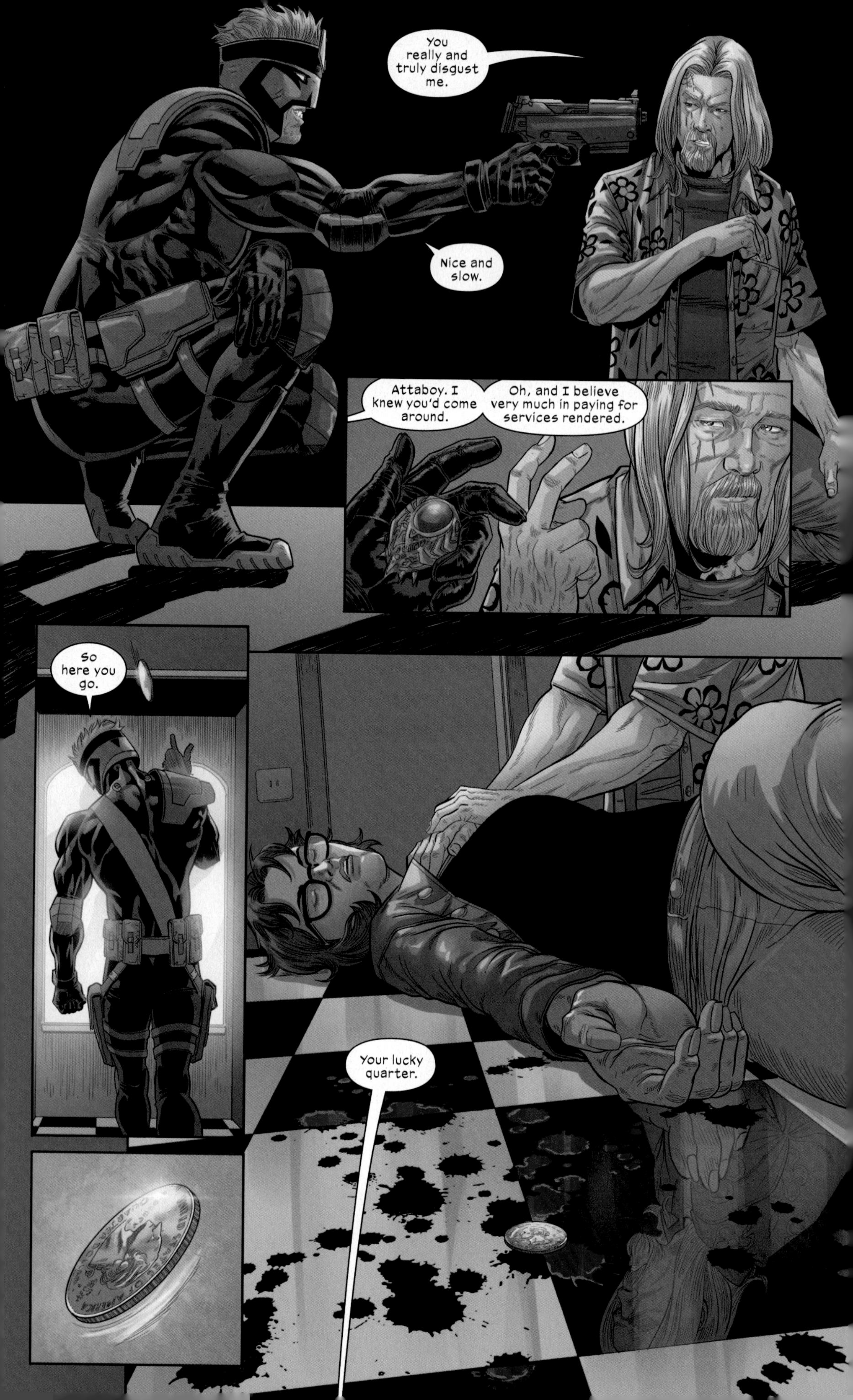
You really and truly disgust me.
Nice and slow.
Attaboy. I knew you'd come around.
Oh, and I believe very much in paying for services rendered.
So here you go.
Your lucky quarter.

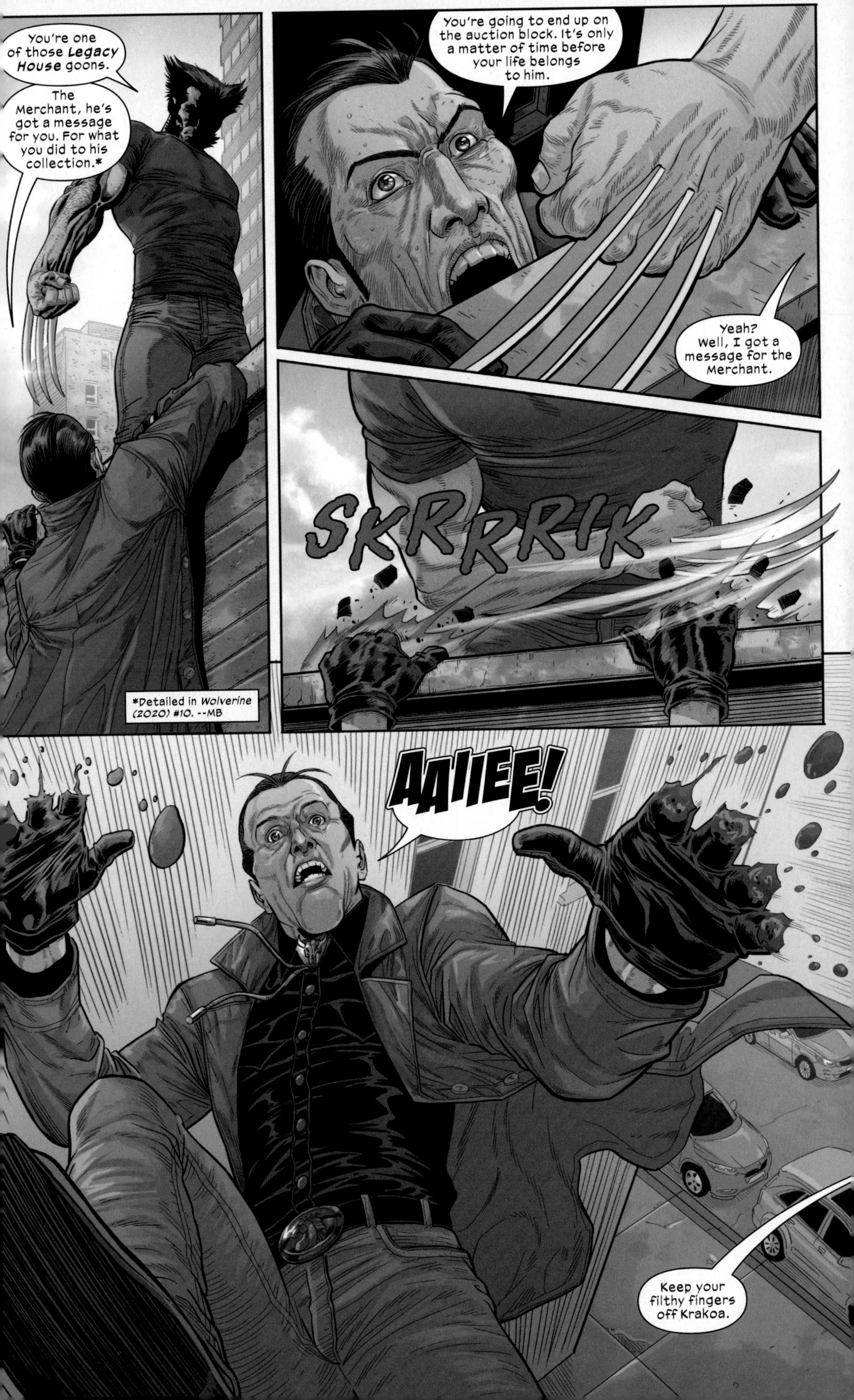
You're one of those Legacy House goons.
The Merchant, he's got a message for you. For what you did to his collection.*
You're going to end up on the auction block. It's only a matter of time before your life belongs to him.
Yeah? Well, I got a message for the Merchant.
SKRRRIK
*Detailed in Wolverine (2020) #10. --MB
AAIIEE!
Keep your filthy fingers off Krakoa.

FORGE'S LOGBOOK: SURVEILLANCE DEVICE

Isolated Audio Sample:

BLACK TOM:

This is a safe space for feelings, yeah? Between us friends and a few nips of whisky?

JUGGERNAUT:

Yeah. Sure, Tom.

BLACK TOM:

Sometimes -- sniff -- sometimes peoples is mistaking Black Tom for Dracula, and it -- sniff -- it hurts our feelings.

JUGGERNAUT:

I know you're not Dracula, Tom.

BLACK TOM:

It's like, hey, whatcha doing out in the daylight, bloodsucker?! Or, hey, you gots dirt and worms in your hair, so's maybe you should clean out your coffin! And har har dee har har and such like.

JUGGERNAUT:

Who said that? You tell me who %^&*$ said that.

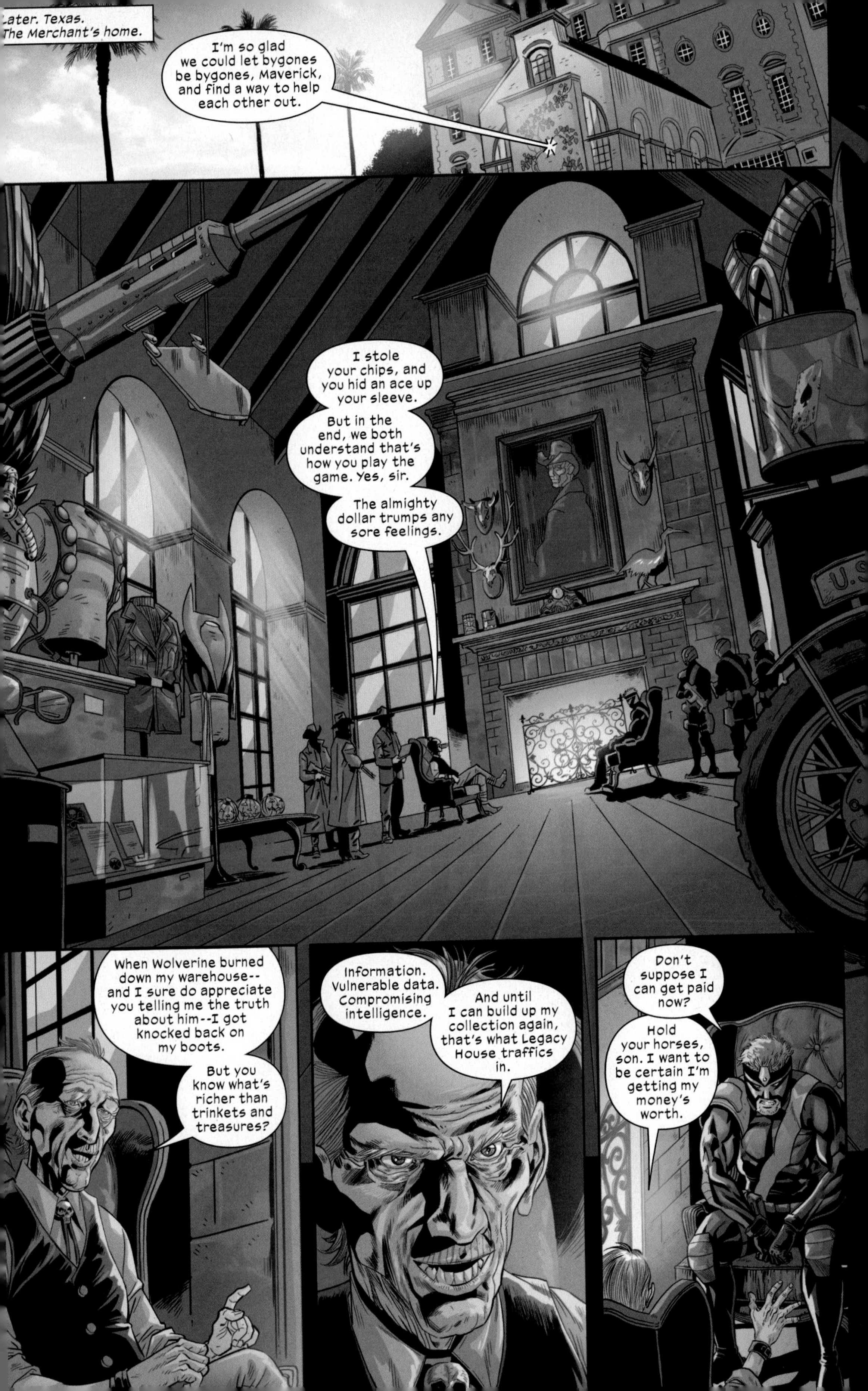
Later. Texas. The Merchant's home.
I'm so glad we could let bygones be bygones, Maverick, and find a way to help each other out.
I stole your chips, and you hid an ace up your sleeve.
But in the end, we both understand that's how you play the game. Yes, sir.
The almighty dollar trumps any sore feelings.
When Wolverine burned down my warehouse--and I sure do appreciate you telling me the truth about him--I got knocked back on my boots.
But you know what's richer than trinkets and treasures?
Information. Vulnerable data. Compromising intelligence.
And until I can build up my collection again, that's what Legacy House traffics in.
Don't suppose I can get paid now?
Hold your horses, son. I want to be certain I'm getting my money's worth.

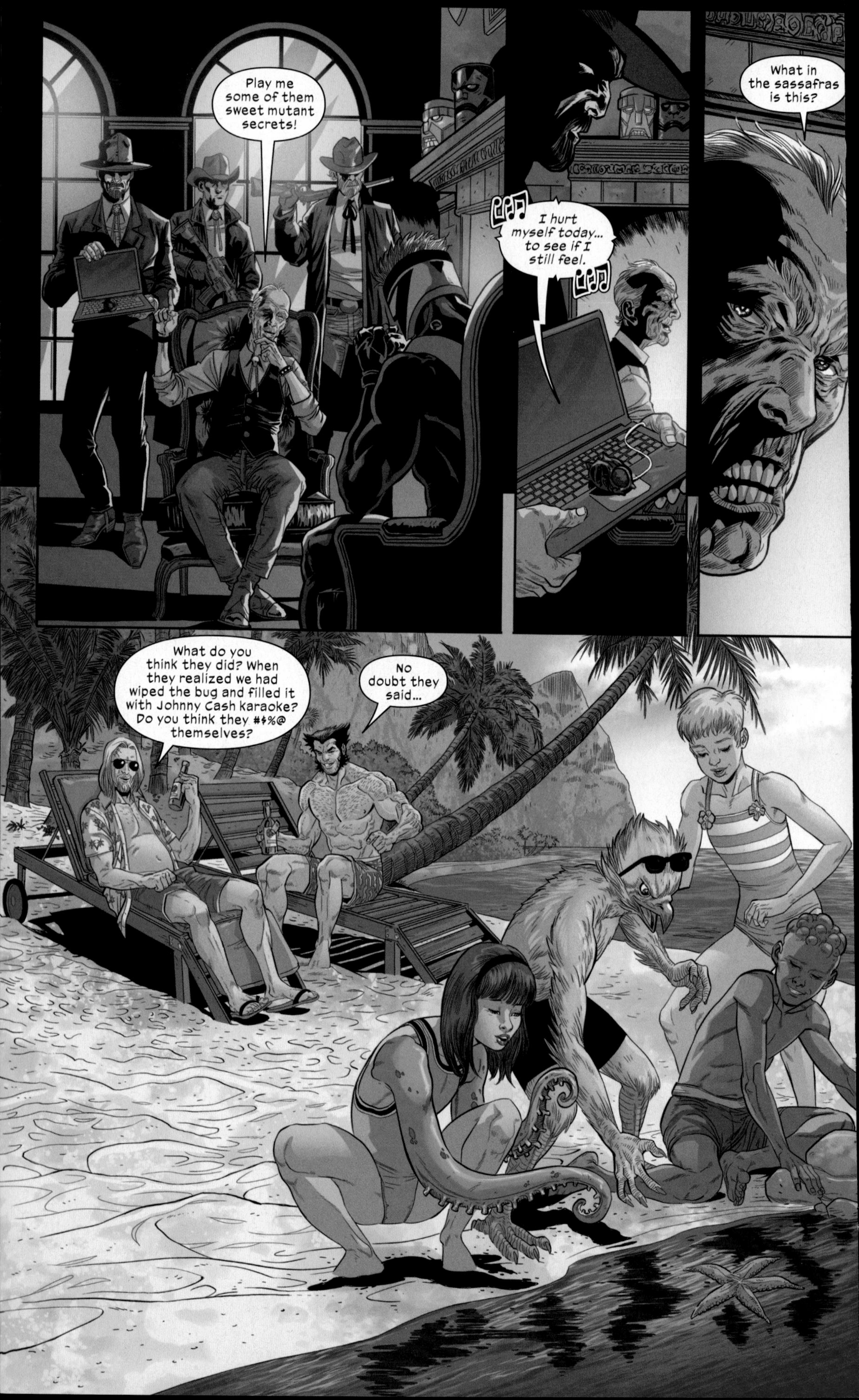
Play me some of them sweet mutant secrets!
I hurt myself today... to see if I still feel.
What in the sassafras is this?
What do you think they did? When they realized we had wiped the bug and filled it with Johnny Cash karaoke? Do you think they #$%@ themselves?
No doubt they said...

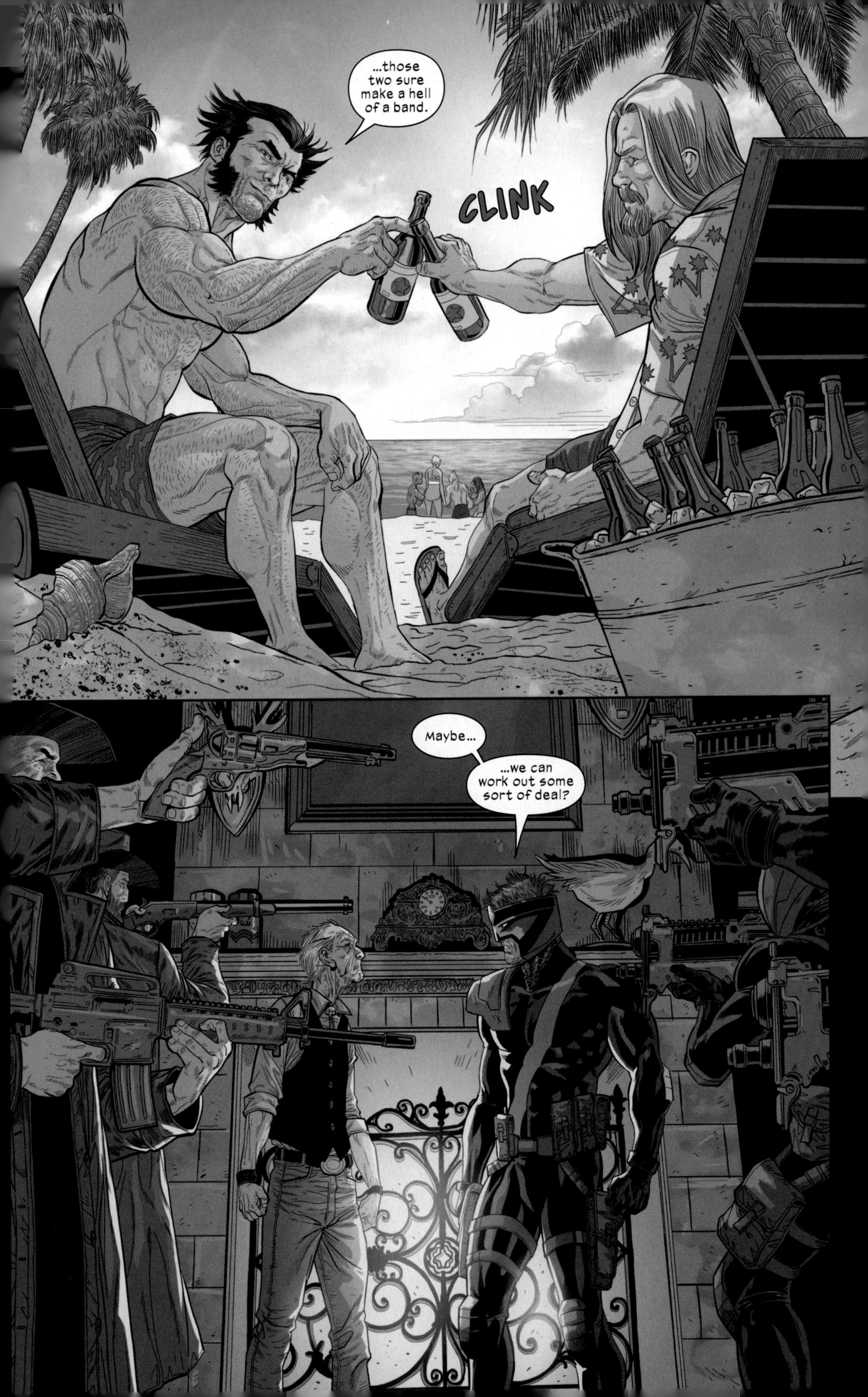
...those two sure make a hell of a band.
CLINK
Maybe...
...we can work out some sort of deal?

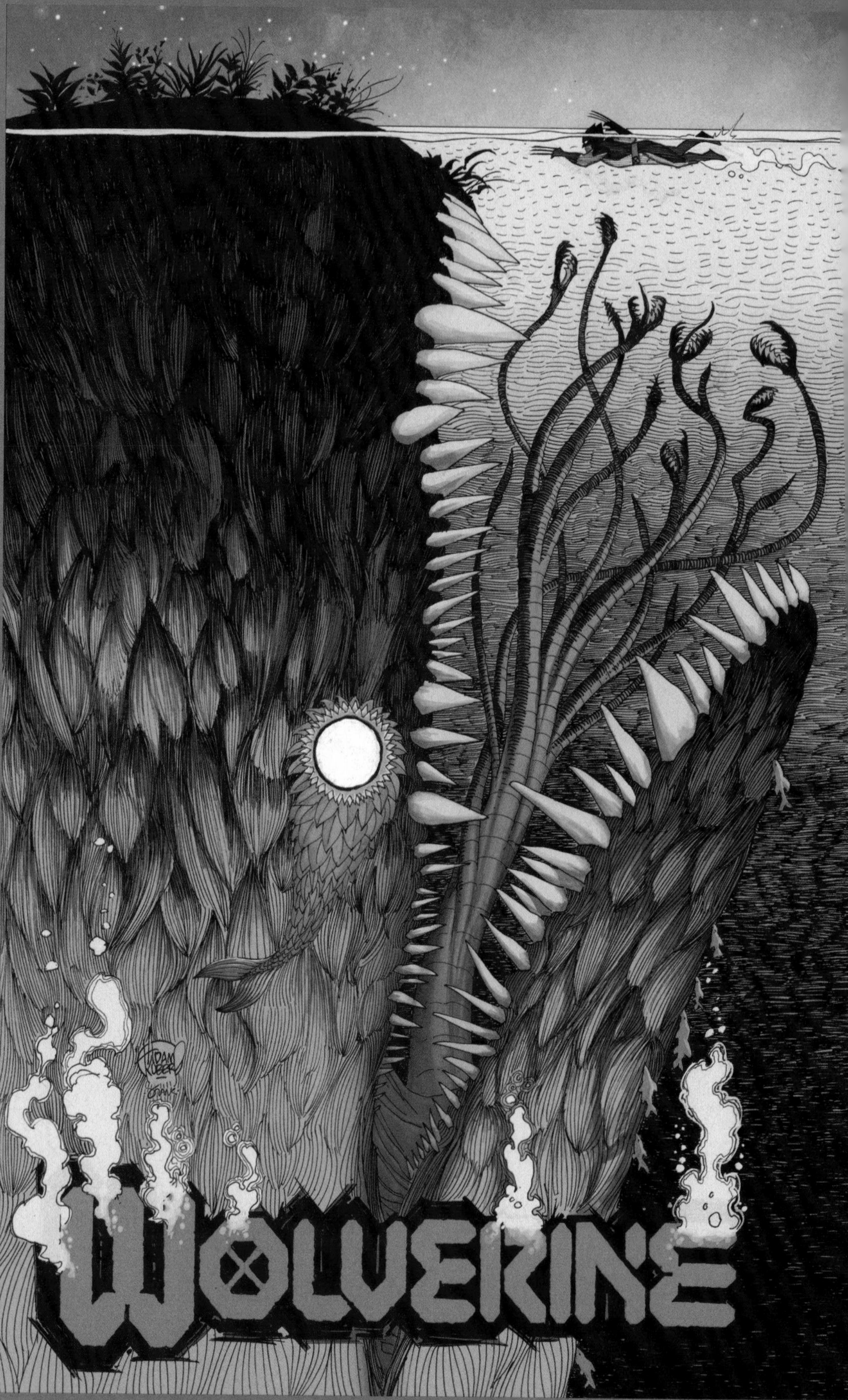
WOLVERINE

The Old Mutant and the Sea

19

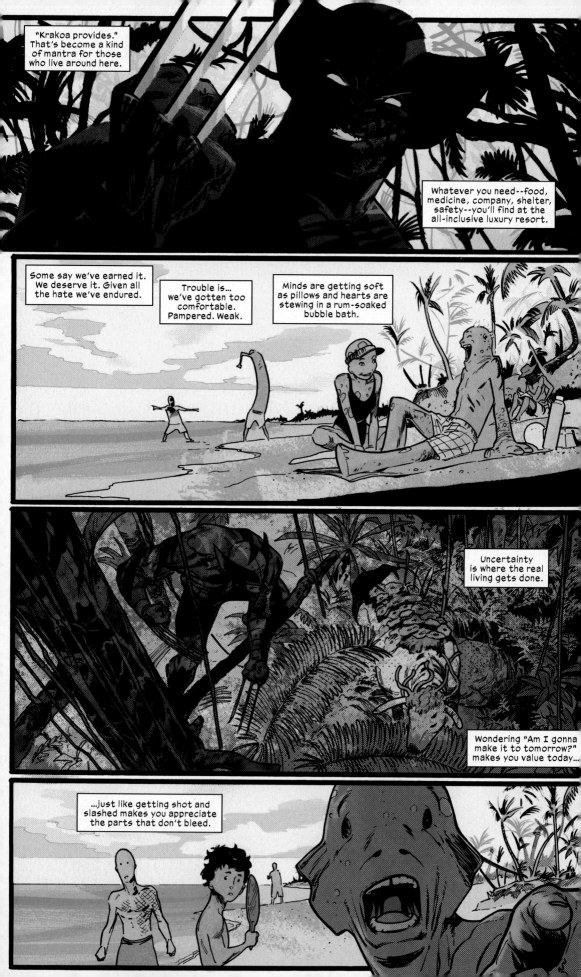

"Krakoa provides." That's become a kind of mantra for those who live around here.

Whatever you need--food, medicine, company, shelter, safety--you'll find at the all-inclusive luxury resort.

Some say we've earned it. We deserve it. Given all the hate we've endured.

Trouble is... we've gotten too comfortable. Pampered. Weak.

Minds are getting soft as pillows and hearts are stewing in a rum-soaked bubble bath.

Uncertainty is where the real living gets done.

Wondering "Am I gonna make it to tomorrow?" makes you value today...

...just like getting shot and slashed makes you appreciate the parts that don't bleed.

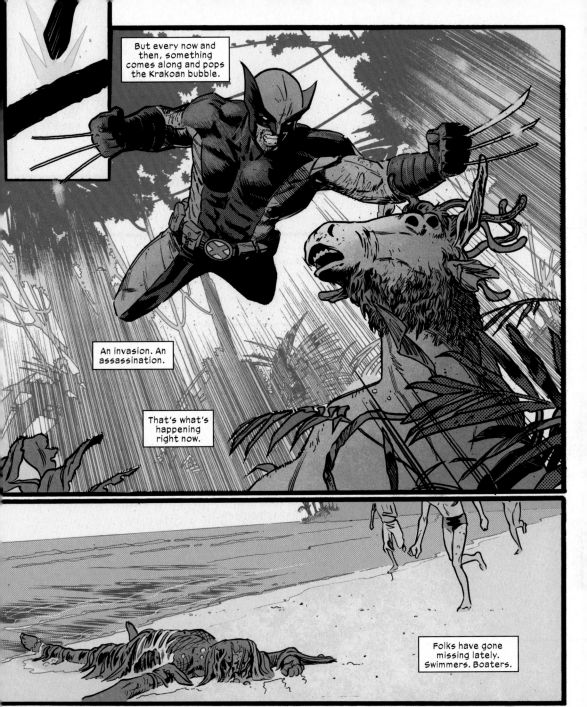

But every now and then, something comes along and pops the Krakoan bubble.

An invasion. An assassination.

That's what's happening right now.

Folks have gone missing lately. Swimmers. Boaters.

Shoreside, we've found severed feet, sea-rotted arms, a chewed-up torso.

Something's out there, circling and stalking the island.

And I think I know what.

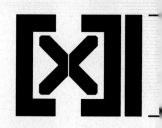

SAGE'S LOGBOOK: NO-PLACE

::BIOMES::

Definition: The No-Place **biomes** are divergent spaces, organically woven into but communicatively separate from the organic grid of Krakoa.

Location: Varied, but all are housed out of view (subterranean, aquatic).

::TUMORS::

Definition: A metastatic offshoot of the No-Place biomes.

Behavior: Defined by parasitic aggression, they seemingly want to spread via attack.

Primary evidence: Infected crew of the *USS SIEGE* battleship
Status: <extinguished>
Ongoing: <naval inquiries//ignored>

Secondary evidence: Infected sea life of trench (geo-pinned)
Status: <extinguished>
Forge testimony:
"Whatever was growing down there, Namor
stomped it out."

Infected whale
Status: <at large; action item>
Wolverine testimony:
"I ain't going to be able to sleep right...
until I kill the leviathan dead."

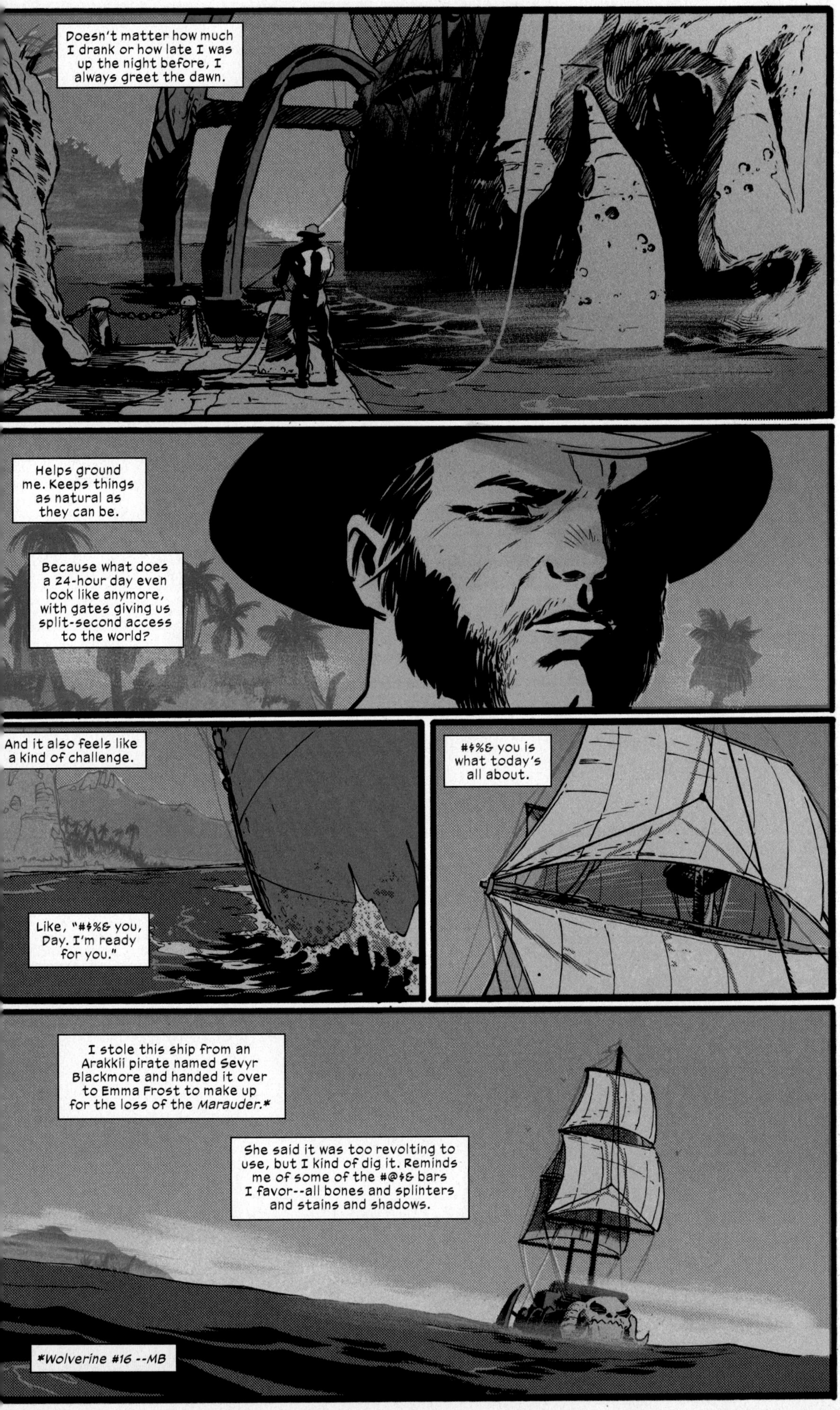
Doesn't matter how much I drank or how late I was up the night before, I always greet the dawn.
Helps ground me. Keeps things as natural as they can be.
Because what does a 24-hour day even look like anymore, with gates giving us split-second access to the world?
And it also feels like a kind of challenge.
Like, "#$%& you, Day. I'm ready for you."
#$%& you is what today's all about.
I stole this ship from an Arakkii pirate named Sevyr Blackmore and handed it over to Emma Frost to make up for the loss of the *Marauder.**
She said it was too revolting to use, but I kind of dig it. Reminds me of some of the #@$& bars I favor--all bones and splinters and stains and shadows.
**Wolverine #16 --MB*

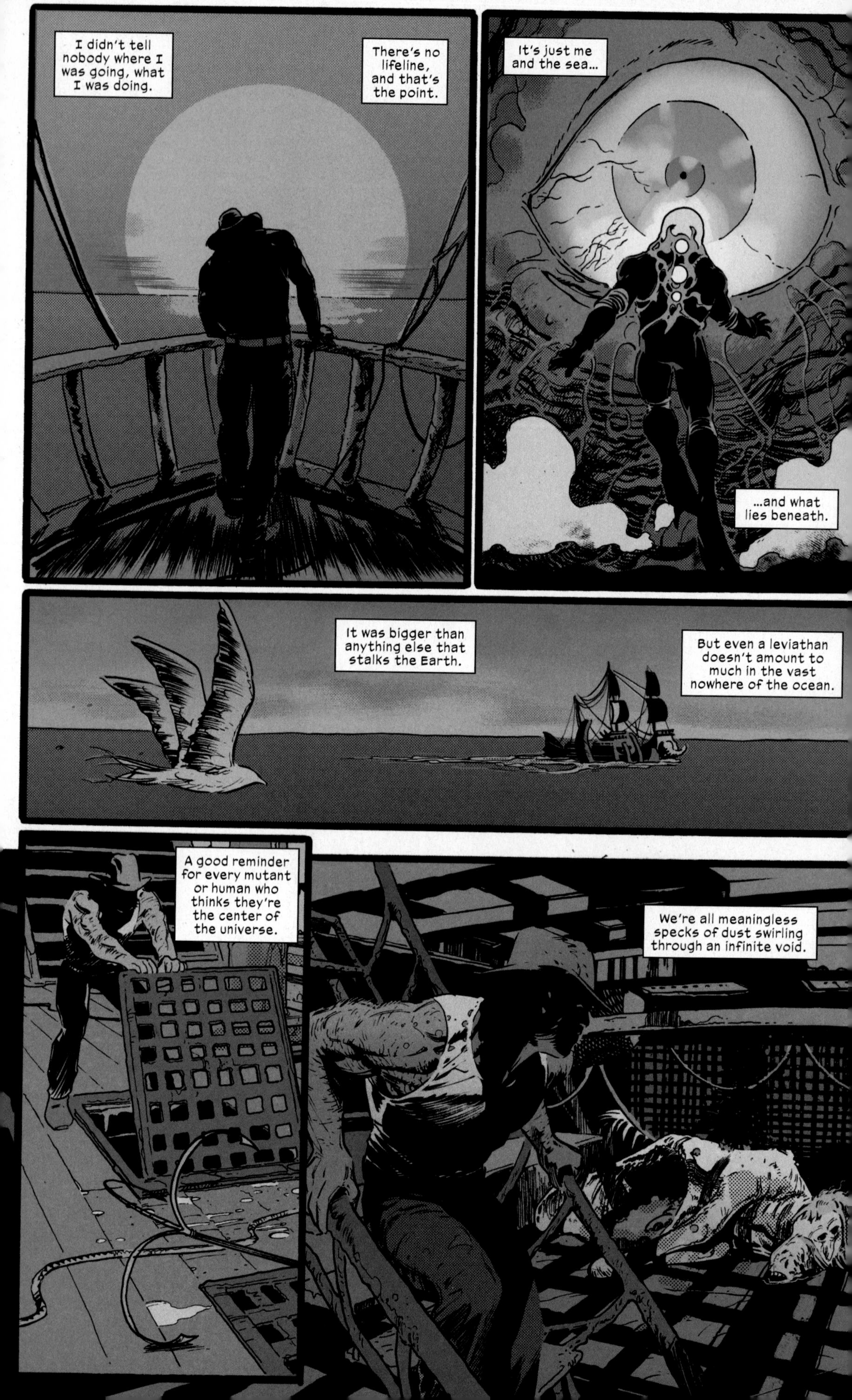
I didn't tell nobody where I was going, what I was doing.
There's no lifeline, and that's the point.
It's just me and the sea...
...and what lies beneath.
It was bigger than anything else that stalks the Earth.
But even a leviathan doesn't amount to much in the vast nowhere of the ocean.
A good reminder for every mutant or human who thinks they're the center of the universe.
We're all meaningless specks of dust swirling through an infinite void.

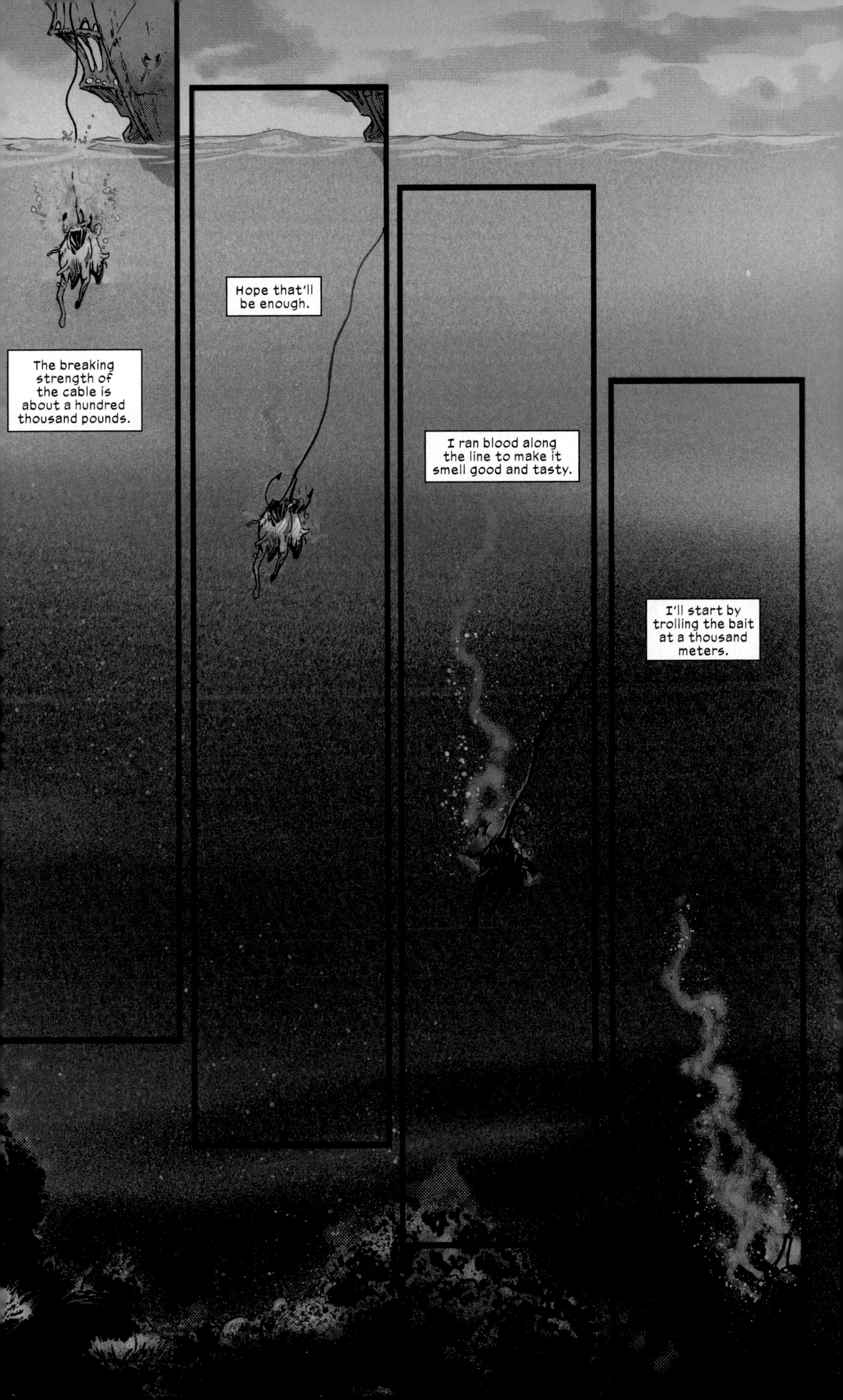
The breaking strength of the cable is about a hundred thousand pounds.
Hope that'll be enough.
I ran blood along the line to make it smell good and tasty.
I'll start by trolling the bait at a thousand meters.

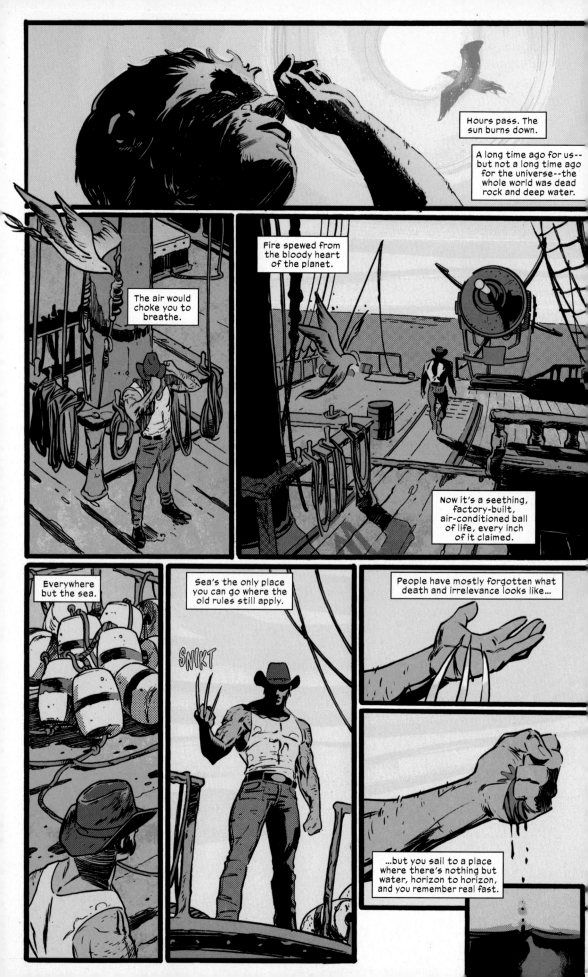

Hours pass. The sun burns down.

A long time ago for us-- but not a long time ago for the universe--the whole world was dead rock and deep water.

The air would choke you to breathe.

Fire spewed from the bloody heart of the planet.

Now it's a seething, factory-built, air-conditioned ball of life, every inch of it claimed.

Everywhere but the sea.

Sea's the only place you can go where the old rules still apply.

SNIKT

People have mostly forgotten what death and irrelevance looks like...

...but you sail to a place where there's nothing but water, horizon to horizon, and you remember real fast.

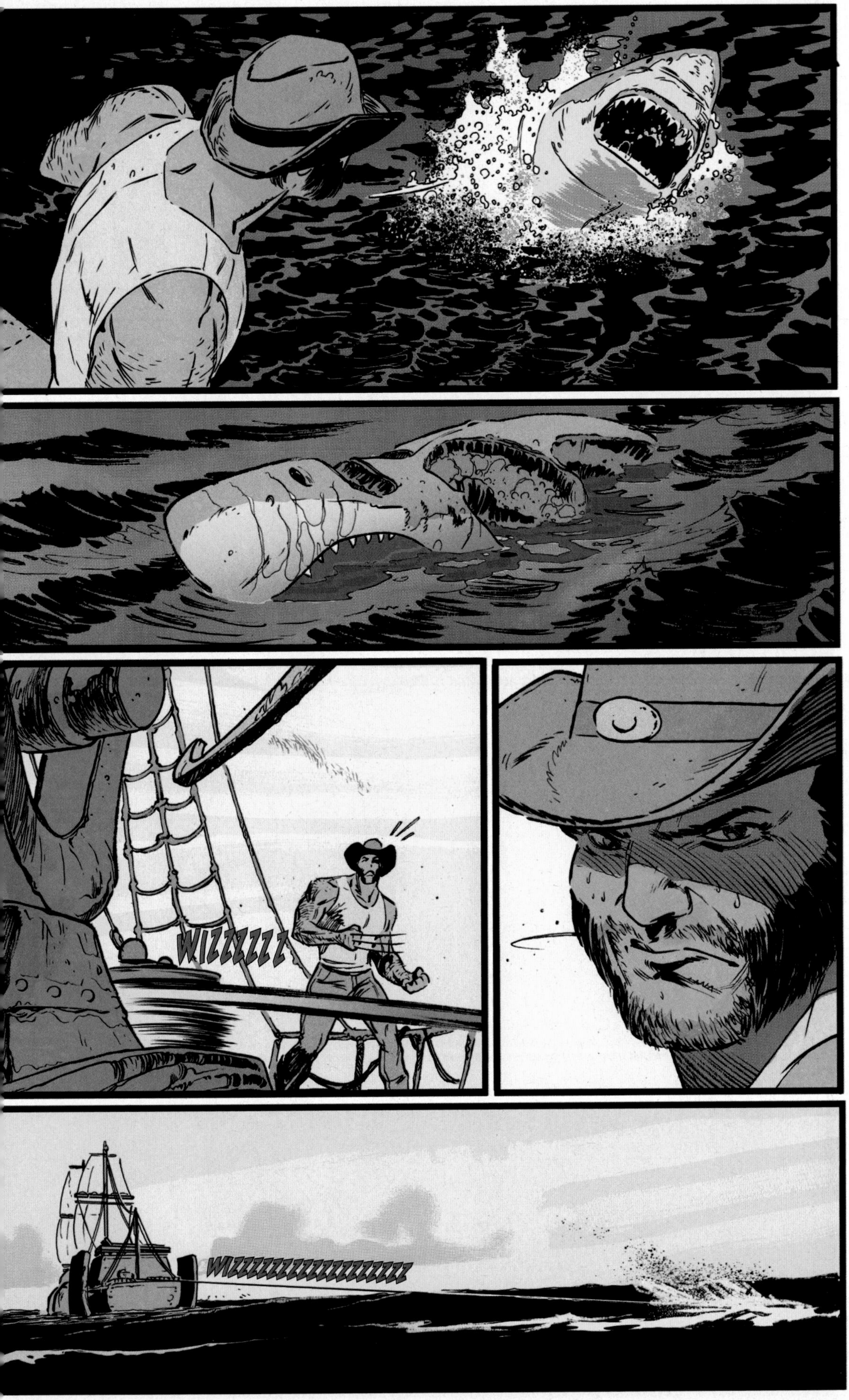
WIZZZZZZ
WIZZZZZZZZZZZZZZZZZZZZ

This reel has high-line capacity...

WIZZZZZZZ

...and a drag set at several thousand pounds.

ZZZZZZZZ

But once I set the hook...

KAK

...I don't think there's any rigging in existence...

CRRRRKK

...that could do anything more than *slow this monster down* in a fight.

SLOSHHHH

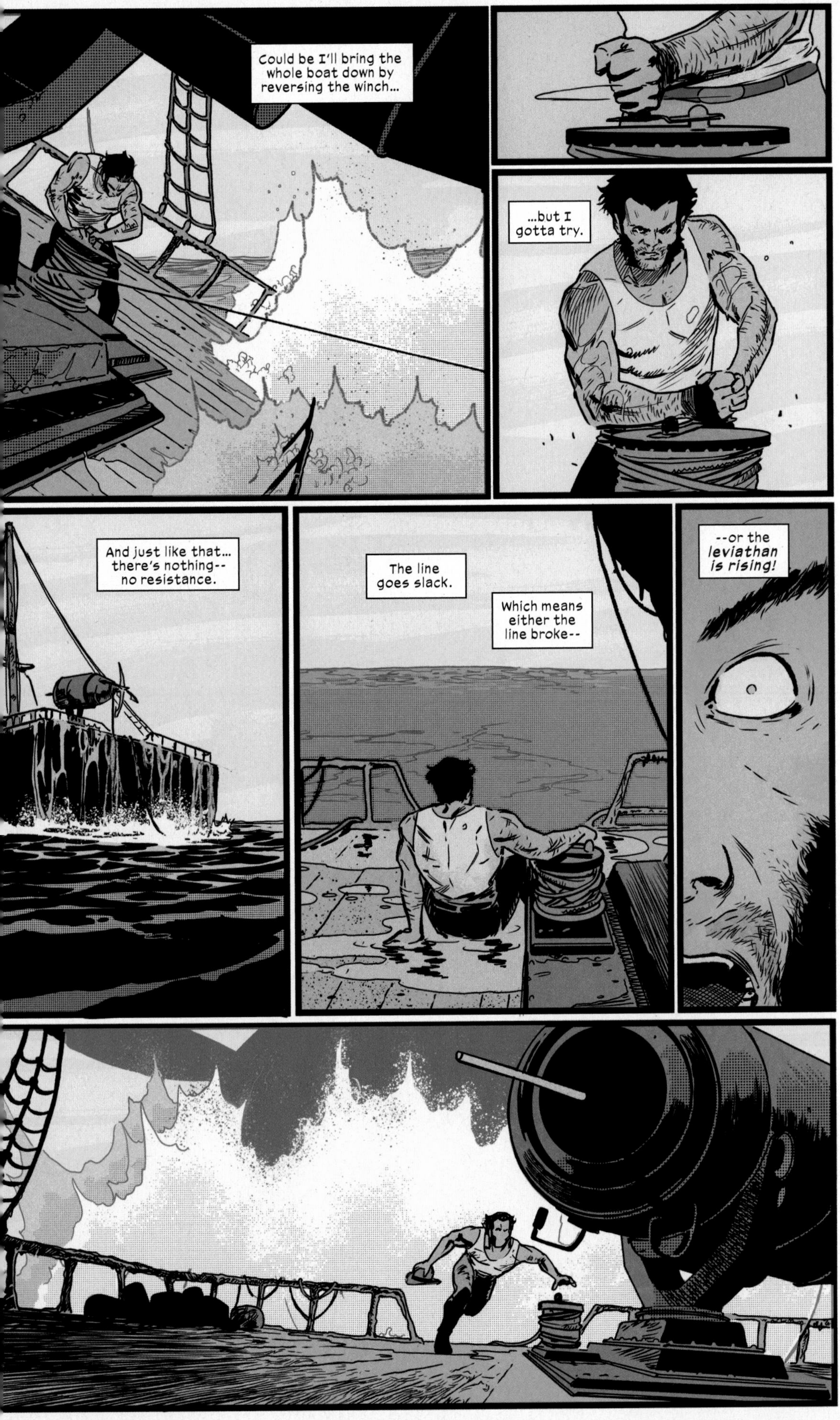

Could be I'll bring the whole boat down by reversing the winch...
...but I gotta try.
And just like that... there's nothing-- no resistance.
The line goes slack.
Which means either the line broke--
--or the *leviathan is rising!*

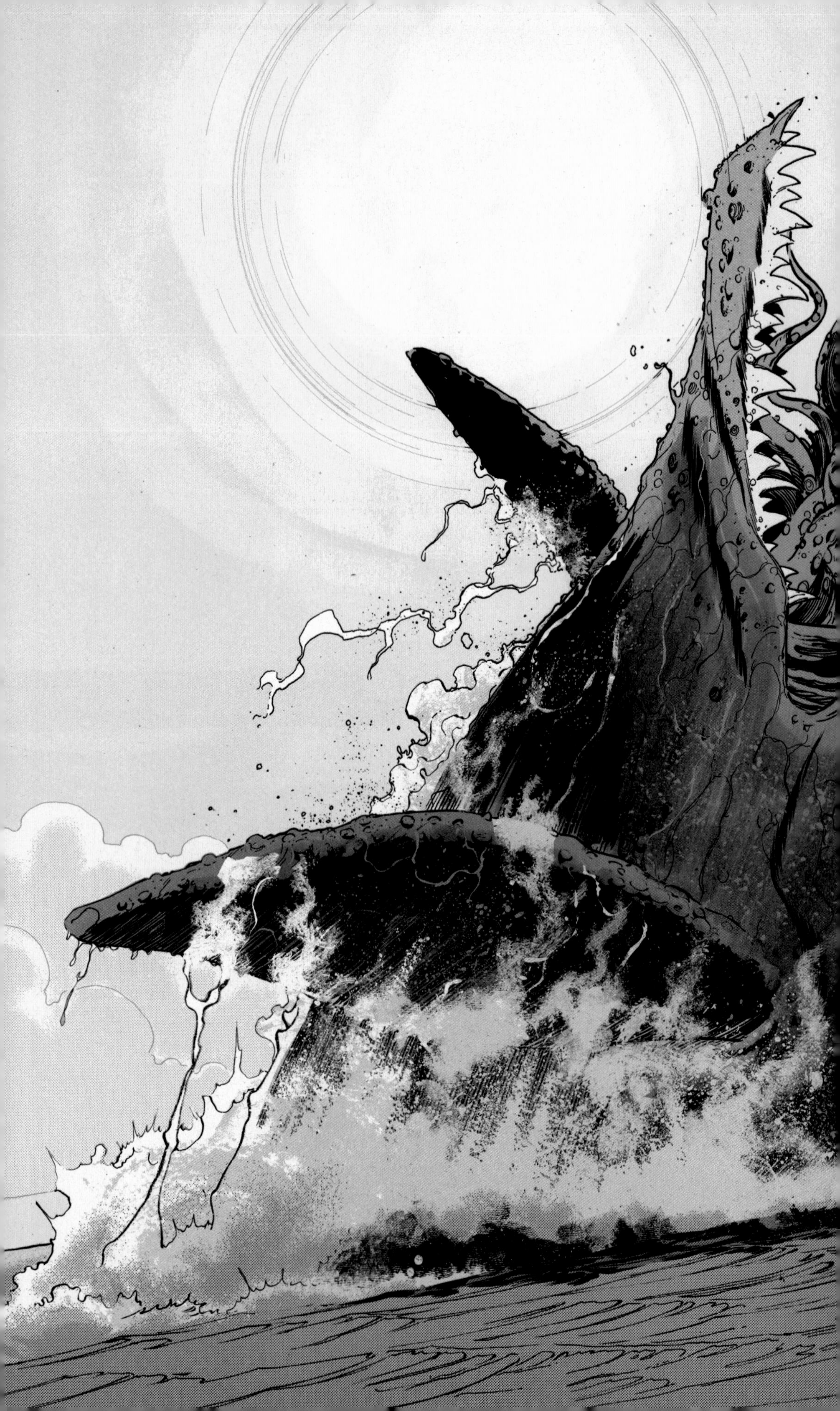

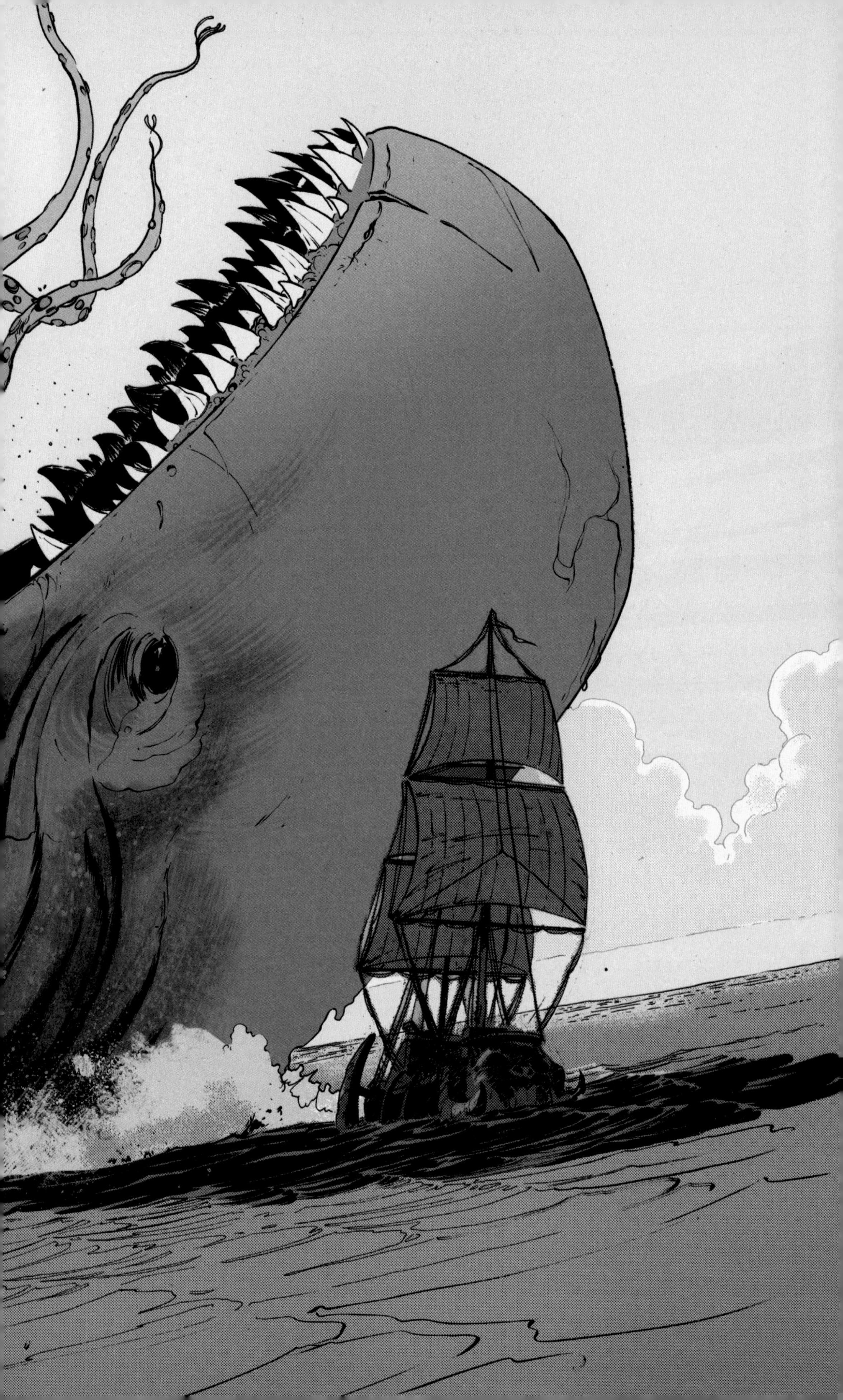

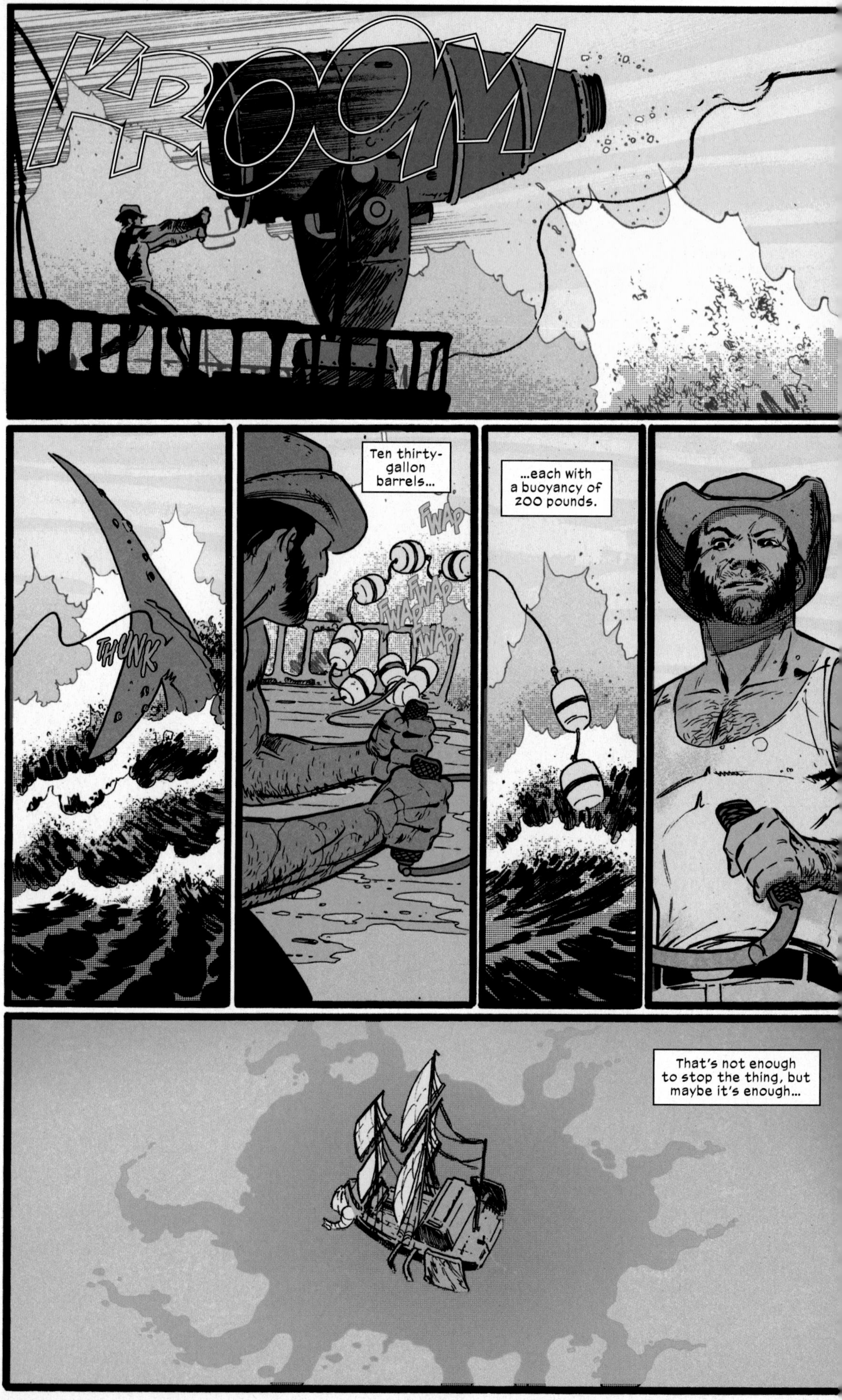
KROOM
THUNK
Ten thirty-gallon barrels...
FWAP
FWAP
FWAP
FWAP
...each with a buoyancy of 200 pounds.
That's not enough to stop the thing, but maybe it's enough...

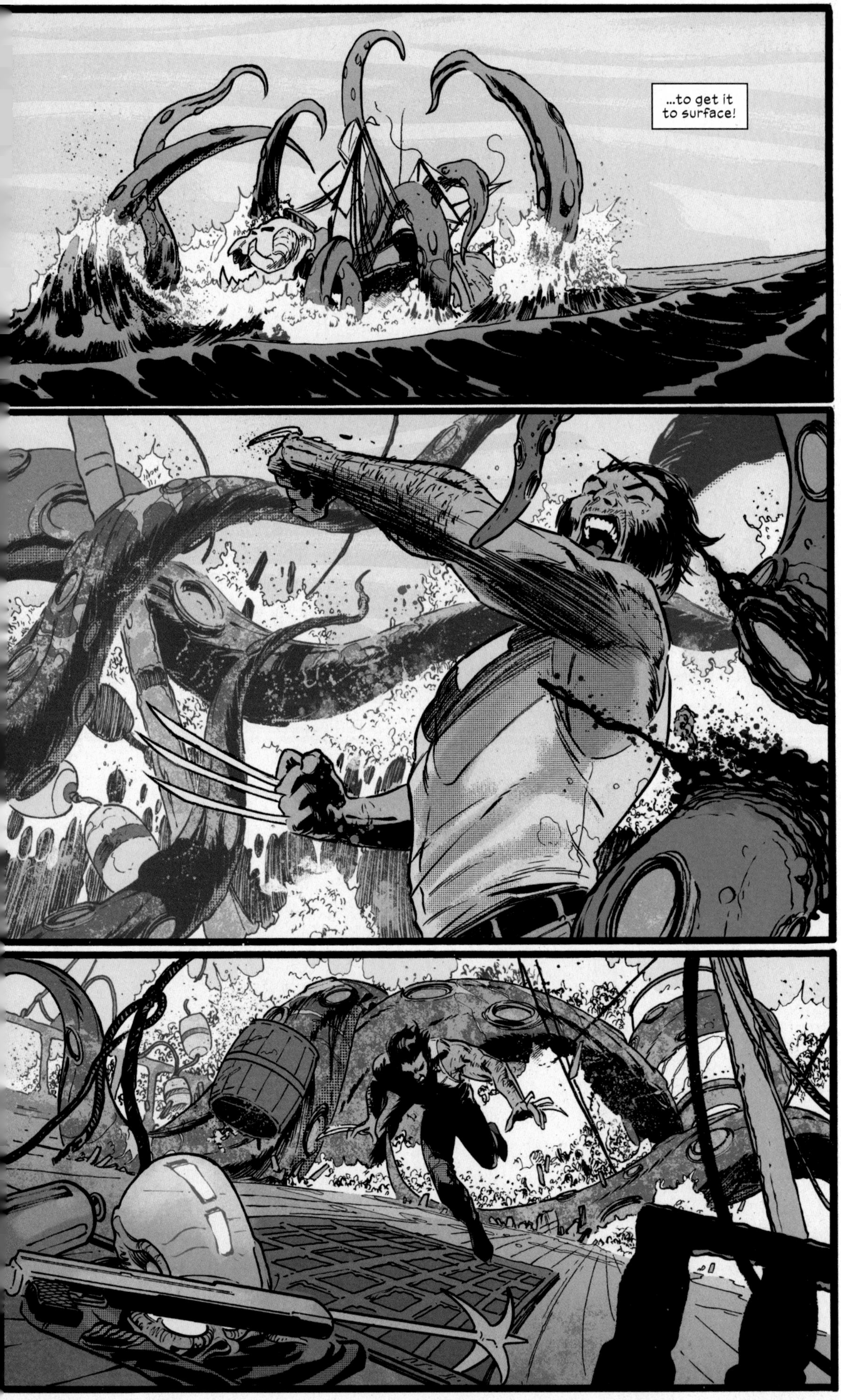
...to get it to surface!

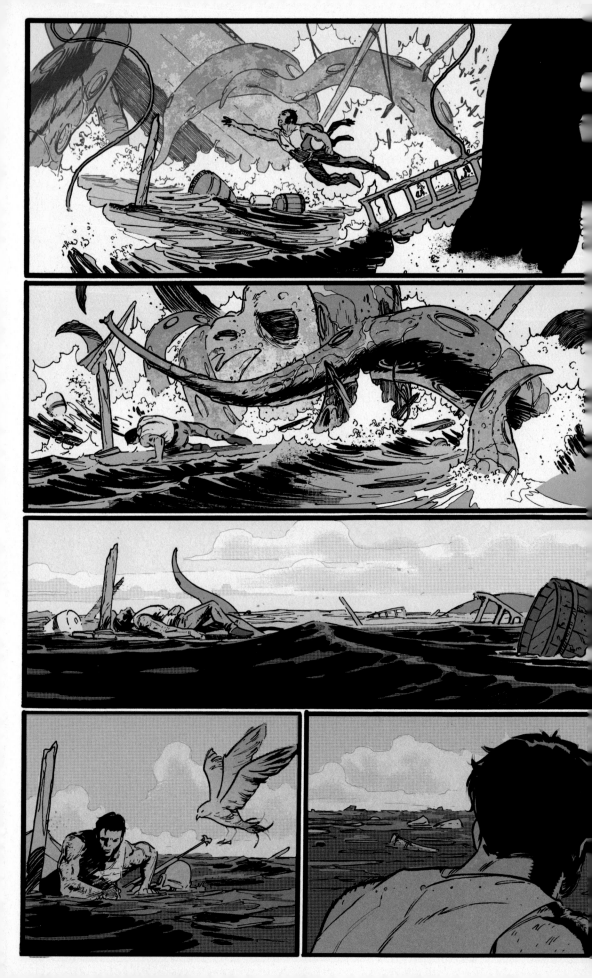

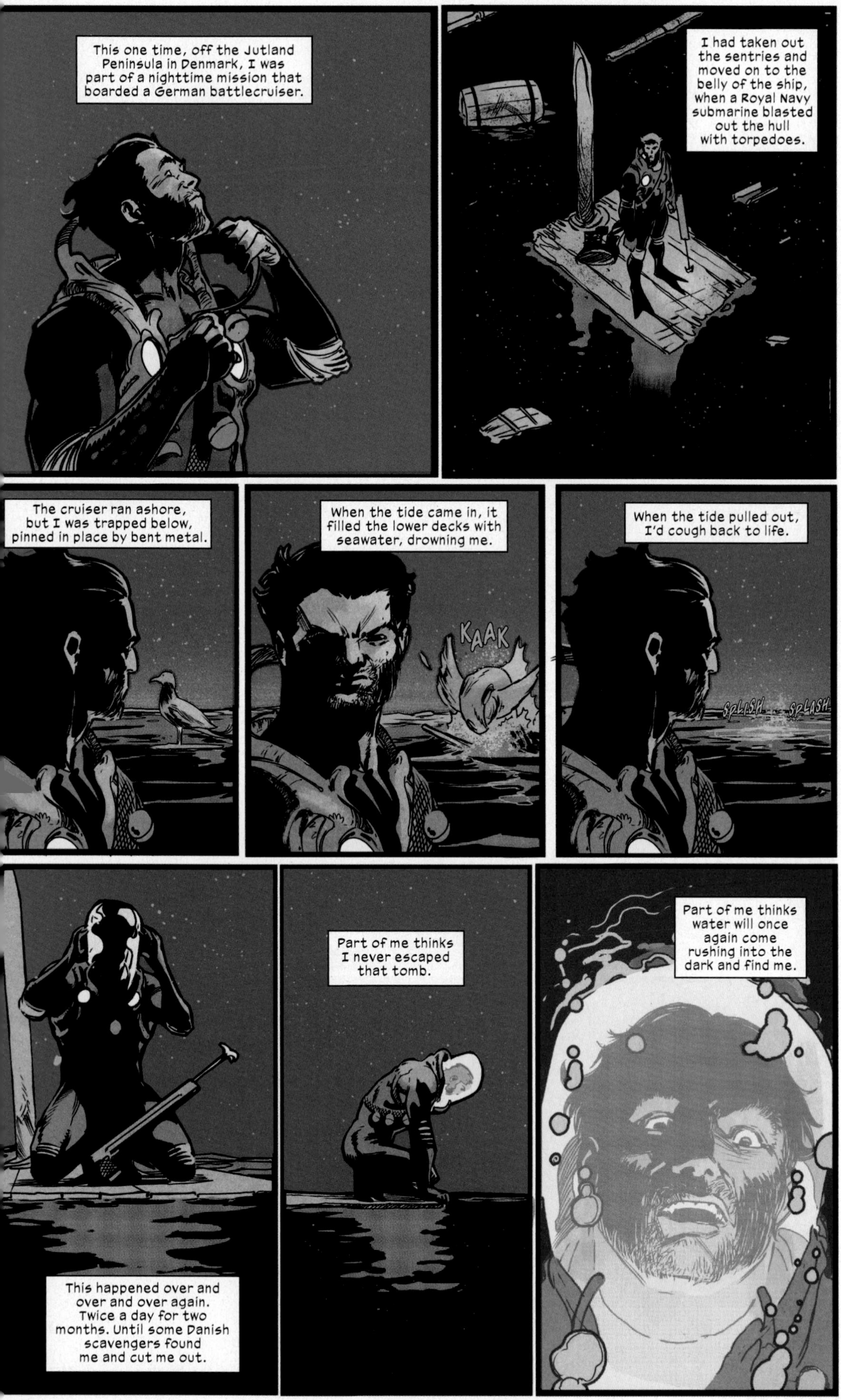

This one time, off the Jutland Peninsula in Denmark, I was part of a nighttime mission that boarded a German battlecruiser.
I had taken out the sentries and moved on to the belly of the ship, when a Royal Navy submarine blasted out the hull with torpedoes.
The cruiser ran ashore, but I was trapped below, pinned in place by bent metal.
When the tide came in, it filled the lower decks with seawater, drowning me.
KAAK
When the tide pulled out, I'd cough back to life.
SPLASH
SPLASH
This happened over and over and over again. Twice a day for two months. Until some Danish scavengers found me and cut me out.
Part of me thinks I never escaped that tomb.
Part of me thinks water will once again come rushing into the dark and find me.

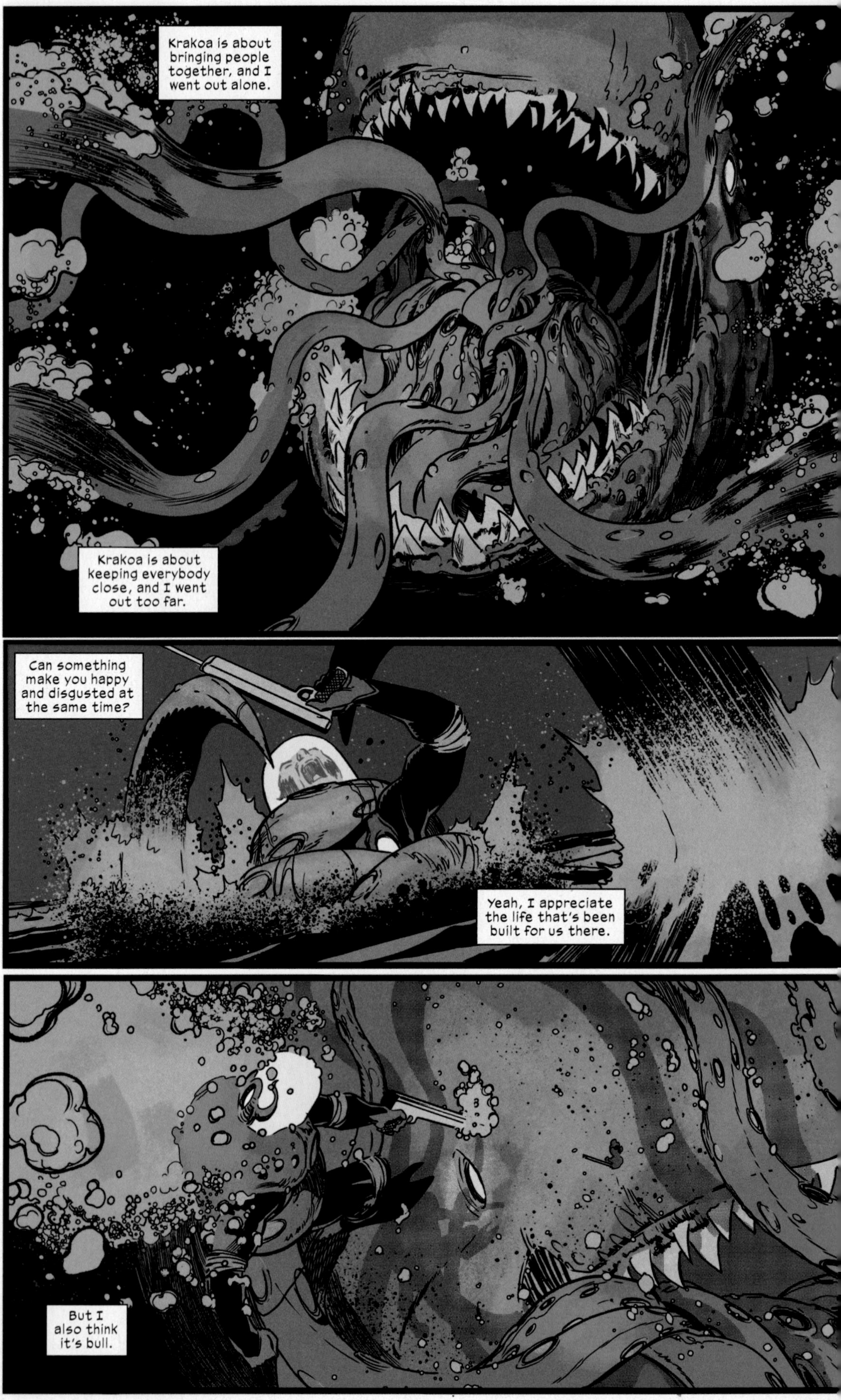
Krakoa is about bringing people together, and I went out alone.
Krakoa is about keeping everybody close, and I went out too far.
Can something make you happy and disgusted at the same time?
Yeah, I appreciate the life that's been built for us there.
But I also think it's bull.

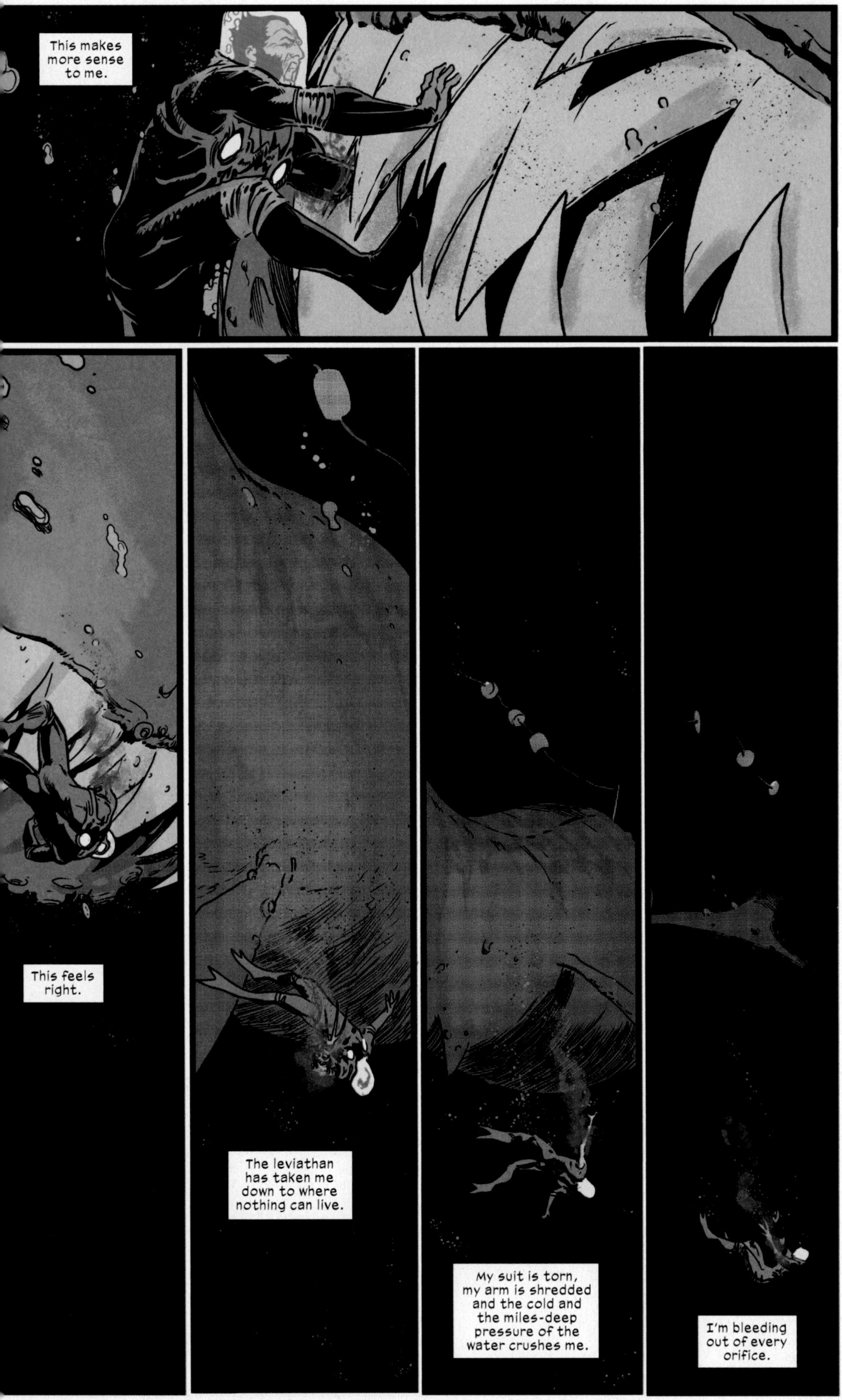
This makes more sense to me.
This feels right.
The leviathan has taken me down to where nothing can live.
My suit is torn, my arm is shredded and the cold and the miles-deep pressure of the water crushes me.
I'm bleeding out of every orifice.

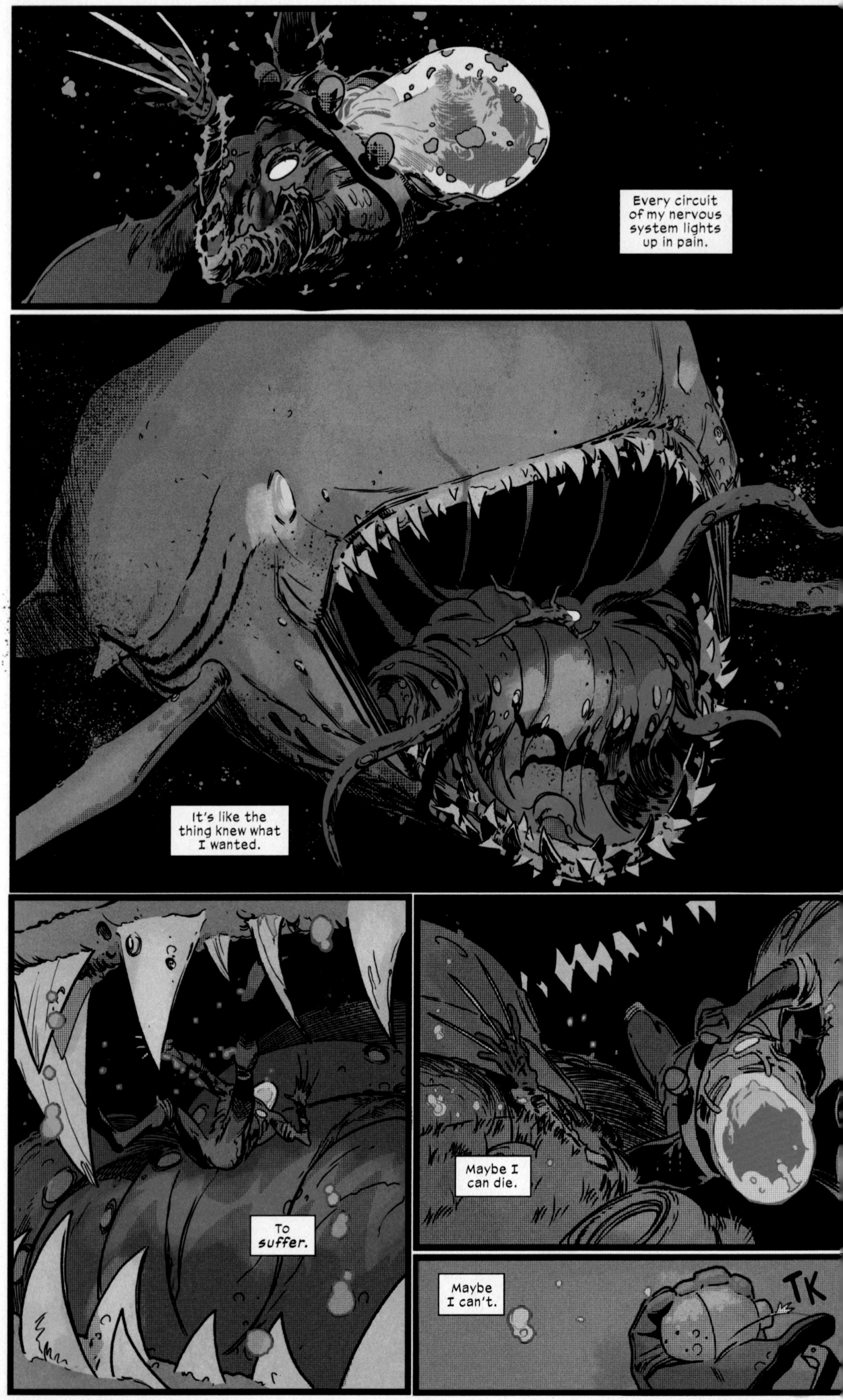
Every circuit of my nervous system lights up in pain.
It's like the thing knew what I wanted.
To *suffer.*
Maybe I can die.
Maybe I can't.
TK

But the hurt helps remind me I'm actually alive.

CHOOOM

Homo superior has become an apex predator.

Seemingly, nothing can touch us.

Which is why we have to remember...

SKELLLCH

...there's always something out there capable of gobbling us up.

I might have won today.

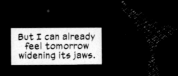

But I can already feel tomorrow widening its jaws.

This morning, another body washed up on Krakoa.

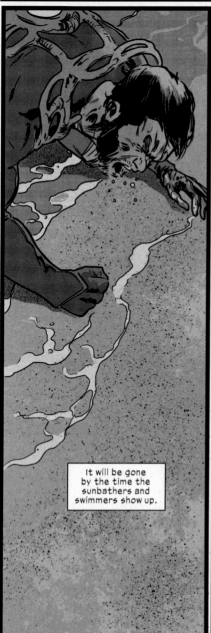

It will be gone by the time the sunbathers and swimmers show up.

They'll live another day without knowing pain.

Because I ate it all for them.

"You can destroy me all day and still not defeat me."

-- WOLVERINE

[wolverine_19]

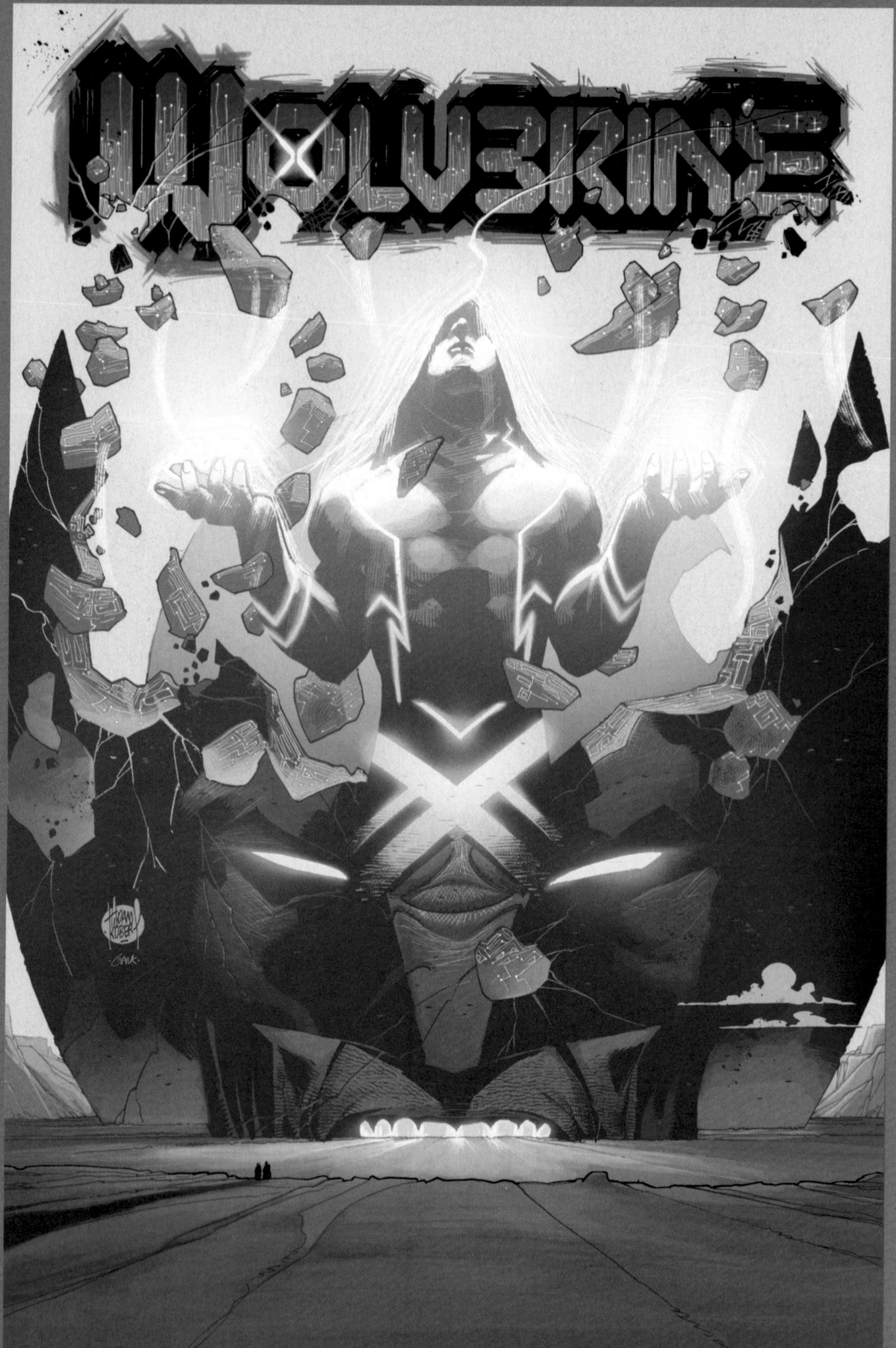
WOLVERINE

Wolverine #14

by Adam Kubert
& Frank Martin

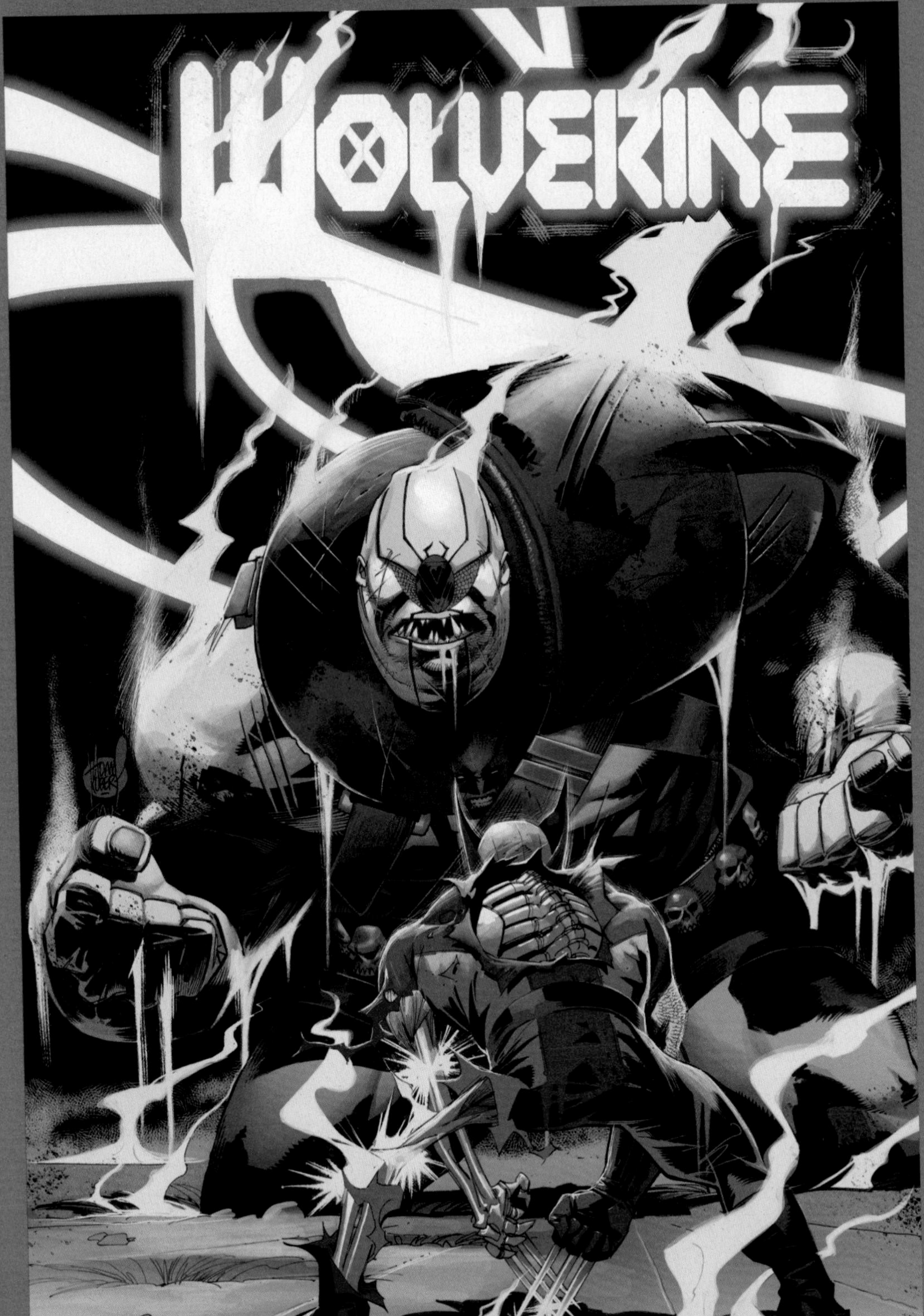
WOLVERINE

Wolverine #15

by Adam Kubert
& Frank Martin

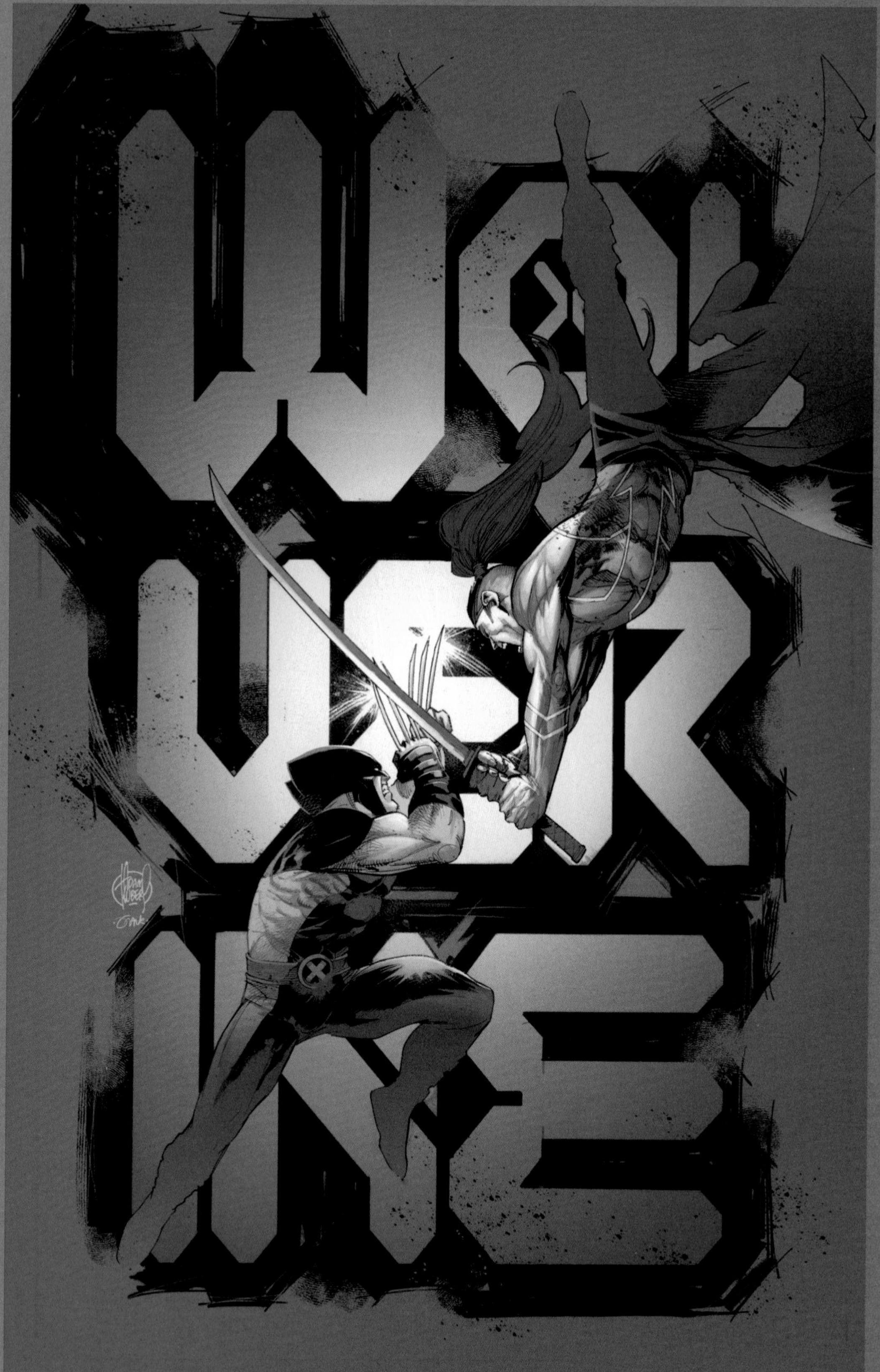

Wolverine #16

by Adam Kubert
& Frank Martin

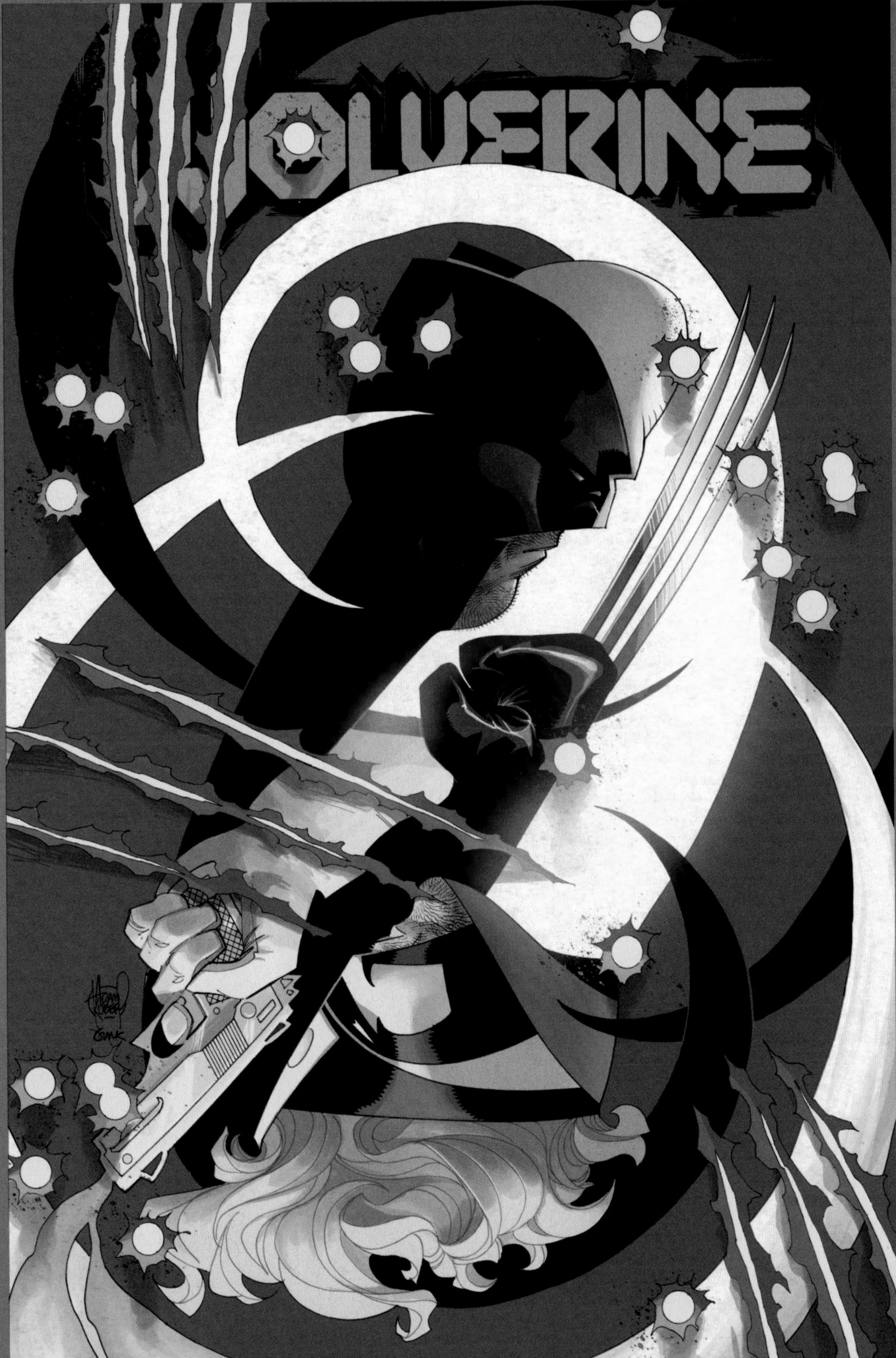
WOLVERINE

Wolverine #17

by Adam Kubert
& Frank Martin

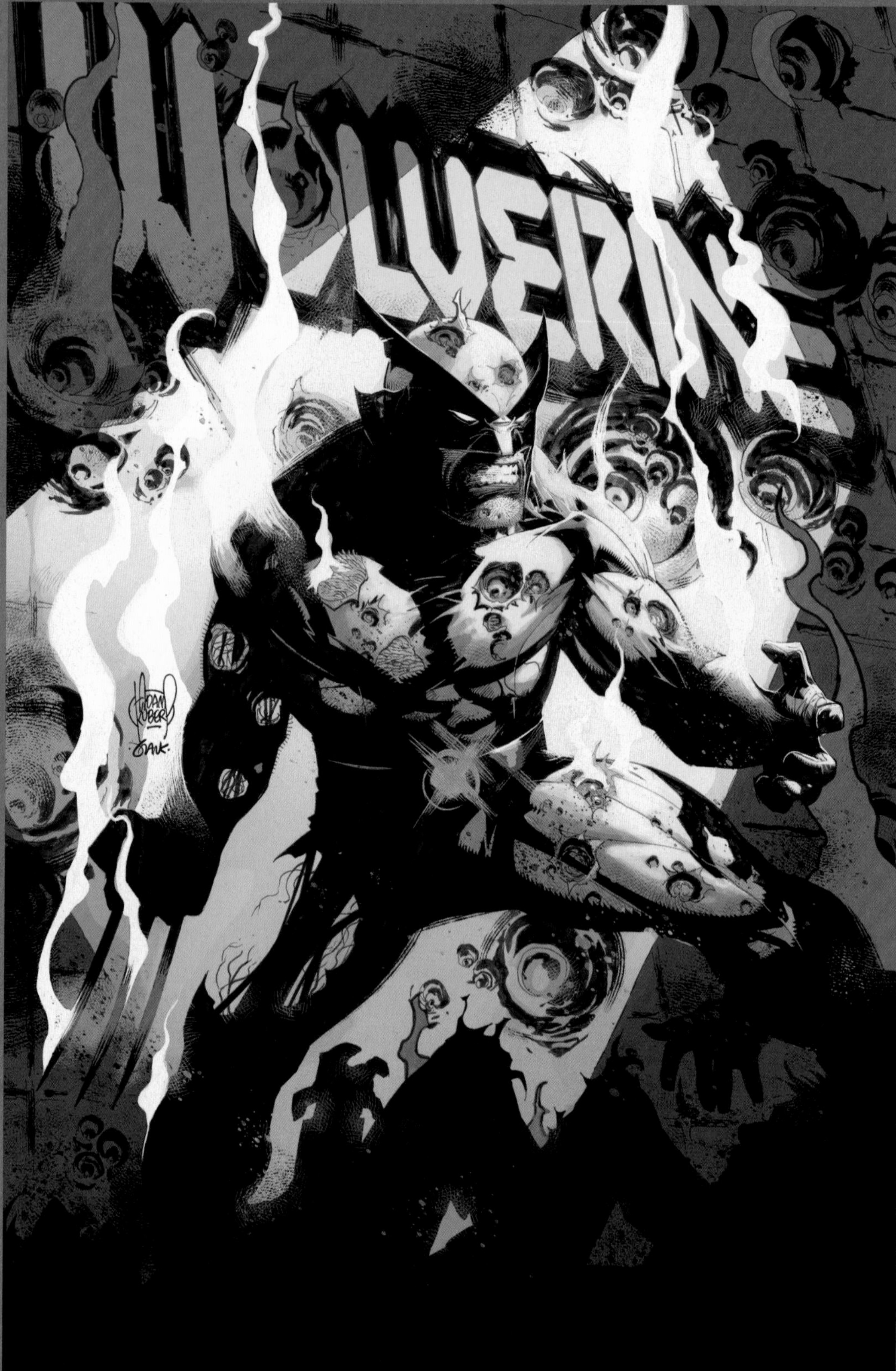
WOLVERINE

Wolverine #18

by Adam Kubert
& Frank Martin

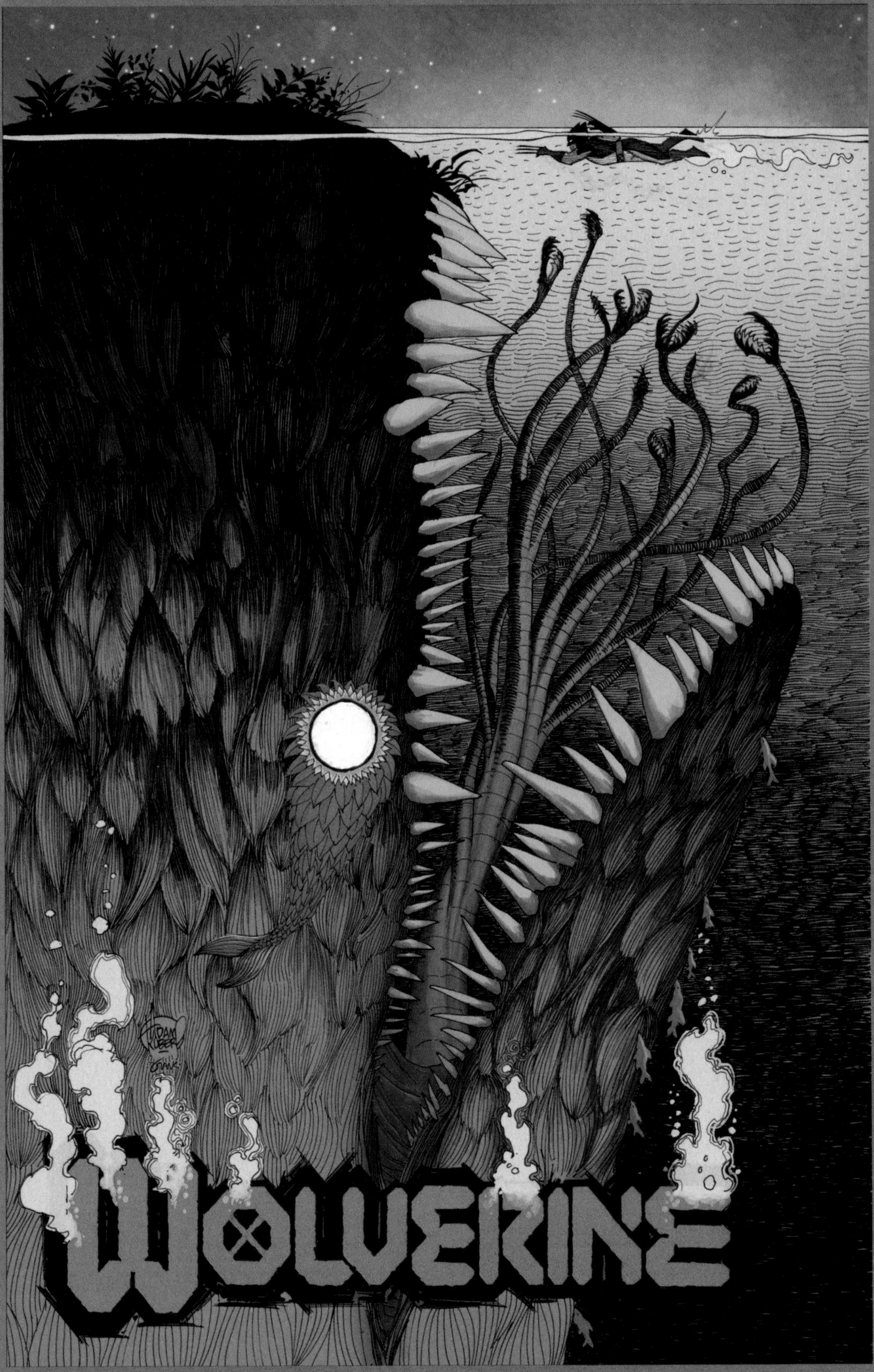
WOLVERINE

Wolverine #19

by Adam Kubert
& Frank Martin

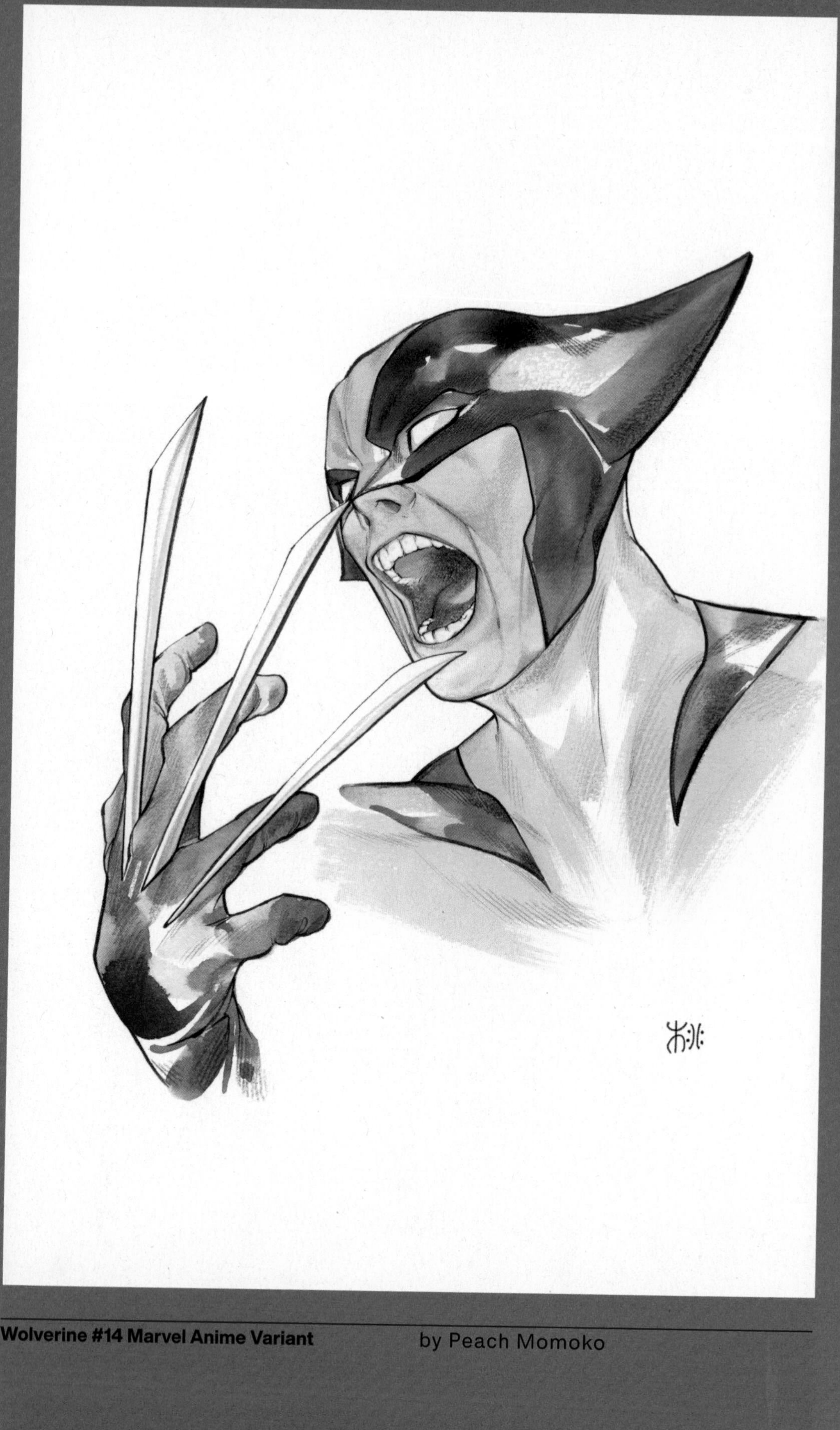

Wolverine #14 Marvel Anime Variant by Peach Momoko

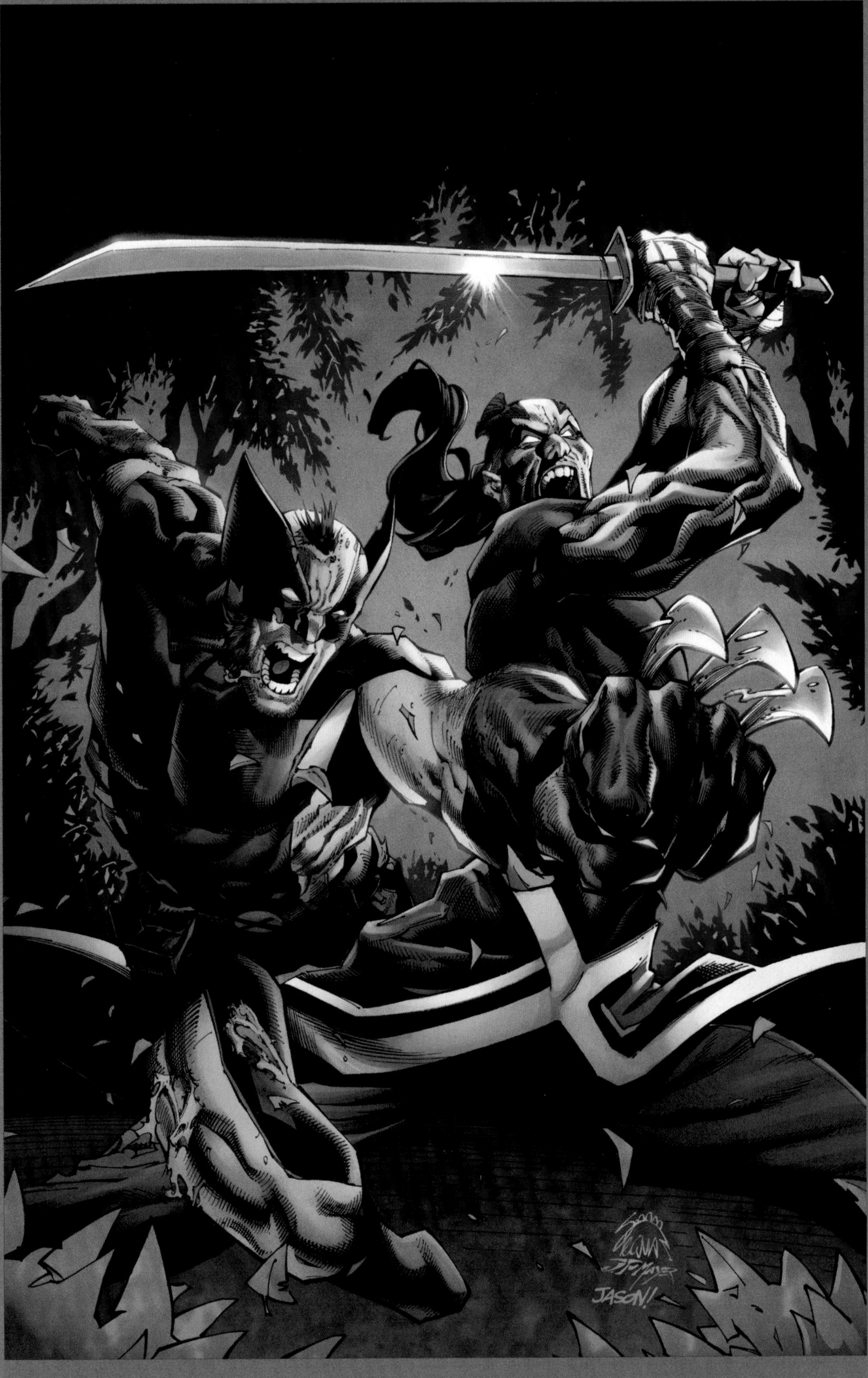
JASON!

Wolverine #14 Variant

by Ryan Stegman, JP Mayer
& Jason Keith

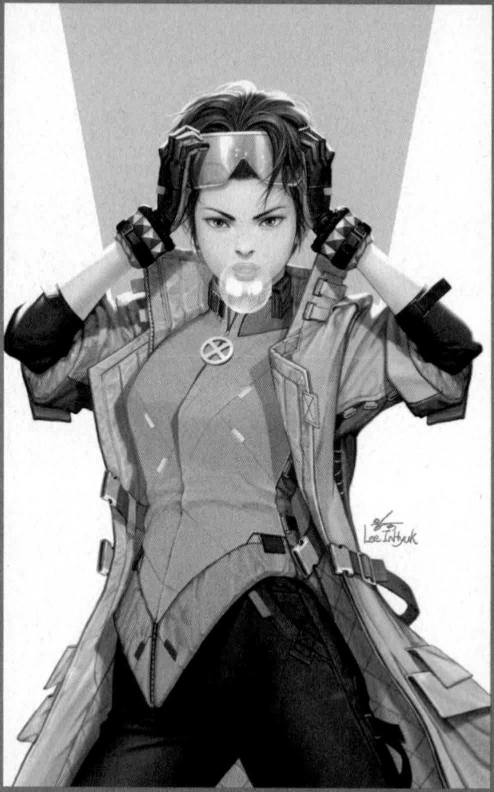
Lee InHyuk

Wolverine #15 Jubilee Asian Voices Variant
by InHyuk Lee

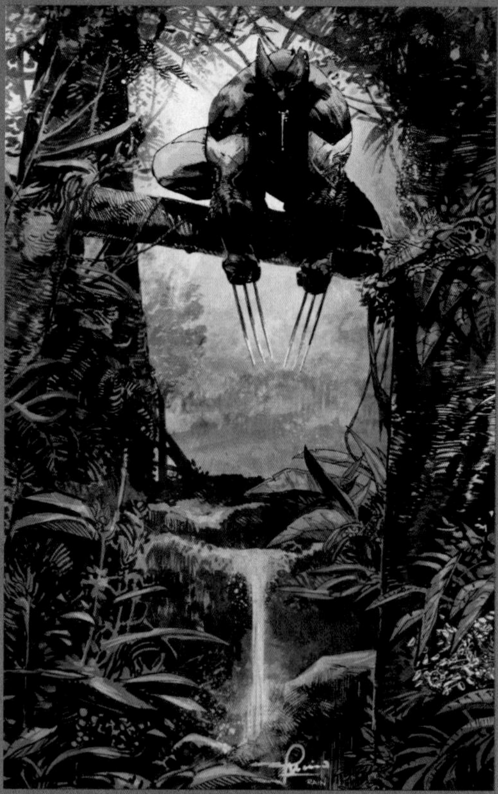

Wolverine #15 Variant
by Gerardo Zaffino & Rain Beredo

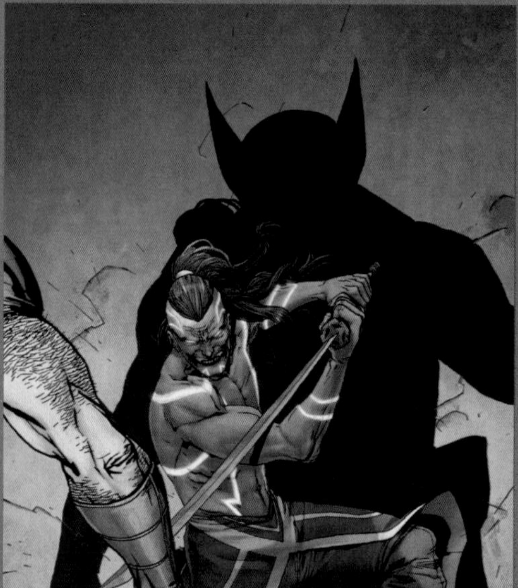

Wolverine #16 Variant
by Giuseppe Camuncoli
& Jean-François Beaulieu

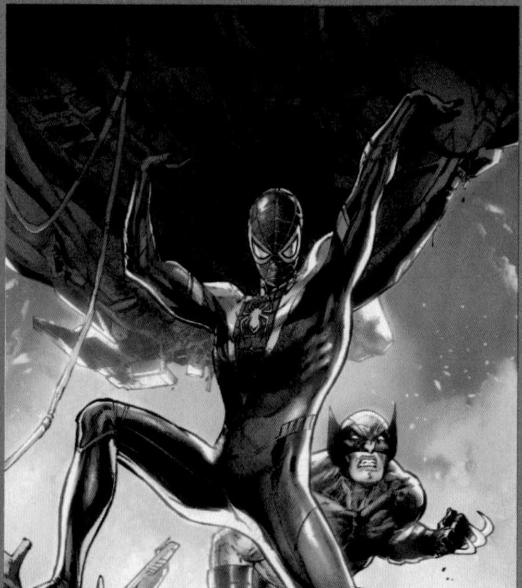

Wolverine #16 Miles Morales: Spider-Man 10th Anniversary Variant
by Tony Daniel & Marcelo Maiolo

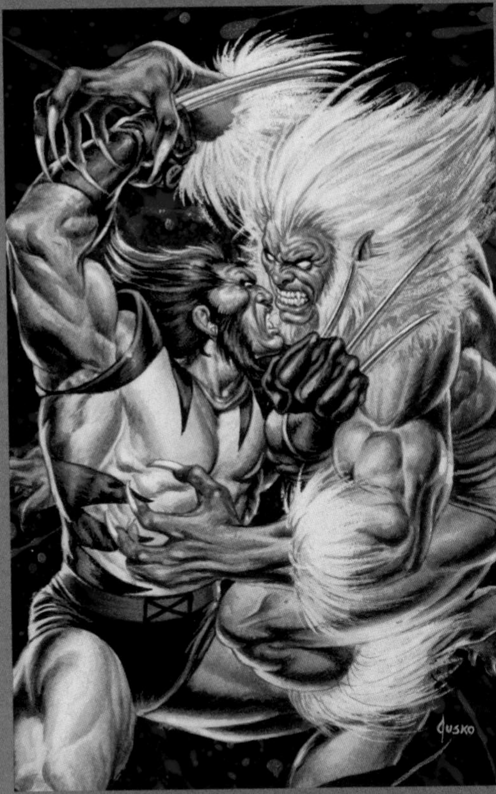

Wolverine #17 Marvel Masterpieces Variant
by Joe Jusko

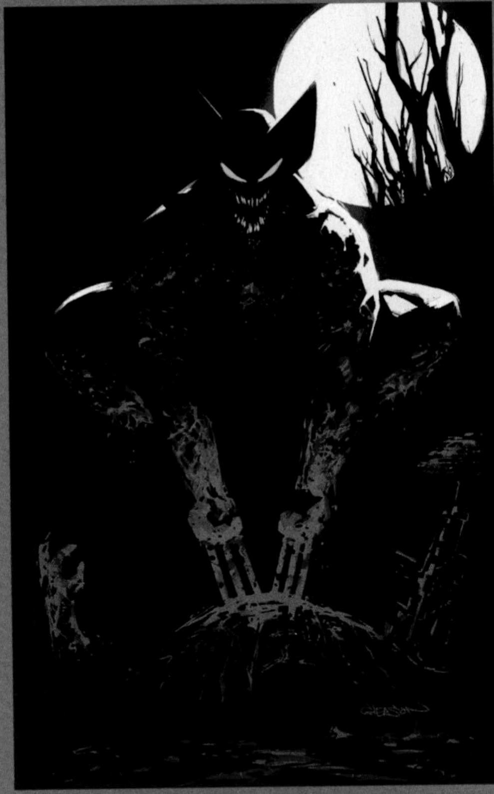

Wolverine #17 Stormbreakers Variant
by Patrick Gleason

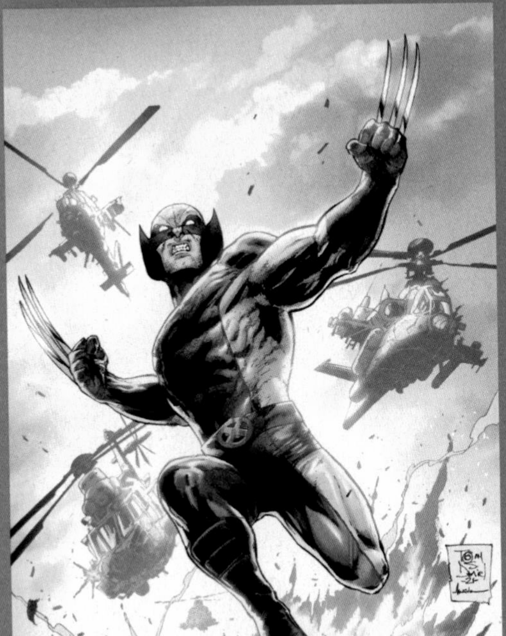

Wolverine #17 Variant
by Tony Daniel
& Marcelo Maiolo

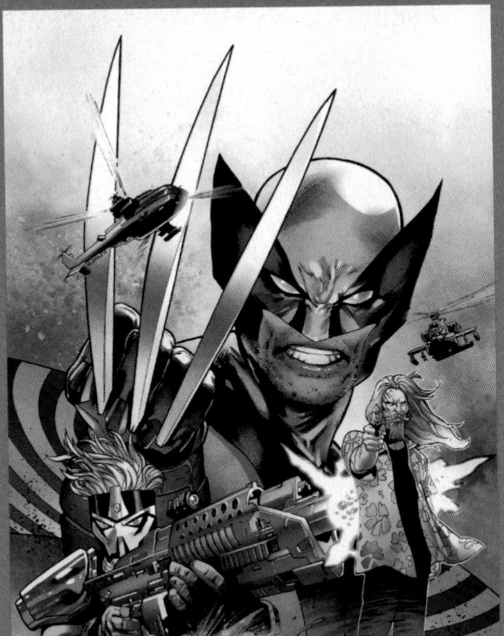

Wolverine #18 Variant
by Greg Land
& Frank D'Armata

Wolverine #18 Variant
by Alex Maleev

Wolverine #19 Variant
by E.M. Gist

Wolverine #19 Devil's Reign Variant
by Tyler Kirkham
& Arif Prianto